Fundamentals of
Educational Research

To: Herbert J. Walberg
   who taught me useful research techniques.
Archie Mackinnon
   who taught me some of the right questions.
Charles Lusthaus
   with whom I enjoy the pursuit of elusive answers.

Fundamentals of Educational Research

Gary Anderson

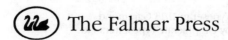

The Falmer Press

(A member of the Taylor & Francis Group)

London · New York · Philadelphia

UK	The Falmer Press, Rankine Road, Basingstoke, Hampshire, RG24 0PR
USA	The Falmer Press, Taylor & Francis Inc., 1900 Frost Road, Suite 101, Bristol, PA 19007

First published 1990   Reprinted 1993

British Library Cataloguing in Publication Data
Anderson, Gary
  Fundamentals of educational research.
  1. Education. Research
  I. Title
  370.78

  ISBN 1-85000-788-8

Library of Congress Cataloging in Publication Data
are available on request

Jacket design by Caroline Archer

Typeset in 11/13 Garamond
by Graphicraft Typesetters Ltd.

Printed in Great Britain by Burgess Science Press, Basingstoke
on paper which has a specified pH value on final paper
manufacture of not less than 7.5 and is therefore 'acid free'.

Contents

Contents

Part IV — Research Tools and Techniques

Acknowledgments

Susan Galt and Mary-Lynne Keenan for tireless efforts at the keyboard.

Norman Henchey for his extensive comments on an earlier draft of the manuscript.

My McGill classes in research methodology of 1987, 1988 and 1989 which provided useful feedback.

Series Editor's Preface

Gary Anderson's book is the first in a broad range of works that will constitute a library for teachers wishing to study education and reflect upon their practice. The intention of this important new venture from Falmer Press is to produce a number of concise and accessible texts which bring the study of education closer to teachers' everyday world — thereby closing the gap between theory and practice. As Gary Anderson points out in his preface, most existing books in this genre are too long. He might also have added that they are normally far too jargon-ridden. The Falmer Press Teacher's Library aims to avoid both of these problems.

Fundamentals of Educational Research successfully brings together a whole range of crucial themes with regard to educational research, research processes and research methods. It is important as an initial statement of the series in that it covers many of the themes and issues which will be investigated in detail in subsequent volumes. In this sense, it provides a vivid and lively "shop window" of the intentions and aspirations of the Falmer Press Teacher's Library.

Ivor Goodson
Series Editor

Preface

Why another book on research methods? The short answer is that existing books do not fulfill the need. The longer answer requires a bit more history. I have been conducting research, and teaching research methodology in various forms for the past twenty years, but my work over the past ten, both in research and in teaching, have opened new perspectives for me which I would like to share.

On the research front, out of a background in mathematics and physics, I began as a quantitative methodologist adept at using multi-variate statistics to explore various types of educational phenomena, but I soon recognized the limitations of such approaches. They did allow great insights into many of the complexities of education, but they were ill-suited to increasing my understanding of the limitations and challenges of educational innovation and reform as I came to experience them as an educational manger. In my role as a manager I became concerned with the development and implementation of new programs and curricula, of educational change and of many forms of education which went beyond formal learning as typically found in schools and universities. I became involved as well in regional and international development and in its forms of research related to planning, evaluation and institution-building. In the course of this work, I experimented with all types of methods: historical research, case studies, ethnography, evaluation and policy research as well as a myriad of special techniques from content analysis to tracer studies. Consequently, I came to appreciate the imperative of diverse approaches to facilitate understanding of highly complex educational phenomena. These approaches taught me a great deal and many of the principles, procedures, tools and techniques which I use routinely are not described adequately in a single source. The desire to share these lessons was one motivation for writing the book.

A stronger motivation was my teaching which focused on a one-semester graduate course, introduction to educational research. I never found a suitable text for the course, though there were many that had important content elements. In the first place, many such books were statistical or at least assumed a sound background in statistics. My teaching revealed that most students know little about statistics even when they have scored high grades in statistics courses. Their knowledge of statistics is analogous to knowledge of an unpracticed foreign language: totally useless in terms of the basic need of the traveller to find directions, food and lodging. I personally learned statistics while addressing real research problems and I suspect that most graduate students, like those I have supervised, also learn them in that way. Consequently, I teach my course with almost no mention of statistics, presuming that beginning researchers can learn such tools as they go along, providing they can be taught to design reasonable studies focused on critical questions.

A second deficiency of existing books and motivation for writing this one is that books on research tend to be far too long. Students in a half course cannot assimilate 800 pages of fine print full of qualifications and caveats all of which serve to mask the basic concepts which generally stay well concealed on the pages of the book. The need was for a short and simple book with clear steps for designing and executing a research study.

Finally, I don't like textbooks in general as I find that they represent a school-based model of learning. I prefer books which talk to people of all types, whether students in a course or professionals trying to do a better job; books which are used in and outside of school to help people of all walks of life understand what a subject is all about. That is the type of book I have tried to write. There are no exercises or drills as the book is intended to help people deal with their research concerns, not mine. Thus, the book is designed to be used by people as they work through their own educational problems and agendas.

I teach my course by having each participant define a suitable problem and then spend the rest of the semester developing a full proposal for conducting the study. However, one of the major problems of teaching research methodology as I do, is that to begin, the beginner must define a problem, but the problem can't be designed without a thorough grounding in how it is to be addressed. Thus, the conundrum is that you must finish my course before you can hope to begin it! This book is seen as a way of re-dressing that dilemma as it permits people to move ahead at their own pace according to their own individual needs. Thus, people can get the big picture before they commit themselves to something which might dictate a type of methodological approach which is of no particular interest.

The final reason for writing the book was because it is fun to write books. They are demanding and challenging as they unfold and are gratifying once they are finished. Research projects are much the same and I hope you enjoy your research endeavors as much as I have enjoyed telling you about some of mine.

Gary Anderson
McGill University

Part I

Introduction to Educational Research

Chapter 1

The Nature of Educational Research

The human species differs from other forms of animal life in that humans are able to learn from the experience of others. Information is collected, analyzed and communicated and over time the body of accumulated knowledge increases, providing the basis for societal progress. There are five main ways in which the human race approaches knowledge. The first is the method of tenacity. In this method people hold to the truth merely because they believe it to be true. They have always known it to be true and so even contrary evidence is dismissed out of hand. This method is nothing more than blind stubbornness, but it is responsible for many prevalent beliefs, some true, others erroneous. It is not an approach to knowledge which need concern us as researchers.

Another of the fundamental ways of knowing is authority based. People rely on experts to gain understanding and guide their behavior. In any family or work setting the views of those endorsed as knowledgeable have credibility and are believed. On the broader scene, certain acknowledged experts are also believed. Thus, if Linus Pauling believes in vitamin C, that is good enough evidence for me. If the Bible says it is true; it must be so. The only utility of this approach to the researcher is that it sometimes poses questions which bear researching: Does vitamin C really cure colds?

The rationalist approach to knowledge adds thinking and deduction which in some instances can lead to useful generalizations or predictions. It is based on the notion of logic which links truths and enables prediction to a situation which may not have been directly observed. If A causes B and B causes C, then A probably also causes C. This is an under-utilized approach in the literature of educational research, but it is a vital one. It helps extend theory and sets up questions which the researcher can then address. It is the fundamental approach of philosophers of education and is also used in evaluation studies and contract research.

A related method might be termed insightful observation. Insightful observation is used by intelligent people who are capable of gathering information from their experience and of drawing useful generalizations and conclusions from it. Unlike the former method, this incorporates some observational basis, albeit unsystematic. This approach is used by some researchers to formulate logical questions and suppositions for more systematic research and analysis. As a way of developing questions, it, too, can be useful to science as demonstrated by the recent research on folk remedies and natural medicines.

Finally, the scientific method incorporates observations and data which are systematically collected and analyzed in order to obtain understanding of phenomena based on controlled observation and analysis. It is this final form which represents research and the research method in its most widely understood meaning. Unlike the other methods, the scientific method builds in self-correction. New evidence is constantly brought to bear and existing generalizations are constantly modified and corrected to accommodate this additional evidence. However, it is also fair to say that most research and especially contract research and evaluation also incorporates some of the useful features of insightful observation and the rationalist approach. Philosophical inquiry does not typically involve systematic observation and relies entirely on a rationalistic approach. For this reason, some people would question whether philosophical inquiry should be called research.

This chapter explores the nature of educational research, the four levels of research and introduces terms which refer to common methodological approaches. It then defines some basic concepts useful for further study of educational research.

The Nature of Educational Research

Research in education is a disciplined attempt to address questions or solve problems through the collection and analysis of primary data for the purpose of description, explanation, generalization and prediction.

Research is fundamentally a problem-solving activity which addresses a problem or tests an hypothesis. I prefer the problem-solving formulation which relies on a series of specific questions addressed by data collected for the purpose. In the traditional research approach, the researcher derives hypotheses which are tested under various conditions and then accepted or rejected, generally in accordance with pre-established conventions. This approach is best suited for certain problems and methods rooted in experimental studies, but is of limited use for the more general problem-solving addressed here. The formulation of research problems and questions is a more general and generalizable approach to research and is the one followed in this text. Succeeding chapters are devoted to the task of formulating researchable problems, suitable research questions and deriving methodologies with which to explore them.

There is another domain of investigation which some scholars consider research. It includes philosophical analysis, especially conceptual analysis, the situation of educational issues within a philosophical tradition, the examination of epistemological and axiological assumptions, criticism and so forth. I view such activities as scholarship, but not as research in the sense in which it is used in this text. The principal difference is the lack of primary data in those approaches which rely entirely on critical thinking and analysis of existing literature and theory.

Figure 1.1 lists ten characteristics of educational research which extend the definition noted above. Unlike other forms of knowing, research relies on systematic and objective observation, recording and analysis. It seeks to answer the questions and address the problems posed by inquiring minds and strives to find general principles and theories which can lead to the prediction of behaviours and events in the future. The goals of research have to do with understanding, prediction and ultimately control (Best, 1977). These notions rely on controlled and accurate observation and the recording of information. Only in this way can prediction be accurately measured and assessed. It is important to understand that the researcher should be unbiased and not have too strong a vested interest in the outcome. It is natural for people to do research in areas towards which they feel a certain value commitment, but it must not interfere with one's ability to preserve objectivity. People with a mission should engage in volunteer work or religion; they should not pursue research to justify their causes.

Research is a scientific process which assumes that events in the world are lawful and orderly and, furthermore, that the lawfulness is discoverable. This is the meaning of determinism and the researcher

Figure 1.1:   Characteristics of educational research

1 Educational Research attempts to solve a problem.
2 Research involves gathering new data from primary or first-hand sources or using existing data for a new purpose.
3 Research is based upon observable experience or empirical evidence.
4 Research demands accurate observation and description.
5 Research generally employs carefully designed procedures and rigorous analysis.
6 Research emphasizes the development of generalizations, principles or theories that will help in understanding, prediction and control.
7 Research requires expertise — familiarity with the field; competence in methodology; technical skill in collecting and analyzing the data.
8 Research attempts to find an objective, unbiased solution to the problem and takes great pains to validate the procedures employed.
9 Research is a deliberate and unhurried activity which is directional but often refines the problem or questions as the research progresses.
10 Research is carefully recorded and reported to other persons interested in the problem.

acts in the belief that the laws of nature can be understood and ulti-mately controlled to at least some degree. In a nutshell, educational research is the systematic process of discovering how and why people in educational settings behave as they do.

The assumptions underlying nature and research are fundamental to our understanding and progress. Very often a shift in assumptions has lead to important discoveries. Jerome Bruner's (1960) assertion that anyone given sufficient time and the right approach can under-stand any concept at some intellectually respectable level is an example of an assumption which thirty years ago called into question what we used to teach in schools at different levels. Acceptance of the principle led to all types of research on the teaching and learning of concepts which had previously been reserved for higher levels of edu-cation. The assumption that learning must be controlled by a teacher who feeds information to students has helped preserve the nature of schooling as we have known it. A shift in such an assumption could lead to fundamental questions about the nature of schools and their usefulness.

Research takes many forms and it incorporates many tools, methods and techniques with which we attempt to understand the world around us. All research relates to questions or problems which present themselves and to which the researcher seeks answers and understanding. Why are school classrooms organized in seats and rows? Why is formal schooling arranged in different levels which take place in different buildings and incorporate slightly different methods? Why do some children learn easily and effectively while others have learning difficulties? Why do some school administrators attend in-

Figure 1.2: The four levels of educational research

Level	I	II	III	IV
Research Type	Descriptive	Explanatory (Internal Validity)	Generalization (External Validity)	Basic (Theoretical)
Major Questions	What is happening? What happened in the past?	What is causing it to happen? Why did it happen?	Will the same thing happen under different circumstances?	Is there some underlying principle at work?
Traditional Associated Disciplines	Anthropology History Physical Sciences Sociology	Anthropology Behavioral Sciences History Physical Sciences Psychology Sociology	Behavioral Sciences Physical Sciences Psychology	Behavioral Sciences Physical Sciences Psychology Philosophy[a]
Methods/ Approaches	Case Study Content Analysis Ethnography Historiography Needs Assessment Observation Policy Research Polling Program-Evaluation Sociometry Survey Research Tracer Studies	Case Study Comparative Correlational Ethnography Ex-Post Facto Historiography Observation Sociometry Time Series Analysis Tracer Studies	Casual-Comparative Experimental Meta Analysis Multiple Case Study Predictive Quasi-Experimental	ABAB Designs Experimental Meta Analysis Policy Research Time Series Analysis

a   While philosophy does not typically incorporate primary source data, empirical evidence, or observation, it is included as an associated discipline since it relies on similar approaches to other forms of theoretical research.

service education while others do not? How do young children best acquire a second language? How can we help developing nations build educational institutions which respond to indigenous needs and reflect indigenous capabilities?

Levels of Research

There are essentially four levels at which educational research takes place: descriptive, explanatory, generalization and basic or theoretical (see Figure 1.2). Descriptive research has two major branches — historical and contemporary. Historical research attempts to describe what was, whereas contemporary research describes what is happening now. While descriptive research is the first and most elementary level of research activity, it is of major importance for understanding and the accumulation of knowledge. A great many contemporary and past educational phenomena are not well understood because they have not been sufficiently described. A great many questions in education are descriptive. How were schools organized in colonial North America? On what activities do principals spend their time? What do teachers actually do in a classroom? What types of programs are offered by leading universities in adult education? What are the backgrounds of teachers of mathematics? What are the concerns of teachers, of parents and of students? What are the learning needs of beginning educational administrators? These and thousands of other questions are not necessarily well understood in the literature and for this reason descriptive research needs to take place if we are to gain understanding of the state of education in our world.

Fundamental to good description are good measurement and observation. Unless we can describe and quantify our observations in objective terms they will have little meaning for others and will be of no general use. Statistics can be used to simplify description by grouping observations and describing in a few words, symbols or numbers what would otherwise take a great deal of prose. In some cases, photographs, videos or films can be used to describe educational situations. Unless we have good descriptions, it is impossible to move to higher levels of research.

Explanatory research asks the question, what is causing this to happen? Why does one school get better results than another? How does a given principal motivate the staff while another is unsuccessful at doing so? Does a French immersion program lead to greater French second language competence than the traditional program? Is a given type of schooling an effective way to expend taxpayers money? Explanation, sometimes called internal validity, focuses on understanding what is happening in a given observable setting. Thus, our interest is in understanding what goes on in a given classroom or school but not necessarily its implications for the world at large. That becomes the third level of research.

Generalization attempts to discover whether similar things will happen in new situations. Building on the explanatory level, an attempt is made to generalize to a new situation. This, of course, begins to lead to prediction and ultimately to control of effects. Our interest is to push the explanation to see how far the results can be generalized. For example, will an approach that taught Johnny to read also help him with mathematics? Will the technique for motivating a school staff apply in another setting? While our interest is in generalization, it does not necessarily try to explain why the generalization occurs. So, for example, if we wanted to predict the level of the tides we could do so easily with a computer model that would enable accurate predication into the future, without any understanding whatsoever of the law of universal gravitation. Discovery of the law leads to the fourth level of research.

Basic or theoretical research attempts to discover underlying principles which are at work. Basic researchers hold that the proper role of science is the study of basic scientific questions regardless of whether their solution has practical application. What are the underlying dimensions of school climate which lead to school effectiveness? What is the relationship of intrinsic and extrinsic rewards to performance? What are the characteristics of educational leadership? Often such basic and theoretical research is conducted in experimental settings, using contrived situations and perhaps even animal experiments in order to isolate the underlying principle. Such basic research has been motivated by a desire to understand theory but as is the case in the natural sciences, such understanding has often had important applied consequences. The study of x-rays and microwaves in physics has led to medical and kitchen applications which were not the primary motivation for exploring the phenomena. Similarly, Skinner's reinforcement theory developed with animals has had profound educational applications.

The Traditional Research Disciplines

Education is a broad field and educational research tends to borrow its many methods and approaches from the various academic disciplines which have longer histories of research. The major disciplines which have affected educational research are listed in Figure 1.2. I have included the physical sciences because they have influenced all of the social sciences through their scientific approach and experimental methodology. As shown in the figure, the physical sciences span all four levels which is important to remember when attempting to work at an educational problem. Good research requires some attention to each of the four levels. Other research traditions such as anthropology, history and sociology tend to be concerned with level I and II, whereas such fields as the behavioral sciences and psychology focus most at levels II, III and IV. It should be stressed, however, that these divisions are by no means absolute. The final row in Figure 1.2 indicates methods and approaches often associated with research at each of these levels and within the various disciplines. These methods and the terms used will be described more fully in Chapters 9–13.

Relationship Among the Levels of Research

The various levels of research are by no means discreet. Furthermore, they often build on one another in an interactive way. It is fair to say, however, that one cannot explain without being able to describe, nor can one easily generalize without being able to explain. Theoretical principles have scant chance of being discovered and understood unless one has a thorough knowledge of relevant generalizations and their limitations.

Generally speaking, educational researchers should attempt to go beyond the strictly descriptive level in their work. Description is the proper domain of pollsters and those who conduct surveys, but in most worthwhile research an attempt is made to explain why the data are as observed. Such explanation relies on a knowledge of theory and prior research and its application is the mark of the experienced researcher. Such a person can relate the present study to others which have taken place in the field and can link sets of findings and extend the basis of general knowledge.

The type of research one does is greatly dependent upon the research culture prevalent in the institution where the research is being carried out. The existence of research teams exploring a similar theme will generally enable one to make a greater contribution than doing an isolated study alone. Furthermore, the higher levels of research require a great depth of experience either in the form of an extensive published literature, successive studies done by an individual researcher or numerous studies done by a research team. In general, the beginning researcher should obtain a thorough grounding in the lower levels before the higher levels of research are attempted. One of the most difficult challenges of all for the beginning researcher is to select an appropriate problem and pursue it at an appropriate level. At this stage, it is fair to say one cannot do the higher levels of research until he or she has mastered the rudiments of the descriptive and explanatory levels.

The Subjectiveness of Objectivity

Research in the social sciences is no more objective than is research into morality. How you see the world is largely a function of where you view it from, what you look at, what tools you use to help you see and what you reflect on and report to others. Thus, an empirical researcher will see only those things which are conveniently measured in empirical ways. A sociologist will only be concerned with patterns affecting groups and will have little chance of learning about individual motivations except as they relate to group behavior. The behaviorist will focus on reporting and controlling behaviors, whereas the anthropologist's concern will be their underlying meaning. Thus, research reflects the values, beliefs and perspectives of the researcher. This is not the same, however, as saying that research is subjective. For valid research, similar approaches should lead to similar conclusions, but different approaches can hardly be expected to lead to exactly the same conclusions. These different approaches cannot even be expected to ask the same questions, let alone realize similar answers. Thus, few researchers are truly unbiased or value-neutral, obviously carrying a baggage of beliefs, assumptions, inclinations and approaches to reality.

Beginning researchers should understand this interaction between the answers, questions and who is asking them. When reviewing previous research attempt to understand the researcher's perspective on the world as well as the results and conclusions. In coming to grips with your own research you must clarify your own preferred way of viewing the world: What questions are important to you? What are your approaches to knowledge? What personal strengths do you have that can help you adopt a particular methodological approach? What types of studies would you prefer to be associated with?

Basic Concepts

Pilot Study

A pilot study is a small scale study conducted prior to the actual research. The entire pilot study is conducted in order to test the procedures and techniques to see that they work satisfactorily. Pilot studies are used to test questionnaires and other instruments and to see whether there is any possibility that worthwhile results will be found. If promising results do not appear in a pilot study, researchers sometimes reconsider the rationale, design or viability of their study. Thus, pilot studies provide an excellent way of avoiding trivial or non-significant research.

Primary and Secondary Data Sources

A primary source of data is one where the person providing the data was actually present whereas a secondary data source is one where the data comes from one who was not present. For example, a child's test results are primary sources whereas a teacher's recollection of how well a child performed is a secondary source. Research studies are primary sources if one consults the original account such as found in a research journal. Descriptions of research studies reported in a book are secondary sources since they are described by the author of the book rather than the person who conducted the research.

Variable

A variable is a characteristic that can assume any one of a range of values. Nominal variables are those which don't have a numeric or quantitative implication such as eye colour, race or gender. Ordinal variables are those where there is a numeric value attached: IQ, age, aptitude score or grade point average are examples. Sometimes these are grouped into intervals such as ages, 21–30, 31–40, etc. These are called interval variables. Ratio variables are those that are created during the reseach by dividing existing ordinal variables. Cost per pupil is an example. In general, nominal variables are used in the construction of frameworks or the division of samples into comparison groups. Ordinal and ratio variables are used for statistical analysis.

Reliability

Reliability refers to consistency in measurement. In common terms the reliability of a test is the extent to which subsequent administrations would give similar results. A test which is not reliable will give different results every time it is taken. Accepted practice uses such measures as test–retest reliability coefficients to indicate reliability. This is equivalent to the correlation (see Chapter 9) of test results obtained on two separate occasions.

The extent to which data relate to objective criteria will improve reliability. When the data are based on personal impressions they tend not to be reliable. However, when they relate to counts or physical measurements or the number of correct math problems, they are generally reliable. For example, it is much more difficult to get agreement on the artistic merits of a work of art than it is on the technical competence of a draftsman. The data used in educational research must be reliable if the analysis is to have any meaning. If we do not have reliable measurement tools, we can't have much confidence in our results.

Validity

Validity is the complement to reliability and refers to the extent to which what we measure reflects what we expected to measure. Thus, an IQ score is assumed to be a measure of intelligence and is assumed to be a valid representation of intelligence in quantitative terms. Similarly, the enrollment of a school is assumed to be a valid measure of its size.

Internal validity refers to the validity of data measures as described above. Internal validity also relates to issues of truthfulness of responses, accuracy of records, authenticity of historical artifacts. There is a related validity problem known as external validity. External validity refers to the generalizability of the obtained results. Are the results obtained with a sample of 100 principals similar to the results expected from all 1243 principals in the province or state? Can the results of studies of school effectiveness in Montreal be generalized to schools in Toronto or Boston? We require internal validity to be confident that the results obtained are true for those participating in a study; we need external validity to be in a position to generalize them.

Unit of Analysis

Researchers must be clear on their unit of analysis. That is, they must decide from the sources of data and sample selection procedures what unit is being selected as opposed to the one which is desired. It is the actual unit which must be used in the analysis. For example, if five classrooms are chosen, the unit of analysis is the classroom, and the study should be of classrooms. It is not a study of individual children, even though many individual children are involved. For that purpose, the unit of analysis would be children and individual children would have to be selected for the study. Even though you have many children involved, if you have selected classrooms you can only legitimately deal with the number of classrooms chosen. This tends to be a great limitation on the generalizability of most research and many researchers violate the principle of unit of analysis by collecting data in one way and then attempting to analyze it and generalize from it in another.

Units of analysis can range from nations or provinces or schools to individual teachers and pupils. Each of these levels has an appropriate place in research, but when the nature of the questions and methods of analysis comprise a collective, such as a nation, then the data used in the study must be overall data for the nation, such as gross national product, population, and so forth. If one wants to use the results of academic achievement tests in referring to a nation, one would have to use the average score for the whole nation.

Statistical Significance

Quantitative research follows the probability laws of applied statistics. These indicate whether relationships and values observed would be likely to occur by chance alone. A trivial example is useful to help understand the concept. If you were researching the question 'Does stereoscopic vision (seeing with both eyes) help score points in basketball?', you might take an expert like Wilt Chamberlain, blindfold one eye and let him shoot from the foul line. If he shot 100 times, he would undoubtedly get some balls in the basket. Now remove the blindfold and let him try again. If he scored fifty with one eye covered and ninety-five seeing with both eyes, we would be inclined to say that stereoscopic sight helps. What if he scored sixty blindfolded and only sixty-five with both eyes? Then we would be less sure. Obviously, there would be variations in performance every time he did the task. These chance variations can be monitored under the two different conditions and the probability of each score can be calculated. Even with no real difference in performance there will be a difference in the actual scores obtained every time the task is performed. The greater the difference in scores, the more likely that stereoscopic sight helps.

A statistically significant result is one which is unlikely to have occurred by chance alone. Thus, the observed relationship or difference is assumed to be a real one. One can never be absolutely sure in dealing with the laws of statistical probability, so researchers generally adopt some level of confidence in their result. The universally used levels of confidence are .05 and .01. These imply that any observed relationship or difference would be expected to occur by chance less than 5 per cent or 1 per cent of the time. In other words, there is a 95 per cent chance that the results observed are real, rather than statistical abberations. In polls, researchers generally describe the confidence in their results by saying that the actual result is within x percentage points 19 times out of 20.

It should be emphasized that statistical significance has little to do with educational significance. Results which might be highly statistically significant may have few implications for researchers or practitioners. Differences can be very small and still be statistically significant, too small to have much practical application. There are other procedures which can be used to estimate how powerful the results are but they are beyond the scope of this text.

Conclusion

There are many routes to knowledge. People learn through observation, reading, discussion and debate. Much of what is to be learned is already known by others and it is a case of accessing this knowledge and learning it. Some things, however, are not known. They must be discovered independently. That is the function of research and is part of its excitement. As a researcher, you are on a quest which despite no small share of frustration and hard work, leads to the discovery of new knowledge which can be passed on to others. The anticipation, the discovery, the potential contribution is what makes it all worthwhile.

While research is a means to discovery of new knowledge, there are many approaches to research. The research approach used tells something of how the researcher views the world. In examining research it is useful to bear this in mind. What assumptions are the researcher using? Out of what traditions have the questions and approaches emerged? What would happen if the assumptions and approaches were changed or traded in for alternatives? These types of questions often generate new avenues of significant research and should be borne in mind when you define a research problem.

For many readers of this text disciplined research is a new activity requiring the learning of many new concepts and skills. Often this is done while one is trying to formulate and develop a research problem and proposal and the challenge is to learn what you need while progressing with your own research. As you develop your interests, consider how each approach to research relates and how it might change the perspective and formulation of your research topic.

For Further Study

BADIA, P. and RUNYON, R.P. (1982) *Fundamentals of Behavioral Research*, Mass, Addison-Wesley.

BEST, J.W. (1977) *Research in Education*, 3rd ed. NJ, Prentice-Hall, Inc.

Reference

BRUNER, J. (1960) *The Process of Education*, Cambridge, Mass, Harvard University Press.

Chapter 2

Research Ethics

All human behavior is subject to ethical principles, rules and conventions which distinguish socially acceptable behavior from that which is generally considered unacceptable. The practice of research is no exception, but like most fields of human endeavor, acceptable standards for research on human subjects have evolved and become more formalized over time (Frankel, 1987). Until relatively recently, many researchers considered their work beyond scrutiny, presumably guided by a disinterested virtue which in their view justified any means by which to reach the hoped-for ends. Thus, in 1932, 399 semi-literate Black men with syphilis in Tuskegee, Alabama had treatment withheld, but were monitored for forty years merely to study the progression of the untreated disease. Although it had become apparent by the mid-1940s that mortality rates for the untreated people were twice as high than for the control group, the experiment went on until its exposure in the *New York Times* in 1972. Closer to home, during the period 1957–60, Ewan Cameron at McGill's Allan Memorial Institute administered psychedelic drugs to fifty-two unsuspecting patients in order to carry out brainwashing experiments for the Central Intelligence Agency of the USA. These experiments were also disclosed publicly for the first time in the *New York Times* in 1977, but it was not until 1988 that the survivors received settlement. Nor are such travesties confined to the medical and psychological fields. In education, countless children have been routinely forced to learn nonsense syllables; native children have been taken from their parents and punished severely for speaking their mother tongue; generations of left-handers have been forced to write with their right hands; most children are at some time asked to participate in questionable experiments in teaching methods; and all of us are called upon incessantly to fill out meaningless questionnaires. What principles are required to protect the innocent from such abuse?

Ethical Problems with the Topic

Ethical problems can relate both to the subject matter of the research and to its methods and procedures. The Kinsey studies on human sexuality, for example, used research to explore personal behaviors some of which themselves were contrary to law, religion or social custom. At the time, no one had valid data on the prevalence of such behaviors and publication of the report caused considerable concern in certain quarters. Ultimately, the researcher must decide the line between what is reasonable to research and the concerns of those who might not want to know.

Sometimes it is not just the topic, but also the sponsor which creates issues. In the early 1960s, the US Department of Defense launched Project Camelot, a research project to uncover the determinants of revolution in various Latin American countries. Once the intent became known, Project Camelot was quickly condemned by social scientists who viewed it as an attempt to intervene in the affairs of other countries through the results of research. In this case the motives of the sponsor were suspect, though by itself the topic may have had scientific merit. Shortly after the outcry Project Camelot was terminated.

The subject matter of research can raise other issues as well. Sometimes evaluation research uncovers practices which range from wastage of public funds to the implementation of harmful educational procedures such as labeling children. In a sense, the decision of a researcher not to conduct and publish an evaluation study might be faulted for not identifying and alerting people to these harmful effects.

Ethical Problems with the Research Procedure

The most prevalent ethical issues relate to the procedures used in conducting human experiments. The most difficult cases often use deception, and the most celebrated example is the series of experiments by Stanley Milgram conducted between 1960–64. Milgram involved volunteers who believed they were administering an electric shock to a learner involved in a learning task. Whenever the learner who was in an adjacent room made a mistake, he was 'punished' with an electric shock. The intensity was increased each time up to levels labeled 'dangerous'. Actually the learner was an experimental confederate, who cried out in pain but was never really shocked. The true purpose of these experiments was to research obedience and explore why some people refused to follow the 'orders' while others carried through. Critics charged that great harm may have been done to those who discovered that they did this terrible thing to another human. Milgram established elaborate debriefing, counseling and follow-up investigations in an attempt to safeguard the participants.

Similar charges may be made against Robert Rosenthal's studies of 'self-fulfilling prophecy' in which teachers were told of the latent talents of selected students who, according to Rosenthal's early reports, did improve subsequent performance, presumably because of the experiment's influence on the teachers. There are issues in this regard even when deception is not used. Terman's long-term study of genius (1954) identified selected individuals who were followed for years. One cannot help wonder how that identification affected their lives.

Codes of Ethics and Controls

The need for regulation and codes of behavior emerged from revelation of the atrocities committed by the Nazis in the name of research. The Nuremberg Code of 1947 for biomedical research is one of the important codes and was the first to focus on the importance of 'informed consent' as discussed later. The Helsinki Declaration of 1964 provided guidance in such areas as the use of animals for research purposes. Perhaps the earliest code in the social sciences was the 1953 code relating to research, teaching and professional practices developed from over 1000 case studies submitted by members of the American Psychological Association (APA) though a research study launched in 1948. The American Sociological Association adopted a formal code of ethics in 1969 followed four years later by the APA whose ethical code for research with human subjects has become the major standard in use by social scientists. The development and adoption of codes and procedures has been an important step mainly because it has alerted people to the problems and issues to consider. The actual judgments involved are still often difficult. Furthermore, the control continues to rest ultimately with the individual researcher and to a lesser extent with a better informed public.

Governments are also involved in controls. In the United States, what is now called the Department of Health and Human Services and the National Institutes of Health have been active in developing regulations for grant recipients. In general, they require that institutions receiving grants provide for an institutional review board to assume the protection and welfare of research participants. There are five general requirements:

1 That risks to participants are minimized by research procedures that do not unnecessarily expose subjects to risks;
2 That the risks to participants are outweighed by the anticipated benefits of the research;
3 That the rights and welfare of participants are adequately protected;
4 That the research will be periodically reviewed;
5 That informed consent has been obtained and appropriately documented.

Most universities have developed review procedures which follow the spirit of these requirements. McGill University's Faculty of Education, for example, has an informed and active Research Ethics Committee which has developed an extensive set of procedures and guidelines governing the conduct of research by McGill students, professors and researchers. The general guidelines are reproduced in Figure 2.1.

Thus, in recent years, an informed public has insisted on professional standards enforced by people other than the involved researchers. In practice, each major research unit must have a research ethics committee charged with the scrutiny of every piece of proposed research. Furthermore, most funding agencies will not fund research unless it has a certificate of ethical responsibility, complete with signatures of all members of the ethics committee. Thus, accountability rests with a group of peers willing to place their names as guarantors of the ethical standards of the research. Such practices now extend to virtually all institutionally-sanctioned research involving human subjects, including that conducted by graduate students.

Ethical Standards

Out of the efforts of professional associations, the regulation by funding agencies and the concerns of professional researchers and the public there have emerged several crucial issues which all researchers need to consider.

Figure 2.1: Ethical research guidelines

Faculty of Education, McGill University

Since ethical responsibility must be assumed by all those who conduct research involving human subjects, members of Faculty are invited to review guidelines proposed by their professional associations as well as the funding agencies from which they are seeking support. Below is a statement of some basic principles governing this subject for our Faculty.

1   The Ethics Review Committee of the Faculty of Education includes representatives from different departments and disciplines.

2   This Committee will pay special attention to (a) research involving children or captive and dependent populations and (b) research projects using deception or involving significant levels of risk.

3   The term 'subject' signifies any person who is used as a source of raw or unformulated data in the conduct of research and who is not acting in the capacity of principal investigator or assisting such an individual.

4   Care must be exercised to protect the human rights of individual groups and large collectivities. Among these are:

   a)   The right to be fully informed about the precise nature and purpose of the research in which participation is sought, so that consent may be given or withheld.

   b)   The right to know of the risks and benefits involved in participation.

   c)   The right to assurance that privacy will not be invaded and that any information disclosed will remain confidential.

   d)   The right of cultural groups to accurate and respectful description of their heritage and customs and to discreet use of information on their daily lives and aspirations.

   e)   Considering the vulnerability of children, special care must be exercised to respect the individual rights of children involved in research protocols and ensure that the research will not bring them psychological or physical harm.

   f)   The right to freely abstain from, enter into or withdraw from a research project on the basis of a fully informed personal decision.

5   No research can be done on human subjects unless they have first provided the researchers with their informed consent. In order for consent to be truly informed, the researchers:

   a)   must provide a full description of the research project including purpose, usefulness, expected benefits, methods, foreseeable effects and risks.

   b)   must explain, relative to such risks and benefits, their nature and duration; they should, further, give to the prospective subjects a careful estimate of the level of the risks inherent in their participation.

   c)   must provide participants with full and frank answers to any questions they may have with respect ot the research project.

   d)   must, with concern for limitations of their comprehension, give potential participants a complete explanation of the purpose of the research and the experimental procedures with a *careful estimate* of the risks and benefits.

   In consequence of this, resource person(s) external to the research group may be approached to answer any inquiry pertaining to the proposed research. Consent of course is considered valid only when freely given, that is, in the absence of any form of coercion, pressure or constraint. Although the consent of parents (or guardians) of minors must be sought for the latter's participation in research, the consent of the minors themselves must be sought in the measure they are capable of providing.

6   Informed consent must be provided in a written form. The form should set out the elements outlined above, to wit:

   a)   the purpose of the research

   b)   the benefits envisaged

   c)   any inconvenience involved

   d)   the tasks to be performed

   e)   the rights of the subject (withdrawal; confidentiality)

   f)   the risks involved

   g)   the names of the person(s), group(s), or institution(s) eliciting or receiving the consent.

7   Participants should be made aware of their right to withdraw their participation at any time.

8   Relative to medico-physiological and animal research, researchers should comply with the recommendations of the Helsinki Declaration.

Informed Consent

The most fundamental principle for ethical acceptability is that of informed consent: the involved participants must be informed of the nature and purpose of the research, its risks and benefits, and must consent to participate without coercion. There are six basic elements to informed consent: (1) an explanation of the procedures used in the experiment and their purposes, (2) a description of any reasonably foreseeable risks and discomforts to the subjects, (3) a description of any benefits that may reasonably be expected, (4) a disclosure of any alternative procedures that might be advantageous to the subject, (5) an offer to answer any questions concerning the procedures, and (6) a statement that participation is voluntary and that the subject is free to withdraw from participation at any time. In practice, many situations require that an informed consent form be duly signed before a participant is permitted to participate. Such a form should describe the purpose of the research, its benefits, the nature of the tasks to be performed, the rights of the participant to withdraw and the names of the person and institution conducting the research. This makes everything clear and provides a degree of proof that the person was informed and consented to become involved. Naturally, the information needs to be suited to the language, culture and age of the participants. Participants who are coerced to get involved, such as prison inmates, or those in search of monetary rewards, are not assumed to have consented voluntarily, so in recent times such groups are rarely used in social science research. The Food and Drug Administration in the United States no longer permits data obtained from captives to be admissible in human trials of new drugs.

Unfortunately, the best intentions behind the principle of informed consent have not necessarily led to more ethically defensible outcomes (Adair, Dushenko and Lindsay, 1985). In practice it is relatively easy to get participants to sign an informed consent form, particularly because of their inherent trust of a scientific leader whose individual attention to the participant becomes a subtle form of coercion.

Use of Volunteers

Most social science studies ask people to volunteer as participants. This raises two major ethical problems. First, the people most inclined to volunteer tend to be the most powerless in society. They look up to the researcher and in some cases, such as when students are involved, the researcher has a position of power over the 'volunteers' who are really subjected to coercion. The second and related problem is that people will volunteer in the expectation that they may be helped. Any new educational program offers hope to those whose problems may not have been addressed in the past, and the risk is that the researcher may lead people on, offering them some hope when before there was none.

A related issue is selection and labeling of participants. By identifying people as having attributes, deficits or potentials, you may unwittingly affect their lives.

Honesty

Investigators should be honest and open. Some experiments call for the use of deception, or telling the subject that the purpose or method of the experiment is one thing when in fact it is quite another. Deception is seldom warranted and in the rare instances when it is, the potential benefits from the research should exceed any known risks. Furthermore, the investigator should take special steps to explain the deception after the experiment and restore a relationship of honesty.

Right to Discontinue

Ethical research practice requires the researcher to respect the participant's right to discontinue at any time. This is an important safeguard particularly when individuals feel that ethical principles have been or may be violated. It is frequently used by people filling out questionnaires (who merely leave offensive questions blank or do not return the questionnaire), but is not as easily exercised by persons who are captive in a group such as a school class. There are also subtle forces between researcher and participant which generally makes it difficult for the participant to stop unless there is good reason.

Debriefing

Once the data are collected, ethical practice suggests that the investigator informs participants about the experiment and clarifies any questions which may arise. The debriefing also permits the researcher to provide additional information which if given in advance may have biased the results. In studies which employ questionnaires or tests it is advisable when possible to offer participants a summary of results.

Confidentiality

Confidentiality involves a clear understanding between the researcher and participant concerning the use to be made of the data provided. Confidential information implies that the identity of the individual will remain anonymous. It assumes as well that the reader of the research will not be able to deduce the identity of the individual. Information may be quoted and reported but the identity of the individual should be protected. While it is the duty of the researcher to protect the identity of individuals there is a distinction between one's public role and private life. It is generally agreed that reports on behavior of someone in public office performing the role of their job can be disclosed but their personal life should be protected.

Right to Privacy

The right to privacy is an important right and implies that the individual concerned should decide what aspects of their personal attitudes, opinions, habits, eccentricities, doubts and fears are to be communicated or withheld from others. There are major international codes of human rights such as the United Nations' Universal Declaration of Human Rights that hold privacy as a basic right. This has been incorporated in all codes of research ethics. One-way mirrors, concealed microphones, video cameras and many other technical devices are all formidable threats to privacy. When these are used special care must be taken for informed consent. It is understandable in the interest of scientific rigor to use such devices but those informed should consent to their use. Note that invasion of privacy cannot be claimed once informed consent has been willingly agreed. The general strategy for protecting privacy is to avoid linking data to the concerned respondent. Many procedures are used generally involving codes and the separation of code keys from the raw data. There are pitfalls ranging from accidental disclosure to legal requirements that certain data be made available to law enforcement authorities. In general, it is advisable to apply and use codes as early as possible in the research process. Researchers should also consider whether it is absolutely necessary to identify individual participants.

Respecting the Participant's Time

Although seldom mentioned in standard works on research ethics, it is unethical to waste the participant's time by asking him or her to complete irrelevant questions or participate in studies which by their nature cannot lead to significant results.

Risks/Benefits

In any social science research the potential benefits must outweigh the risks to individual participants. There are occasions, such as in medical research, when the risks are high but are tolerated because of the potential to aid great numbers of people. While difficult to assess, this benefit is an essential consideration in certain types of research.

Vulnerable Populations

Certain groups of people are particularly vulnerable to damage as research subjects due to their age, limited mental capacity or their psychological disposition. Special care is required in dealing with such populations.

Risk to Cultural and Proprietary Values

Special care must be taken in dealing with sensitive populations whose cultures are fragile. Removing of archaeological artifacts, the inappropriate storage or display of sacred objects, the taking of photographs in certain cultures are examples. Common courtesy dictates a need to understand what one is doing and to go as far as possible to protect cultural values. Similarly a researcher should not impose foreign values or introduce disruptive ideas when performing a research role. There is a place for educating people of all cultures, but it is not a legitimate part of the researcher's role.

Different Cultures

Research involving people of different countries and cultures requires special care (see Hamnet, 1978). Informed consent is difficult, both because of linguistic barriers and because it is often difficult for people in other cultures to understand the nature of research and its uses. Researchers operating in other cultures generally have an advantage of wealth and power and it is easy, therefore, willingly or unwillingly to coerce subjects to participate. An important safeguard is to involve researchers from the other culture to assist in explaining the research and in interpreting its results.

Conclusion

When developing a research proposal, consider the methodology you intend to employ and its relationship to the various principles articulated here. You should be able to answer the questions raised by each of the issues listed. You should also find out the rules and procedures governing ethical approval at your own university and take early steps to fulfill the institutional requirements. These procedures often take considerable time, so it is wise to think ahead and not jeopardize your research on the failure to comply with a technical requirement.

No listing of principles of ethics can cover all eventualities. However, the above principles provide a framework within which proposed research may be examined. Ethical responsibility, of course, begins with the individual researcher and the researcher is the main determinant of ethical standards. As well, both in their professional practice and as potential subjects for research, educators have a responsibility to know ethical principles and help ensure that they are followed in their schools and with their students.

For Further Study

KIMMEL, A.J. (1988) *Ethics and Values in Applied Social Research*, Beverly Hills, Sage.

References

ADAIR, J.G., DUSHENKO, T.W. and LINDSAY, R.C.L. (1985) 'Ethical regulations and their impact on research practices', *American Psychologist*, 40, pp. 59–72.

HAMNET, M.P. (1978) 'Ethics and Expections in Cross-cultural Social Science Research.' Paper presented to the Second Annual Conference on Intercultural Communication, Tampa, Florida. ERIC ED 162372.

FRANKEL, M.S. (Ed.) (1987) *Values and Ethics in Organization and Human Systems Development: An Annotated Bibliography*, American Association for the Advancement of Science.

TERMAN, L.M. (1954) 'The discovery and encouragement of exceptional talent', *American Psychologist*, 9, pp. 221–30.

Chapter 3

Defining a Research Problem

The old cliché that a problem well stated is half solved, applies perfectly to educational research. It may be easy to decide on a general area of research interest and to have some idea of the general thrust of a research study, but it is not nearly so simple to state the problem in terms which limit the problem without robbing it of its significance. Many graduate students spend months refining a problem, only then to abandon it as once it has been adequately articulated it loses its appeal. The task of defining a research problem requires a combination of experience and intuition, and efforts spent in developing the required skills are useful even though a specific problem may be abandoned.

Developing research problems and conducting the study is analogous to attempting to build your own house. While we all have at least a general idea of the kind of house we would like to live in, we are differentially equipped to build it. Some people will have a very clear idea of the specific requirements for the house — of how it will be sited, of its proportions, space allocation and style. Others will have only vague ideas and will require considerable assistance from professionals in order to come up with an appropriate design. Needless to say, basic building skills, experience in the use of tools and the ability to develop and follow a plan are essential if the task of construction is to be accomplished. The first effort, of course, should be more modest than later efforts because it is a learning experience and training ground in the necessary skills. The most successful beginning house builder will follow the established models and will break new ground in only minor ways.

To put the task of writing a thesis in perspective, there are more than 20,000 articles published in educational journals each year and there have been over half a million masters and doctoral theses written in North America alone. The next thesis will add one more small contribution to a vast and expanding universe of knowledge. Despite the vast quantity of work, there are rarely major individual breakthroughs. Thousands of studies add up to very little in the way of concrete knowledge. Rather, there tend to be modest advances which together, over time, add up to a better understanding. In this context, a graduate student thesis should not be viewed as a vade mecum. It will not be the definitive work that will revolutionize the field of education, and if viewed as such, the author can only be disappointed. Treat your thesis for what it is: a good if modest contribution to the advancement of knowledge, but one of the most significant steps in your own education. The purpose of this chapter is to help graduate students define a research problem that will do this for them.

Approaches to Thesis Research

There are essentially three general approaches to an education thesis. One involves a prescriptive method which follows established models adding some small nuance of difference to work which has gone on previously. This often assumes a 'building block' notion of knowledge: that numbers of studies on a similar topic will together add up to a complete fortress of knowledge about the subject. More importantly, it is a good way of teaching and learning basic research skills while making a more useful contribution to the advancement of knowledge than would be made by creating totally new questions, methods and research tools. This, in its most disciplined and highly developed fashion, is closest to the approach of the physical sciences. It is used most often in educational psychology. In many universities, research shops attack a given theme and do so over a period of years. Generations of graduate students follow similar procedures and each adds a new bit to the accumulated wisdom. As previously noted, this prescriptive approach is a good way to learn about research. Having been walked before, the path is clear. One knows the limits of the field, the preparation which must precede formulation of the problem and what type of problem will be accepted. As for the research itself, models are there to follow. Furthermore, other researchers are interested in the problem and there are generally funds and support which see the problem through to a logical conclusion. For those who do not join a research team such an approach is still partially possible by referring to exemplary published studies and existing models from the literature.

A second approach is a more individualized approach, often followed by students to address a topic of individual interest. Most students are inclined to develop research interests out of their experience rather than through a base in the research literature, so many adopt problems without regard to their standing in the field. They select the problem and work back to the literature trying to find studies which support their interest. Problems so defined may integrate various methods, fields of study and sources of data and are generally less likely to be at the higher levels of research (generalization and basic) than those following the prescriptive approach. In its best form this approach borrows the procedures and methods of the prescriptive model, but does so over time and across space. The individual approach lends itself well to explanatory research and a wide range of descriptive studies. Its difficulty is in its lack of boundaries and lack of focus. It is very easy under this approach to take on too large a problem and never get closure on it.

The third approach which is not really an approach at all might be termed muddling-through. I have included it because it tends to be one of the most common ways in which graduate students write their theses. In short, the muddling-through approach takes a general topic area, begins doing research and collecting data, and probably does not define the problem sharply until after the study is almost complete. Then it must be rewritten and recast in terms that relate to the problem which has now been defined. It is recommended only for those who have unlimited time and resources and who thrive on inductive solutions to life's problems.

One should not assume by the foregoing that research is merely a static and deductive process. On the contrary, good research is characterized by an evolving dynamic such that the research problems and questions may only be articulated fully when the study is far advanced. The ongoing process of collecting and analyzing data, endless discussions with others who bring new perspectives to bear and limitless personal thought and deduction may transform a routine problem into something new and different. In an extreme example, I was conducting research on the letters of nineteenth-century Canadian Governors General when I uncovered in the National Archives a previously unrecorded diary which led me in a totally new direction on a new problem (Anderson, 1984).

Asking the Right Question

What is an appropriate research question? This is the fundamental issue for most researchers. There are two considerations, the topic and the scope. With respect to topic, you need a question which will sustain your interest and one in which your colleagues or supervisors can assist you. You should also consider its relevance and potency in the field of research at this point in time. This is where a sound review of the research literature is important (see Chapter 8). It should tell you whether your topic is timely or whether interest in it has waned. You might also want to review recent theses in your university to see whether others might have begun related explorations which suggest the utility of continuation.

Once you have defined a general topic area, the problem is to formulate the specific research problem or questions with just the right scope. It is easy and tempting to 'research the world': That is, it is simple to ask a question so broad that it will always contain more meat. For example: 'What is an effective school?' Such questions are good topics for a speech or a book, but they are too big to be useful research questions. By the same token, a question which is overly specific can easily be addressed, but it may have no relevance beyond the immediate situation and little interest except to those directly involved. The challenge is to ask a question at the right level of breadth or abstraction.

It is relatively easy to generate research questions but less easy to generate questions at the right level of abstraction for your resources and abilities. To choose a problem which is overly specific is to rob the research of any generalizability. To select a problem which is overly broad will prevent you from getting any closure on its resolution. How does one choose a problem at the right level of abstraction?

It is useful in thinking of research questions to think in terms of a ladder of abstraction as summarized in Figure 3.1. The illustration shows that a given area of interest can be expressed on a continuim from the highly specific to the very general. You will find it useful in defining research questions to learn how to change the level of abstraction. Take any researchable question and make it one level more specific or one level more general. You may continue this exercise until you have a whole hierarchy of questions ranging in specificity. In general when you define a research problem, you will have sub-questions. Experience and counsel from those who know about

Figure 3.1: Research questions at different levels of abstraction

1 What major factors enhance the transfer of training from school to daily living?
2 What major factors enhance the transfer of second language learning to daily living?
3 What major factors enhance the transfer of French learned as a second language to daily living?
4 What major factors enhance the transfer of correct usage of the subjunctive tense in French to daily living?
5 What major factors enhance the transfer of correct usage of the subjunctive tense of the French verb 'to be' to daily living?

research will enable you to choose the level of abstraction suitable to your capabilities and resources. It will also show you that even though you may have a fairly narrow and specific interest it relates to a more general sphere of research interest.

Characteristics of a Good Thesis Research Problem

Figure 3.2 summarizes ten important characteristics of a good research problem for a thesis. The list enables one to examine any research problem and see the extent to which it measures up. Obviously, few problems will achieve all ten characteristics but good problems should fulfill most of these requirements. A few words are in order about each of them.

1 *The problem can be stated clearly and concisely*
 Unless the problem can be stated clearly and concisely it is probably a poor problem or a non-problem. The best way to test the problem statement is to write it into a concise sentence or paragraph and to share it with others. If the problem cannot be stated in a clear paragraph it has difficulties and will not endure as a suitable problem. Of course, it is not easy to express complex issues in simplistic terms and it may take many weeks and countless drafts before the statement is satisfactory. Good critics are essential. If your spouse or mother can't understand it, it is probably flaky.

2 *The problem generates research questions*
 The problem should generate a number of more specific research questions. These turn the problem into a question format and represent various aspects or components of the problem. The research questions make the more general statement easier to address and provide a framework for the research. Formulation of such questions can be challenging,

particularly the specification of questions at the right level of abstraction.

3 *It is grounded in theory*
Good problems have theoretical and/or conceptual frameworks for their analysis (see Chapter 5). They relate the specifics of what is being investigated to a more general background of theory which helps interpret the results and link it to the field.

4 *It relates to one or more academic disciplines*
Good problems relate to academic disciplines. The disciplines might be sociology or psychology or management science, or whatever, but problems which do not have clear links to one or two disciplines generally are in trouble. Without a discipline it becomes impossible to determine where in the universe of knowledge the problem lies.

5 *It has a base in the research literature*
Related to the former points, a well-stated problem will relate to a research literature. Tight problems often relate to a well-defined body of literature written by a select group of researchers and published in a small number of journals. With some problems it might at first be difficult to establish the connections and literature base, but there should be a base somewhere (see Chapter 8 for a further discussion of this issue).

6 *It has potential significance/importance*
This is the important 'so what' question: Who cares once you solve the problem? Assume that you have solved the problem and answered the questions and then ask yourself whether you are then any further ahead. At the very least the problem must have importance to the researcher, but ideally it should also be of consequence to others as well.

7 *It is do-able within the time frame, budget*
There are logistic factors in terms of your ability actually to carry out the research. There is no point pursuing a problem which is not feasible to research. Don't do a study of education in India unless you have the means to go there and collect data — which may require years to collect. This factor helps explain why few theses relate to longitudinal data. The only exceptions come from research shops where there is a long history of collecting and studying data on a defined population. Terman's study of genius (1954) in which a defined sample was traced over thirty years, is a good example.

Figure 3.2: Characteristics of a good thesis research problem

---

1 The problem can be stated clearly and concisely.
2 The problem generates research questions.
3 It is grounded in theory.
4 It relates to one or more academic disciplines.
5 It has a base in the research literature.
6 It has potential significance/importance.
7 It is do-able within the time frame, budget.
8 Sufficient data are available or can be obtained.
9 The researcher's methodological strengths can be applied to the problem.
10 The problem is new; it is not already answered sufficiently.

---

8 *Sufficient data are available or can be obtained*

In some cases, there are insufficient data to address the problem. Historical persons may have died, archival materials may be lost, or there may be restrictions on access to certain environments. As noted, it is difficult to conduct research on a distant country unless you can go there and collect local data. One under-used approach is to use an existing data base. Some data banks have been developed over many years and contain many opportunities for exploration of new questions and issues.

9 *The researcher's methodological strengths can be applied to the problem*

As well as being grounded in a discipline, a good problem is generally related to some sort of standard methodology. This might be historical, or comparative or empirical, but it should build on the strengths of the investigator. There is no point conducting research on a problem that is best addressed with statistics if statistics are not your strength. Consider your problem carefully and ask whether your background is appropriate to tackle it.

10 *The problem is new; it is not already answered sufficiently*

While this is often a concern to new researchers, it is generally not an insurmountable problem. Once one knows the field, it becomes clear what has been done and what needs to be done. The danger applies mostly to problems which are stated prematurely without adequate knowledge of the field. If you know and can analyze the relevant literature you can often easily identify the most logical steps which need to be researched.

Some Finished Examples

The suggested approach to defining a research problem is to develop it to the stage where it can be written in a concise paragraph or two followed by specific research questions which can further define the study. I have found that four to eight questions are about the right number, but these are generally broken down into many more sub-questions (See Chapter 5 for further discussion). While it often appears straightforward once it has reached its final form, the problem definition process can take many months. Often the problem gets changed and refined as the study takes place, so the final form does not emerge until the study is finished.

Over the last several years, I have worked with my students to express their research problems in the suggested format. All types of problems incorporating all sorts of research approaches lend themselves to this type of expression. I have found that it forces you to define your problem precisely and eliminates the frequent pattern of lengthy rambling around the problem without ever coming to grips with its essence.

Figures 3.3–3.8 present six problem statements from recent graduates who have worked under the author's supervision. The desired format is for the researcher to introduce the problem by providing a paragraph of rationale for its study which might include reference to prior research and theory, followed by a concise paragraph on the purpose of the study, followed by research questions and sub-questions.

Students find it difficult to define the purpose and are encouraged to do so by completing the sentence 'The purpose of this study is to ...'. It is not easy to express the purpose in a single sentence in this way, but if you can do so you generally know what you are doing.

The particular examples shown here have been abstracted from more lengthy proposals or completed theses and in some cases I have omitted the rationale and reference to previous research.

The examples represent various levels of research as defined in Chapter 1. The study by Beals (1987) was restricted to description and explanation. It was motivated by a desire to understand and explain recent historical events and there was little interest in or opportunity for generalization. This is often the case with historical studies which are justified solely on the basis of understanding and explanation. The studies by Rice (1986) and Hatfield (1987) move to the generalization level and consider possible extension to broader populations. Another

Figure 3.3: The role in elementary and secondary education of the federal Office of the Secretary of State

The purpose of this study is to describe the involvement of the federal Office of the Secretary of State in elementary and secondary schooling during the period 1970–1985, and to identify both the goals, and the source of the goals, of these initiatives in education.

Research Questions

1 To what extent is the federal Office of the Secretary of State (OSS) involved in elementary and secondary education, and how has this involvement evolved during the period 1970–1985?

   1.1   What are the specific education programs administered by OSS?

   1.2   Which programs are directed toward the public school system, and which towards non-formal education?

   1.3   What is the funding pattern for these education programs?

   1.4   How has the funding pattern changed during the period under study?

2 During the period 1970–1985, did the government of Canada have what might be construed as national goals for elementary and secondary education?

   2.1   If national goals existed, what were they?

   2.2   Where did these goals originate — i.e., what fundamental philosophy or agenda gave rise to these goals?

   2.3   Were these goals clearly defined and articulated, or were they concealed?

   2.4   Did these goals have a basis in legislation or policy documents and papers?

   2.5   How did the educational programs administered by the OSS relate to the national goals?

3 To what extent were the educational goals of the federal government, during the period 1970–1985, a reflection of the political agenda of P.E. Trudeau, Prime Minister of Canada?

   3.1   What were the fundamental philosophical and political principles which guided P.E. Trudeau?

   3.2   How were these principles reflected in his political agenda?

   3.3   To what extent were the educational goals of the programs administered by the Office of the Secretary of State a reflection of P.E. Trudeau's political agenda?

(Beals, 1987, pp. i, 10–12)

interesting point is how the studies by Rice, Hatfield and Rona interrelate. Those by Rice and Hatfield were similar in design though they used two entirely different populations. They provide an example of how a subsequent study can borrow methodological approaches from an earlier piece of work. Both describe and explain relative to the group under study and suggest some areas of potential generalization. Rona (1988) later extended Hatfield's study through an in-depth analysis of one school in Hatfield's sample. The study of Algranti (1988) spans all three levels and also begins to examine more general principles related to the transfer of training to the job. That by Jones (1988) relates to an evaluation type study, but one with profound general and potentially generalizable implications.

Figure 3.4: Factors which influence older adults to participate in education: The Elderhostel experience in Atlantic Canada

The provision of educational opportunities specifically for the 'aged' began in the 1960s, and research has identified characteristics of older adults which may predict participation in such activities. Though opportunities are provided, the rate of participation of persons over the age of 60 years in these programmes remains low. The factors which influence registration in popular programmes (i.e., those which attract older adults) become of interest to planners and organizers of such activities, as well as to administrators of institutions faced with declining enrollments.

The purpose of this study is to determine the factors which motivate decisions to participate in Elderhostel programmes. The personal and background characteristics of the participants, their needs and situational circumstances, the content and organization of the educational experience, will be examined in an attempt to determine the effects these have on participation in Elderhostel. In addition, previous participation in education will be examined in an attempt to determine the influence on participation in education in general, and in Elderhostel in particular. Also of interest is whether situational and organizational factors influence participation differently according to personal and background characteristics of participants.

It is expected that the investigation will provide insights into the types of programmes which attract older adults, and the motivational factors which influence participation of this population in education.

Research Questions

The study was defined by the following questions with specific areas of interest noted as sub-questions:

1   What are the personal characteristics of Elderhostelers?
   1.1   What are the characteristics of hostelers with respect to citizenship, age, sex, marital status, educational background, previous participation in a variety of activities and health?
   1.2   Do hostelers attend programmes alone or in the company of a spouse or companion?
2   What reasons do hostelers state as primary motivators of participation?
3   What general categories of subject matter attract Elderhostelers?
4   What are preferred organizational characteristics in educational experiences?
   a)   To what extent do the travel and residential components attract participants to Elderhostel programmes?
   b)   Do non-traditional models of education attract the older population? (e.g., media, distance, non-credit, mini-course).
   c)   Does cost influence decisions to participate in such courses?
   d)   Does the frequency and form of contact by Elderhostel administrators (national and campus) influence decisions to participate in Elderhostel programs?
   e)   What is the time lapse between learning about and participating in Elderhostel programs?
5   To what extent are motivators, subject matter, preferences and desired organizational characteristics different according to personal and background characteristics (e.g., citizenship, age, marital status, attending alone or in the company of another, educational background)?
6   Do different sub-groups have different preferences in organizational characteristics?

(Rice, 1986, pp. 12–13, 34)

Fundamentals of Educational Research

Figure 3.5: Return motivation and subsequent satisfaction among former high school dropouts

The purpose of the study is to examine motivation for return to school, subsequent satisfaction, and the relationship between motivating factors and subsequent expressed satisfaction among students enrolled in Outreach schools in the Montreal area. These schools are defined as autonomous institutions catering to the needs of students who have dropped out of the regular high school system.

The following research questions were addressed:

1   What reasons do Montreal students state as primary motivators for returning to school?
2   Do differences in motivation exist between sub-groups which differ in background characteristics?
3   To what extent are Montreal Outreach students satisfied with their present school experience?
4   To what extent is satisfaction different according to background characteristics?

(Hatfield, 1986, pp. 11–14)

Figure 3.6: The effects of training on job performance: A study of the factors affecting the learning transfer process in Employment and Immigration Canada (EIC)

The purpose of this study is to examine the effects of a training program on the subsequent performance of operational tasks. This study goes beyond the course itself, the content, the teaching methods used in presenting the subject matter, the course design and so on. It traces the transfer of learning from the course to the job, and offers an analysis of the factors which influence transfer.

The characteristics of the participants and their ability to comprehend and experiment with the new learning are examined as are the motivational factors which influence the transfer of learning. It was expected that the value placed on the course and the learning gained by the participants, as well as the encouragement offered in the workplace, would affect the participant's perceptions and attitudes in the matter of learning transfer. The job of identifying some of the organizational elements that appear to inhibit or encourage the transfer of training is both an important and difficult one.

The question which is particularly difficult to answer and which this study addresses is what difference, if any, did training make back on the job? Since the aim of job-related training is to improve performance on the job, transfer failure obviously defeats the purpose. When trainees return to their jobs after participating in a training program, how do we know whether or not they are doing anything differently, or anything better?

This study investigated general considerations in the field of training through specific reference to EIC and employment counselors trained in employer services:

1   Do the participants achieve the course objectives?
2   Which skills developed and knowledge acquired by participants in training are transferred to the job?
    2.1   What is the effect of the training on the experimenters' jobs?
3   What is the importance of learner characteristics in enhancing transfer?
4   What is the importance of participant perceptions of training in enhancing transfer?
5   What roles do the work environment and the supervisor play in the transfer process?
6   Are there any other factors which enhance transfer?

(Algranti, 1988, pp. 11–12, 26)

Figure 3.7:   Characteristics of effectiveness of an alternative high school: A follow-up study of its graduates

---

The high school dropout is a source of serious concern for educators and society at large. For educators, the dropout represents not only a sense of personal failure for teachers but also a failure of the school system as a whole to meet the needs of its clientele, not to mention the potential loss of jobs for teachers and funding for school boards. Dropping out of high school also incurs a wide array of individual and social costs. For the individual, failure to complete high school is linked with limited occupational and economic prospects and a rejection by society and its institutions. On a societal level, premature school leaving results in increased expenditures for government assistance, higher rates of crime, and the maintenance of costly special programs for employment and training (King, 1978; Levin, 1972). Recent statistics indicate that one-third of young people who enter high school in Quebec drop out prior to completion (Blouin and Martino, 1986). Given the magnitude of the problem, the question that must be addressed is what solutions are being sought to alleviate this growing concern.

Although much research has examined the characteristics of dropouts and the causes of dropping out, very few studies have considered alternative programs designed to help high school dropouts to complete their secondary education. One large urban school board in the Montreal area has developed a network of independent publicly funded schools dedicated to the education of dropouts who wish to continue their high school education. Hatfield (1987) studied student satisfaction in these alternative schools and found that students are generally experiencing more satisfaction in them than in their previous high schools. It seems that the key to curbing the dropout problem is to provide programs that are attractive enough to hold these students and effective enough to promote their learning and development. In an attempt to understand better the nature of effective schooling for dropouts, this study examines the characteristics of effectiveness of one such high school for dropouts from the perspective of its graduates and of students currently enrolled. It looks at the extent to which students currently enrolled perceive their school to be effective. It also examines the extent to which the school is effective and identifies its factors of effectiveness. It seeks to answer the following questions:

1   What are the characteristics of effective schools?
2   To what extent do Options II students perceive the effectiveness characteristics as found in the literature?
3   To what extent is Options II effective as measured by:
    3.1   Achievement of school objectives
    3.2   Success of its graduates
4   What factors made Options II effective for its graduates?
    4.1   What is the relationship between the impact of Options II on its graduates and its factors of effectiveness?

(Rona, 1988, pp. 1–2, 42–43)

The Evolution of a Problem

The problem statements of the previous section represent the finished product. They all went through various stages of evolution before they reached their penultimate formulation. Figure 3.9 shows a much earlier form of a problem (Maonga, 1988). In this case, the student submitted two problems in roughly the same stage of development and asked my advice about which he should pursue. I recommended the one shown in Figure 3.9 and suggested how it might be developed. After considerable work, Timothy submitted a second draft

Figure 3.8: The foreign language program at the Episcopal School of Dallas: A case study

The place of foreign languages in the school curriculum has been, at best, equivocal and tentative in the history of traditional Western education. Before the thirteenth century, languages other than Greek and Latin were not formally taught (Kelly, 1976). Only in the latter part of the nineteenth century were modern or foreign languages attributed the status of academic subjects in British secondary curricula. Their evolution from a social skill to a mental, academic discipline worthy of competing with Greek and Latin developed out of the social and educational climate of the time; and according to Bayley (1987), their inclusion in the curriculum was largely a result of royal commission policies. Now, it seems that the pendulum has swung back towards the social skills with curricular goals of communication in foreign language teaching.

The purpose of this study is to examine the place of the foreign language program in the general curriculum of the Episcopal School of Dallas, where the Board of Directors has recently approved a recommendation by the Academic Council for changes in graduation requirements in science, history, foreign languages and physical education. The major issues of this investigation will be concerned with how the new foreign language requirement of three years instead of two will affect existing curriculum. It is expected that this study will provide insights into what kinds of educational contributions the foreign language program makes to the school and how these contributions match up with the school community's expectations of a foreign language program. Because this is essentially a study of curriculum development, fundamental questions will be raised: what languages can and should be taught, to whom, when and how? An initial investigation of policy and curriculum will serve as a background in which to situate the study. More literature will need to be reviewed as the process unfolds.

Research Questions

This study will address the following questions.

1   What considerations led to the change in graduation requirements?
    1.1   What is the stated philosophy of the school, and how do the new requirements reflect this philosophy?
    1.2   Has the student population evolved since the early years of the school?
    1.3   How do language teachers interpret the curricular implications of the new requirements?
2   How do students feel about learning a foreign language?
    2.1   What reasons do they state for choosing a particular language to study?
    2.2   What are student expectations about learning a foreign language?
    2.3   How do students rate their language experience at the school?
3   What implications does the new requirement have on the existing foreign language curriculum?
    3.1   Which students have typically fulfilled just the minimum requirement of two years, and why?
    3.2   Is the new minimum requirement of three years feasible for students with learning problems in the existing curriculum?
    3.3   Which students typically continue in advanced courses?
    3.4   Will the new language requirement increase enrollments in advanced placement courses?
4   How does the middle school language program articulate with the upper school curriculum?
    4.1   Are exploratory courses in Spanish and French preferable to Spanish or French only?
    4.2   Does the curriculum favor Latin in the 7th and 8th grades to the detriment of the modern languages?
5   What are reasonable goals for the foreign language program?
    5.1   Is a proficiency-based curriculum feasible within the context of the 'seat' requirement of three years?
    5.2   Are goals generalizable from language to language?

Figure 3.8:   *(cont.)*

---

6   Can the success of the program be determined by upper school – college
    articulation?
    6.1   How many Episcopal students continue studying the same language at
          university in the projected sequence?
    6.2   How many Episcopal students are *faux-debutantes* in language courses at
          university?
    6.3   How many students choose to study a new language, and what are their
          reasons?

(Jones, 1988, pp. 1 – 2, 16 – 18)

Figure 3.9:   The implication of the 8:4:4 system of education to the teaching of geography in Kenyan secondary schools

---

In 1985 the Kenya government changed its education system from the 7:4:2:3 System to the 8:4:4 System of education. This meant the change of the duration and academic content at every level of the school system.

The purpose of this study is to assess to what extent is the new geography curriculum different from the old and assess the perceptions of the teachers and students to the new curriculum. Finally the study will examine how effectively the new geography curriculum is being implemented in schools.

Figure 3.10:   The effectiveness of the new geography curriculum at secondary school level in Kenya.

1.0 INTRODUCTION

In 1985 the Kenya government changed its education system from the 7:4:2:3 System to the 8:4:4 System of education. This meant a change of the duration and academic content of all subjects at every level of the school system. As with many educational reforms, the goals of the 8:4:4 curriculum are sometimes different but rarely radically new by comparison with the alternatives it has replaced. The most noticeable difference is that the new curriculum put more emphasis on practicals. That is, each subject area should be geared at making learners self reliant.

Fullan and Pomfret (1977), identified four different, but related reasons for studying implementation. They are (a) the documentation of the features of the curriculum change, (b) the identification of important variables associated with installation of a new program, (c) the determination of which curriculum features are related to the outcome measures, and (d) to understand some of the reasons so many education changes fail to become established. Revicki and others (1981) believe that the measurement of implementation of the attributes of programs allows for a more accurate evaluation of the program. Investigation of the relationship between level of implementation of program attributes to relevant outcome measures provides program developers with the necessary empirical information for fine tuning innovative programs. The collection of implementation information by program users should thus serve a diagnostic function.

1.1 STATEMENT OF THE PROBLEM

This study will determine and assess how successful or effective the implementation of the new secondary school geography curriculum (syllabus) is, within the context of the 8:4:4 system of education. In particular the study will look at how the teachers understand the new geography curriculum, how they are implementing it, and how they have and are being assisted by the curriculum developers in implementing it. The students' attitudes towards the new geography curriculum will also be assessed. Finally this study will deal with determining how the effective implementation of the geography curriculum meets the needs of the 8:4:4 System of education.

41

Figure 3.10: (cont.)

1.2 THEORETICAL FRAMEWORK

Most curriculum developers and evaluators have normally considered the adoption of innovation in a curriculum to be linked to the input-ouput model. They had neglected the process, which is the implementation part. Therefore in focusing on curriculum implementation, we are saying that the process is also important, and it actually influences the outcome. In fact, to borrow from the well-known distinction of curriculum levels proposed by Goodlad et al (1979) one might argue that it is implementation which is key to the teachers and students, who play a major role in success of any educational innovation. Goodlad's levels of curriculum are: a) ideal curriculum, b) perceived curriculum, c) operational curriculum, and d) experiential curriculum. Of these four levels, the teachers and pupils are involved in the last three. The success of the curriculum implementation will be determined by the effective application of the three levels.

A look at the input-output model will show that the process aspect in curriculum innovations has always been neglected. The determinants of curriculum implementation will be the ones that might suggest some conceptual framework for this study. The determinants of curriculum implementation as cited by many scholars are: characteristics of the innovation, strategies, characteristics of adopting units and characteristics of macro-sociopolitical units (Fullan, 1972; Cole, 1971; and Siebber, 1973). These factors are empirically derived from most recent studies on curriculum implementation. And as Fullan and Pomfret in 1977 said, these factors can guide us in the study of curriculum implementation for there is no comprehensive and coherent theory of implementation.

1.3 RESEARCH QUESTIONS

1 How is the new geography curriculum organized?
    a) Does it clearly state and describe the content?
    b) Is the curriculum balanced and of intellectual and social worth?
    c) Does it clearly state the methods to be used in teaching?
    d) Does it clearly show the methods of evaluation?
2 How were teachers prepared to implement the new geography curriculum?
    a) What strategies were suggested by curriculum developers for use in implementing the new curriculum?
    b) Are these strategies effective in terms of achieving the curriculum objectives?
3 How is the subject being implemented in class?
    a) Do teachers use relevant teaching techniques appropriately?
    b) Do they use fieldwork, case studies, systems and models, simulations and games to help students understand problem solving techniques?
4 Do teachers and curriculum developers in geography have the same viewpoints about the new curriculum?
    a) Is their understanding of the goals and purposes of the new curriculum the same or different?
5 What are the teachers' and students' attitudes towards the subject?
    a) Do teachers think that the course content is over-inflated or under-inflated?
    b) Are the teachers satisfied with the new geography syllabus?
    c) Are students motivated and how does their performance compare to the previous performances at the same level or grade?
6 How effective is the geography curriculum implementation within the context of the 8:4:4 System of education?

(Maonga, 1988, pp. 1–4)

---

which essentially expanded the introductory paragraph and added research questions. The third version is shown in Figure 3.10 which added the second paragraph relating it to the literature and the theoretical framework. The research questions were refined only slightly from those in the second draft. It should be emphasized that what is shown in Figure 3.9 is merely the proposal. It will be further refined and probably trimmed as the study takes place. The important thing is that the problem statement has potential and that subsequent versions are directional. If you begin with a fairly clear area it is relatively easy to refine it. A problem which is ambiguous in the first instance is difficult to refine.

Conclusion

There is probably nothing in one's university education that can compare to the preparation of an original research thesis. It involves a lengthy commitment and difficult challenges. One not only learns a great deal about a narrow area of content, but more importantly, one learns how to write a coherent and purposeful report. Most people learn new things about themselves, their strengths and limitations and develop their self-confidence. At its best it is a rewarding and exhilarating experience. At its worst it is an unbearable chore. In large measure the particular research problem is what makes the difference. You must live with the problem a long time, so make sure you choose it well.

References

ALGRANTI, C.A. (1988) 'The Effects of Training on Job Performance: A Study of the Factors Effecting the Learning Transfer Process.' Unpublished MA Thesis, McGill University, Montreal.

ANDERSON, G. (1984) 'The Diary of James McGill Strachan: A Trip to the Mingan, 1849', *Atlantic Salmon Journal*, 33, 2, pp. 12–14.

HATFIELD, D. (1987) 'Motivation to Return and Subsequent Satisfaction among High School Students enrolled in Montreal Area Outreach Schools.' Unpublished MA Thesis, McGill University, Montreal.

JONES, J.G. (1988) 'Statement of Research Proposal', Course Assignment, McGill University.

MAONGA, T. (1988) 'Statement of Research Proposal', Course Assignment, McGill University.

RICE, K. (1986) 'Factors which Influence Older Adults to Participate in Education: The Elderhostel Experience in Atlantic Canada.' Unpublished MA Thesis, McGill University, Montreal.

RONA, S. (1988) 'Characteristics of Effectiveness of an Alternative High School: A Follow-Up Study of its Graduates.' Unpublished MA Thesis, McGill University, Montreal.

TERMAN, L.M. (1954) 'The discovery and encouragement of exceptional talent', *American Psychologist*, 9, pp. 221–230.

Chapter 4

Sources of Research Literature

Educational research should never take place in a vacuum. It should begin with a preliminary analysis to see what in the particular field has been researched before, what types of study have taken place, when they have been conducted, how and by whom. Educational research is a cooperative field and contributing researchers are obliged to know their field and its previous research. Research is a cumulative process whereby knowledge is developed and added to. Just as it would be ridiculous for a biologist to go into a strange environment and begin applying his or her own names to flora and fauna, it is folly for an educational researcher to embark on a study without first becoming familiar with prior research. Any scientist attempts to find out whether the territory has been covered before and whether there is previous knowledge and experience to guide new investigations. In education, it is surprising that so many graduate students begin developing problems and going forward with research plans without an adequate understanding of what has gone on before. The purpose of this chapter is to provide a quick reference tool for beginning graduate students interested in finding information in their field of potential research. It begins by discussing the types of research knowledge. It then outlines where to look for previous research and how to search it out and will help you prepare for the all-important review of research discussed in Chapter 8.

The challenge for the beginning researcher is to cut through a great quantity of previous knowledge and find out what has been done and the major conclusions. In this sense, searching out previous research is an important aspect of data collection and is therefore a legitimate research activity. It involves the collection of data, weighing its importance and relevance and classifying it for future use. This process of discovery should be a significant learning activity as it should help in redefining and reshaping our particular view of our own research problem. Very often, as a result of the search, the problem is recast and sharpened. Thus, long before a formal review of research takes place, exploration of prior research and its interaction with the research problem is a crucial step in the overall research process. How, then, does one find out what has been researched before?

The Six Types of Knowledge

Chapter 1 pointed out five main ways of knowing. There are also different types of knowledge, and it is important in looking for literature to understand the type of knowledge that is being pursued.

Historical knowledge of research is the history of investigation in a particular field. In various eras educators have different views of the world, different concerns, and their research reflects these views. In psychology, for example, the study of intelligence evolved from a philosophical analysis on the nature of man to a systematic approach to measurement of peoples' abilities. Any researcher working on intelligence should be familiar with this historical evolution in the field. So it is with any research topic. Many topics have their popularity at a given point in time after which interest wanes, and the topic remains relatively dormant until another era when it is picked up and different frameworks and approaches are used. When you look at published research, keep its historical context in mind and be aware of the need to understand how the topic and approaches to learning about it have evolved over time. This will give you possible insights into your own problem and will protect you from embarking on a path which has been pursued and abandoned in some previous era.

The second important type of knowledge is **axiological knowledge**, what might be called the theory of experience. It is what was termed in Chapter 1, insightful observation. Axiological knowledge is found in the literature written by practitioners whose many years of experience lead to important conclusions and generalizations. Many educational research journals are written by practitioners for practitioners. They talk about the problems of school discipline, how to implement curriculum, ways of organizing schools and so forth. These articles tend not to be based on previous research but rather on the experience of the author. Beginning researchers should recognize that this literature is not, technically speaking, a research literature. It is a literature from the world of practice; it bears some relationship to research but should not be the sole source of prior information leading up to your research problem. Thus, you should recognize axiological knowledge for what it is and not use it as if it were theory or prior research.

Theoretical and conceptual knowledge provides the structure within a particular field of inquiry. It generally results from critical analysis of prior research and theory and provides the constructs leading to pursuit of interesting research questions. Research not based on theory is generally utilitarian and is often suspect in academic circles. Thus, in your study of prior knowledge you should attempt to identify appropriate theories and theoretical frameworks which bear relation to your problem.

Prior research studies are an essential starting point for any research investigation. There are countless such studies and the challenge is to identify those which are valid and have particular relevance to the specific type of problem you wish to investigate. Such studies often further illustrate theory and conceptual literature and are important in showing the sequence of studies and how they have evolved historically. Often you cannot identify previous research studies that relate directly to your interest but there are studies which are related to part of the problem and within its general boundaries. You may need to move to a higher level of abstraction (see Chapter 3) but you should be able to locate research studies which are in the same area as your interest.

Reviews provide another indispensable type of knowledge. Other researchers have reviewed many of the significant prior studies and critiqued them. You should identify sources which enable you to become familiar with these reviews. They have the advantage of pulling together a lot of specific pieces of research and casting them into frameworks and levels of generalization which might be more helpful than any specific study alone. Reviews exist in most fields of investigation but here too you may have to change the level of abstraction to find one which is relevant to your needs.

The final type of knowledge identified here is **academic debates**. Very often new lines of research inquiry give rise to debates in the literature. Some journals publish these debates which typically take the form of critiques of prior articles. In some cases, journals will over the course of a year or two publish critiques accompanied by rebuttals from the original researcher. The academic debate, therefore, goes back and forth and moves the thinking forward in the field under discussion. In areas where these debates exist, unless you are familiar with them, you might find yourself embarking on a direction which has already been well discussed and rejected.

In your search for knowledge about your topic, you should pay attention to these six types of knowledge. You should identify relevant literature pertaining to each of the six types. If you do so, you will have a complete perspective on your problem and be in a good position to know where you can move forward with your particular research contribution. The remainder of this chapter outlines the sources of information related to these six types of knowledge.

Sources of Knowledge

Ask an Expert

Even in this technological age, the best overall source of information continues to be people. The smart researcher will consult an expert in the field and find out from him or her where to go from there. By asking someone who knows the field, you can find out the significant books and articles, the important researchers, the key conferences and places to look for information. This will save a great deal of time and will help you in the difficult process of evaluating the quality of the research you review. Some experts maintain bibliographies in their field which can be most helpful. However, to provide good guidance the expert will require a clear idea of the particular problem you would like to pursue. As a start, I suggest you ask for recommendations of a small number of key writings. By seeing what an expert considers the best work in the field you will develop a notion of whether or not it is for you.

Books as Sources of Information

University libraries contain vast numbers of books on every conceivable topic and they are often the starting point of people looking for previous research. Unfortunately books are not generally a good source of information on prior research. In the first place, books, with rare exceptions, are dated and much of the information they contain was written at least five years before the publication date. Secondly, research information tends to be current and directed to a more specific audience than is generally the case for books. Thus, books tend to give summaries and general backgrounds of research information but they do not provide the primary research material which is so crucial to someone exploring research in a given field. However, they are excellent sources of information about broad areas of study. They are a good source of theory which is essential in determining the nature of a conceptual framework and thus the structure of a research review. For these reasons, one should consult books for general background, but should not spend too much time searching books for research findings.

There are, of course, exceptions to the general rule. Encyclopedias and handbooks, for example, summarize information and the summaries are generally written by leading authorities in the discipline. *The Handbook of Research on Teaching* is one such publication. It is published every five years and summarizes the research on all aspects of curriculum, instruction, supervision and the teaching of specific subjects. It is an excellent source of information on who is doing what type of research and it provides a general framework for the important research trends over the half decade. *The Encyclopedia of Educational Research* is another example. One advantage of these publications is that they distill countless research contributions into generally more interpretable and digestible summaries and they often project emerging directions and areas for further research. A number of other books and periodicals provide excellent sources of information about the more important journal literature and they will be discussed later.

Journals as Sources of Information

There are currently upwards of 1,000 journals in the field of education. These are published a number of times a year and are sent to subscribers, including libraries. Journals provide the major source of research literature for researchers and graduate students. Journals vary greatly in nature however, and only some of them provide more than token treatment of research. Most journals are devoted to articles of fact and opinions about a topic — axiological research. Such articles reflect mainly a rationalist approach to knowledge and are of limited use to the researcher. They may inform you about trends and points of view but their substance is useful only to help define questions. Some journals offer conceptual pieces which are based on theory and research. These are helpful in defining frameworks and providing rationale for a study, but they too are deficient in conveying what has been learned in previous research on a topic. The most significant journals are those which report on research studies and their findings. They present research studies which include brief reviews of prior research, methods and procedures used, results and conclusions. Enough information is provided for the reader to assess the quality of the research design.

One of the major advantages of journals is that they are published periodically and more frequently than books, and thus the information they contain is much more recent. Most research journals have a publication cycle of about a year so that articles appearing there represent papers written about a year earlier. Be forewarned, however, that such papers often reflect research conducted a year or so before that, so journal information may be two years old as compared to book information which is likely to be five years old.

Like anything else, journals vary in quality. Graduate students should be aware that many of the journals are of low standard. They publish much of what is submitted and its quality is mediocre at best. The best journals are refereed, meaning that an editorial board or group of professional peers reviews each article and decides on its quality and suitability for publication. It is common practice to have blind reviews; that is, the reviewers do not know who submitted the paper. The most prestigious journals in the field will publish as few as 3 or 4 per cent of the submissions. When you realize that most submissions are by established researchers with doctorates and academic positions, you can understand that the articles which appear in those journals are certainly superior to those in less rigorous journals. Figure 4.1 lists some leading refereed journals and describes what they publish. Note that most of these journals are supported by universities or professional associations which help ensure their overall quality and continuity.

Students often learn of articles in obscure journals which are difficult to obtain. Chances are that if the journal is for a localized audience it will not be as consequential as will a national or international journal. In general, my advice would be not to bother with lesser journals unless one's topic is exactly matched by an article there. There are, of course, small circulation journals catering to highly specialized audiences which are also noteworthy. This is certainly the case for some foreign journals which may be difficult to find. When in doubt about the quality and relevance of a journal, ask an expert in the field.

Figure 4.1: Some significant journals for educational researchers

Journals	Comments
Administrative Sciences Quarterly	The major theoretical journal about organizations. Includes some research on educational organizations.
Adult Education Quarterly	Publishes research and theory in adult and continuing education.
Alberta Journal of Educational Research	One of the few good quality Canadian journals dealing with research. Mix of methodologies and topics related to all aspects of education.
American Educational Research Journal	One of the most rigorous journals devoted exclusively to research articles in all areas of education. Many articles esoteric, empirical and multivariate statistics are generally used.
American Journal of Education	Pursues themes and general issues emphasizing theory and research.
Australian Journal of Education	Contains largely research articles related to a wide range of topics related to Australia and education in general.
British Journal of Educational Psychology	A high quality British journal containing largely empirical research on a wide range of topics in educational psychology.
British Journal of Educational Studies	Contains largely theoretical and axiological articles on contemporary issues related to Britain and the Commonwealth.
Canadian and International Education	Contains high quality articles, reviews, reports with some research on development.
Canadian Journal of Education	A major national refereed journal for professors and researchers in education. Publishes mixture of general articles and research of interest to Canadians.
Comparative Education	Provides information for general readers on significant trends throughout the world.
Comparative Education Review	The major research journal in comparative education.
Curriculum Inquiry	Publishes studies of curriculum research, development, education and theory.
Educational Administration Quarterly	Elementary and secondary schooling focus with mixture of conceptual studies and those with a traditional research focus.
Education Evaluation and Policy Analysis	Mixture of theoretical, analytic and research articles related to policy and evaluation.
Elementary School Journal	Publishes original studies, reviews of research and conceptual analyses for researchers and practitioners interested in elementary schooling.
Harvard Educational Review	One of the most influential journals containing occasional research studies which tend to be milestones. Published by students.
History of Education Quarterly	A leading American journal on history of education.
Journal of Applied Behavioral Science	Emphasis on soft research such as case study, conceptual and opinion articles and action research.

Figure 4.1 (cont'd.)

Journals	Comments
Journal of Educational Psychology	One of the many psychology journals of most interest to educators. Contains research studies, mostly empirical and many experimental.
Journal of Educational Research	Emphasizes research with practical application to elementary and secondary schools.
Journal of Reading	A forum for current theory, research and practice in reading.
Review of Educational Research	Most significant quarterly devoted to reviews of research in all areas of education. Excellent conceptual and meta-analysis.
Journal of Research in Science Teaching	A leading journal devoted to research on science teaching.
New Zealand Journal of Educational Studies	Publishes essays, research studies and critical comment in all areas of education.
Research in the Teaching of English	Publishes research and discussion related to the teaching of English and the language arts.

Note: This summary is not intended to be definitive but rather is indicative of the range of journals of interest to researchers.

Dissertations as Sources of Information

Previous student theses and dissertations are a natural source of research information. Doctoral students generally explore new areas and if they are on a similar topic they provide great insight into research questions, methods and findings. Their limitation, of course, is that they represent student work, albeit work conducted under supervision. In many cases, they are lengthy, cumbersome and are of variable quality. While there are quality control procedures, these vary from institution to institution and from student to student. Although each study must be examined on its merits, in general, one index of quality can be the university where the study was conducted. Mass degree mills tend to turn out poorer dissertations than those with traditional student selection procedures, programs of study, dissertation committees, and formal thesis defence.

The major source of doctoral studies is *Dissertation Abstracts International*, a monthly periodical which includes titles, key words and author indices for doctoral dissertations in over 350 institutions in North America and abroad. Abstracts of the dissertations are provided in the publication and complete copies of dissertations may be ordered on microfilm or hard copy from University Microfilms of Ann Arbor, Michigan.

The best starting point is to review the theses and dissertations done in your own university. They will indicate the types of research emphasized in the institution and the types of approaches considered acceptable. Knowing what has gone on locally is also very helpful in enabling you to define a topic which builds on previous studies in your department. If you can find out which are considered the best dissertations it will be worthwhile reviewing them even when their topic differs from your own. Recent dissertations are often more timely than either journals or books and they are also more complete. Every dissertation should contain copies of the research instruments which otherwise are often difficult to find.

Conference Proceedings

A number of associations of educators and researchers including the *American Educational Research Association (AERA)* and the *Canadian Society for the Study of Education* (CSSE) hold annual conferences. Their published programs indicate the name of re-searchers and papers to be presented. When they first come out, these have the great advantage of representing work done within the year and, thus, are a good indicator of what research is in vogue. Once the program is received, you need not attend the conference. It is acceptable to write to selected presenters asking for a copy of their paper. This often yields access to a research paper a year or more before it reaches the pages of a journal.

Previous Reviews of Research

In general terms, the fields are so vast and there is so much infor-mation that it helps to use the work of those who have already accessed and evaluated it. Often leading scholars review previous research. Such research reviews assemble the information, put it into context and often order it in ways which are helpful for someone attempting to conduct a study. These reviews may be published in handbooks and encyclopedias or they may be found in journals or other publications devoted to the purpose. The most significant of these is the *Review of Educational Research*. Of course, every research article, dissertation or research report normally contains a review of prior research, so this aspect of previous studies should be especially noted. If a relevant review is found, one needs to devote most energies to updating it, working from the date of publication, or a year or two before, until the present.

Searching the Literature: The Manual Search

Knowing where to look for information is only part of the problem; you must also know how to search out research literature. Perhaps the best way to get a feeling for the field and the type of research done is to conduct a manual search. Attempt to locate the significant journals and other periodicals which report on research in your field of interest, and manually flip through the tables of contents and indexes to find articles related to your topic. It is useful to take recent issues of the journal and work backwards to find other articles that relate to the topic being explored. Many journals publish annual indexes to previous issues. Once you locate one of these, you can merely consult that issue each year and this saves you from examining each individual copy.

Another approach with which you should be familiar is the ancestry method. Once you find an article of relevance, check its references and in detective-like fashion trace down the various journals and articles cited there. The journals identified may provide other sources of articles related to your topic. Search out reviews, dissertations and other sources of bibliographies which can be used in similar fashion.

Computer Assisted Information Acquisition

As information in libraries becomes computerized, such libraries are increasingly compiling banks of references useful to the researcher. These data bases are inventories of information which are assembled and centrally stored in computers. Most of the information exists in hard copy form in journals and such places but the data bases provide a way of tracking down most previous research related to a topic. This can be accessed by users for a relatively small fee.

The general strategy is to identify key words or descripters which limit the topic being searched for. A descripter like 'school principal' will yield a great number of research references. It can be limited and refined by using other descripters such as 'elementary school principal' or 'female principal' or 'teaching principal'. By combining descripters it is possible to limit the access to studies which bear directly on your chosen topic. You can also limit the search by date. To do a

Figure 4.2: *Major data bases for computer-assisted literature searches in education*

Data Base	Description
Bilingual Education Bibliographic Abstracts	Covers various aspects of bilingual education in the USA with some international coverage. The scope includes such topics as classroom instruction, teacher education, ethnic and minorities, linguistics, second language instruction and culture.
British Education Index	This file indexes the literature of education, covering not only traditional facets of primary, secondary, tertiary and further education but also adult and continuing education, student counseling, special and vocational education, and women's studies.
Educational Index (EDI)	EDI indexes 350 of the key English language periodicals in all areas of education.
Educational Resources Information Centre (ERIC)	The major education data base. Consists of two files, *Current Index to Journals in Education* (CIJE) covering over 700 education and education-related journals, and *Resources in Education* (RIE) covering 16,000 non-journal materials including research reports, surveys, program descriptions and evaluations, curriculum and teaching guides, and instructional and resource materials. Printed equivalent: CIJE and RIE.
Educational Sciences	Provides coverage of the history and philosophy of education, educational policy, teaching organization, educational research, teaching methods, teachers, orientation and goals and the sociology and psychology of education.
EDUQ	Analytical bibliography on Quebec education. Provides information on elementary, secondary and post-secondary education. Contains research documents, literature on pedagogy, statistical studies and bibliographies. Includes all French and English documents printed in Quebec or dealing with Quebec.
Exceptional Child Education Resources (ECER)	Provides coverage on exceptional child education.
International Development Research Centre (IDRC)	This file is a merger of several data bases related to international development. Among these data bases are the USAID data base, and the UNESCO data base.
	USAID data base: contains technical research and development material produced by aid programs. Among the subject fields covered are education and human resources.
	UNESCO data base: includes worldwide coverage of literature written by or for UNESCO. It deals with a broad range of educational, scientific, and cultural programs with an increasing emphasis on development issues.
PsycINFO	Refers to a group of publications, data bases and services from the PsycINFO division of the American Psychological Association. It's the major resource for information on behavior sciences and related fields.

Figure 4.2 (cont'd.)

Data Base	Description
PsycFILE	This file is a portion of the PsycINFO data base. PsycFILE contains citations and summaries on such topics as personnel management, selection and training, managerial practices and characteristics, organizational behavior and changes, and occupational attitudes.
Social Sciences Citation Index (SSCI)	Contains references from more than 1,500 of the most significant journals in the social sciences. SSCI contains relevant source items in the social sciences from approximately 3,000 additional journals in the biomedical, natural and physical sciences. Amongst other social sciences, SSCI covers education, psychology and sociology. Printed equivalent: Current Contents SSCI.

proper computerized search you need a good delimitation of your area of interest. The reference librarian is invaluable in helping to limit your search. Once you feed in the descripters you will be given the number of studies related to the topic and can obtain a printout of their titles, and in some cases, short abstracts describing what they contain. You can then go on and search out or request copies of the full document.

Perhaps the most useful data base in education is the Educational Resources Information Centre (ERIC) which indexes over 700 periodicals and hundreds of thousands of research papers, projects and reports in education. The International Development Research Centre (IDRC) in Ottawa has a similar data base related to international research. Many other such data bases exist and are summarized in Figure 4.2.

The Social Sciences Citation Index (SSCI) is a unique indexing service because it categorizes documents based on the works cited in them as well as their topical focus. Using SSCI you can look up an author and find out which articles have cited that author. This is, in effect, the reverse of a manual ancestry search as it works from an article forward to others which refer to it and presumably build on its research. The identification of a definitive study can therefore lead to all kinds of spinoffs.

The major difficulty with computer-assisted methods is that they do not evaluate the information they contain, so you often receive lists of many in-house documents and reports which are of limited validity and limited use for your purposes.

What to do with the References you Locate

Previous studies located should be photo-copied and classified in a system for future reference and retrieval. Such photo-copying is legal for research purposes and saves considerable time over making notes by hand. Be sure that the full reference source is on the title page, and if it is not there be sure to write down the particulars in order to refer to it later. Your time in the library should be spent in scanning and retrieving information. Later it can be fully read and digested.

Conclusion

In conclusion, a thorough knowledge of the field being investigated is essential if your research is to make a significant contribution. You cannot do justice to a topic in the absence of knowledge of what has gone on before. By using the significant efforts of others you can design a better study and make it more grounded in the field which you are investigating.

Part II
Research Processes

Chapter 5

Research Frameworks

Much of good research follows a framework developed from prior theory and research or by thought and rational deduction and this framework serves to clarify the problem and help determine the best approach to its solution. Thus, the work of an excellent researcher is organized inquiry. The questions, the way they are framed, the combinations of concerns are not random. They represent approaches which help the researcher do significant research and which enable the reader to understand the point. Educational research is not the only activity organized in this way. Education itself follows organized models. There are concepts and objectives and activities, assignments, tests and exams all of which fit together in a coherent fashion. While the approach can be inductive or discovery-oriented, the result should relate to some established framework.

Frameworks range from simple one-dimensional lists to elaborate multi-dimensional models with layers of intersecting parts. Even a simple scheme is better than none at all. In selecting a principal for a school, it is better to rate the applicants on a list of characteristics than it is merely to accord each a global rating. Such a list leads to improved agreement among various raters (reliability) and also more precise estimations of background and performance on each characteristic (validity). More elaborate and improved frameworks would take into consideration which of the characteristics are most important for the particular position available. So, for example, bilingualism might be very important in one setting and less so in another. The purpose of this chapter is both to emphasize the importance of conceptual frameworks and to provide examples and knowledge of the types of framework which have proved successful in the past. For any researcher, the development of a suitable framework is part of the process of planning and clarifying the research problem and conducting the analysis. As in any problem-solving endeavor, problems which seem overwhelming can often be tackled once they have been broken into their constituent parts and the interrelationships among the parts have been graphically and conceptually arranged.

Some theoreticians use paradigms to explain their theories. These are often elaborate diagrams with flow paths and arrows. They often clarify relationships among loosely coupled systems and can suggest research questions and lines of inquiry. They sometimes have the advantage of situating research into a theoretical context, but in my experience, they are generally unhelpful in tightening the questions and level of understanding. This is why I use the term framework. A framework is a model which allows the researcher to explore the relationships among variables in a logical and prescribed fashion. It clarifies questions by relating questions and their constituent sub-questions and it summarizes the overall concept being investigated. This chapter restricts its treatment to simple one and two dimensional frameworks which are generally adequate for most research purposes.

Whatever framework one uses for a research study, the development of research questions and sub-questions will facilitate the task of conducting and writing it. My experience suggests that conceptually sharp research questions can serve as the foundation for most types of research. If the study relates to a conceptual framework the questions will fit into such a structure; if there is no other research framework, then research questions become the framework. Examples of such questions have been provided with the sample problem statements outlined in Chapter 3. Let me emphasize that such questions are difficult to resolve and phrase. Often they evolve and get refined as one grapples with the analysis of data and the writing of results. Thus, they may not merge in final form until the study is virtually complete. Sharp questions indicate the potential of a good study; weak questions suggest a study that may not have been worth conducting. Let us move on now to various other types of frameworks.

The Importance of Definition

Some researchers do not do justice to their studies because they fail to define their terms. This is not necessarily a simple matter because concepts in education are often expressed in non-technical terms making them difficult for the researcher to deal with. It often takes considerable research just to break a concept into components which can be clearly described and more work if the researcher desires to express such components in measurable terms. Furthermore, complex concepts and the imprecision of language sometimes result in confusion about research results. The findings might appear clear when expressed in words, but the words used by the researcher might apply to different concepts than those in the minds of the readers.

In research, even seemingly simple concepts may, after a little thought, be found to be complex. For example, school effectiveness seems simple at first glance but the concept of effectiveness as it applies to schools has many meanings. There have been thousands of studies on school effectiveness, but much of this research is hard to compare since conceptions of effectiveness are not defined or not subject to reliable and valid measurement. By definition, the effectiveness of something is the extent to which its objectives are achieved. The many types of objectives for schooling leads to many meanings for school effectiveness. Is it the proportion of students who achieve high school graduation? Does it imply a qualitative dimension and the acquisition of certain competencies? Does it include the school leaver's success in further education, employment and life in society? To study a concept like school effectiveness, one must clarify what is meant. A school may be highly effective in some respects and deficient in others.

This notion of defining a concept by sub-dividing it into components is a common practice in educational research. The components can be defined and measured more validly than the overall concept. For example, it is relatively easy to establish the dropout rate in a secondary school, as the answer can be expressed in a per cent, number or ratio. It is slightly more difficult, but feasible, to determine whether graduates of the school can read and at what level, since there are reasonably reliable and valid tests to measure such a component of effectiveness. It is more difficult still to assess the development of morals, values or character, but even that can be defined and measured to some degree. The impossibility is to attempt to apply a single score to the global effectiveness of the school. To do that requires you to apply a set of educational values to the issue. I might prefer a school where everyone graduates; you might favor one where only some graduate, but with high academic standing; someone else will prefer the school which instills certain religious beliefs in those who attend; others might value athletic development.

The solution to this problem is to define your terms carefully and work with a multi-faceted definition of effectiveness. Thus, effectiveness becomes a multivariate concept with a variety of components which can be joined together or not depending on your purpose. It then becomes possible to analyze various components of effectiveness and to obtain understanding of relationships derived from research.

It is folly to assume that all important concepts have been defined in this way. Recent research on the development of universities in Third World countries (Lusthaus, Anderson and Adrien, 1989) indicated that millions of dollars were being spent to develop universities without a clear understanding of what is meant by university development. Does development mean more buildings? More staff? More courses and programs? Does it imply greater research productivity? An enhanced reputation? A better employment record of graduates? Clearly it means all of these things but our investigation showed that little attention had been paid to the components of university development or to the different ways to support development of these components. Our solution was to define the components of institutional development as shown in Figure 5.1. This is a simple, intuitive definition essentially emerging from axiological research. This seems to cover the major components of university development and is the least one must do when confronted with a concept ill defined in the literature.

Sometimes definitional frameworks have a more theoretical or research base. For example, in the late 1960s, I conducted a series of research studies on classrooms, processes and environment. Until that time, there had been little significant research relating the processes in classrooms to learning. Herbert Walberg and I examined classrooms and classroom processes by taking the significant psychological and sociological writings on groups, classrooms and schools and analyzing the various dimensions which that literature revealed (see Anderson, 1970a and 1970b; Anderson and Walberg, 1968, 1972 and 1974; Walberg and Anderson, 1968 and 1972). We obtained a number of dimensions which were then developed into an instrument which could be used by pupils to describe perceptions of what went on in their classrooms (see Figure 5.2).

The theoretical analysis led to components of the classroom environment which were adapted into measurement tools. These were then tested, refined and validated using empirical data. Student perceptions along fifteen dimensions enabled us to make unprecedented predictions of student learning based on the processes within their classes. The important contribution here was that the theoretical framework on classrooms and social groups gave rise to measurable dimensions which were clearly more important than a single score on the classroom environment. The first level of research was to attempt to describe classrooms according to this framework

Figure 5.1: *Components of institutional development of Third World universities*

Development Dimension	Outputs
1 Development of University Management Capacities	Management is an important dimension of institutional development. This might concentrate on building an institution's capacity to manage its programs, finance, students and so forth through, for example, the development of financial and information management systems, systems for personnel and student management or systems for enhanced communication or coordination.
2 Development of Curriculum	This dimension could focus on building the institution's programs through, for example, curriculum and program development which could include faculty training related to curriculum development, development of course materials and the provision of equipment and texts.
3 Enhancement of Teaching	This aspect could include such things as faculty training, the development and implementation of new teaching methods, and/or the provision of equipment to extend the practical relevance of teaching.
4 Enhancement of Research	This dimension could concentrate on building the institution's capacity to perform research in support of national development priorities, teaching programs or community-based programs. It might also provide opportunities for collaborative research of this type or for research dissemination.
5 Enhancement of Accessibility	This refers to building the institution's capacity to increase access to its services, for example, by developing outreach activities such as non-degree courses and programs, extension services, consultancy expertise for use with government and industry and other such means of reaching new and underserved clienteles.
6 Enhancement of Institutional Capacities for Dealing with their External Environment	This refers to the institution's capacity to develop policies and plans to help the institution relate to its environment. A project might help build an institution's capacity to develop mechanisms for shared services in teaching, research and community service.
7 Development of Physical Plant	This refers to building construction.

and to see whether students could differentiate one class from another based on the fifteen dimensions. That phase established that through our instrument pupils could discriminate one class from another and that there was agreement among the pupils within a given class. This was the descriptive phase. We next related the differences among classes to such things as teacher characteristics and class size, the explanatory phase. Having established descriptive and explanatory phases we then explored the effects of the differences on student learning, the predictive and generalization phases. The first

Figure 5.2: Scale description and sample items for the learning environment inventory

Scale	Scale Description	Sample Item
Cohesiveness	Extent to which students, know, help and are friendly toward each other.	All students know each other very well. (+)
Diversity	Extent to which differences in students' interests exist and are provided for.	The class has students with many different interests. (+)
Formality	Extent to which behavior within the class is guided by formal rules.	The class is rather informal and few rules are imposed. (−)
Speed	Extent to which class work is covered quickly.	Students do not have to hurry to finish their work. (−)
Material Environment	Availability of adequate books, equipment, space and lighting.	The books and equipment students need or want are easily available to them in the classroom. (+)
Friction	Amount of tension and quarreling among students.	Certain students in the class are responsible for petty quarrels. (+)
Goal Direction	Degree of goal clarity in the class.	The class knows exactly what it has to get done. (+)
Favoritism	Extent to which the teacher treats certain students more favorably	Every member of the class enjoys the same privileges. (−)
Difficulty	Extent to which students find difficulty with the work of the class.	Students in the class tend to find the work hard to do. (+)
Apathy	Extent to which students feel no affinity with the class activities.	Members of the class don't care what the class does. (+)
Democracy	Extent to which students share equally in decision-making related to the class.	Class decisions tend to be made by all the students. (+)
Cliqueness	Extent to which students refuse to mix with the rest of the class.	Certain students work only with their close friends. (+)
Satisfaction	Extent of enjoyment of the class.	There is considerable dissatisfaction with the work of the class. (−)
Disorganization	Extent to which classroom activities are confusing and poorly organized.	The class is well organized and efficient. (−)
Competitiveness	Emphasis on students competing with each other.	Students seldom compete with one another. (−)

Notes: a) Items designated (+) are scored 1, 2, 3, and 4, respectively, for the responses Strongly Disagree, Disagree, Agree and Strongly Agree. Items designated (−) are scored in the reverse way.
   b) From Fraser, Anderson and Walberg (1982. p. 5).

investigations were overall studies, examining classroom perceptions and student learning. Once we established the predictive value of student perceptions, we then developed more elaborate frameworks which began to divide the students into different types. That research ultimately showed that different types of environment are suited to different types of students for different types of learning outcomes.

The process used in developing frameworks and models for that line of research are indicative of how researchers build frameworks, how they extend and refine them and how such frameworks assist in providing common understanding of the phenomena under investigation.

As the above examples illustrate, many concepts can be clarified if they are broken down into components which convey a shared meaning. The components are derived through the analysis of the literature and what people have said about the concept, as well as by rational logic which breaks up the concept into its constituent parts. As the process develops, the researcher then attempts to define the concept in words which incorporate these components. The purpose of research is to convey understanding to others and the only way of doing so is to provide clear definitions which enable other researchers to understand what is meant by the concept being researched. Even if others use different definitions, they will at least be able to compare and see where the results might converge and where they might differ. Thus, in all research, it becomes important to define the crucial terms related to the research being carried out.

One-Dimensional Frameworks

Clarification of definitions by breaking concepts into their constituent parts represents the most basic type of framework. This is a one-dimensional framework and it can be made to apply to many types of description. For example, the size of a school can be described in many ways — the number of pupils, the number of classrooms, the size of the physical plant, the number of staff and so on. Each convey part of the notion of size, but collectively they communicate a clearer understanding of the size of an educational institution than any one of them in isolation. Major advances in research often rely on something as simple as defining concepts in such a uni-dimensional fashion. Even in this day and age, many complex concepts have been treated globally and therefore clear research results have not been forthcoming.

Thus, the starting point for the research is often the formulation

Figure 5.3: Input – process – output framework

| Inputs | ⟶ | Processes | ⟶ | Outputs |

of a one-dimensional framework. Definitions are one way of sub-dividing concepts; time is another. Chronology in historical research is a good example. If events are arranged by dates, one can analyze and interrelate events, causes and effects.

Undoubtedly the most common one-dimensional time-based framework is the pre-test–post-test experiment in which something is measured before an educational intervention and again afterwards. One might assess arithmetic performance, provide a special teaching program and then measure the performance again in an attempt to attribute any change in scores to the teaching program.

Figure 5.3 illustrates another type of one-dimensional time-based framework, the input-process-output model which is applicable to all types of education. This model simply takes the educational process and breaks it into what goes in, the process of education, and the outputs achieved. Some researchers have done major work merely by examining the input and output sides of the framework. Called a black box model, it avoids the complex job of trying to define and quantify terms like curriculum and instruction. My own Masters study (Anderson, 1966) used just this model to relate such inputs as teacher qualifications and salaries and the socio-economic characteristics of communities to school outputs defined in terms of high school leaving marks and pass rates. This was done using the school as the unit of analysis. Naturally, the inputs, including finances, qualified teachers and so forth have a direct relationship to the processes that go on in schools but in the black box model one need not describe or quantify these processes.

The one-dimensional model can either take a concept and break it into its constituent parts or it can examine a process such as that described in Figure 5.3. In either case, understanding can be attained by conducting research within the structure provided by the framework.

Two-Dimensional Frameworks

While often helpful, one-dimensional frameworks are limited in that they do not permit analysis of the interrelationships between sets of

Figure 5.4:   Typical two-dimensional framework for cross-tabulations or analysis of variance

Nominal characteristic (e.g., gender)	Ordinal Characteristic (e.g., Socio-Economic Status)		
	Low	Middle	High
Male	Data for low male	Data for mid male	Data for high male
Female	Data for low female	Data for mid female	Data for high female

related variables. Two-dimensional frameworks are among the most common in educational research.

One of the most common and useful frameworks is formed by dividing the data sample into groups with like characteristics. Figure 5.4 outlines a typical framework of this type. In this example, one dimension is formed by grouping the sample into a useful number of groups, in this case formed by splitting the sample into three groups representing high, middle and low socio-economic status. The other dimension in the example is a two-level nominal variable, gender. The data in the six cells formed by the intersection of these characteristics are the averages for people in that cell. For example, a cross tabulation candidate might be the relevant data permitting exploration of the question 'How does the candidate appeal to people of different gender and socio-economic background?' If one were to use analysis of variance, it would be necessary to have the mean and standard deviation of the groups assigned to each cell. That type of analysis would be necessary if the data were more complex such as performance scores where the variability within the group as well as the mean is important.

You can make your own two-dimensional frameworks to serve the particular needs of your research. Figure 5.5 provides a simple example. It combines the categorizations of the concept of university development illustrated in Figure 5.1 with the input-process-output framework of Figure 5.3. The intersection of the two one-dimensional frameworks creates a series of boxes or cells in which two conditions exist. This example illustrates how one can focus clearly on what is going on with the benefit of such a framework. It enables us to conduct research on changes in the state of institutional development over time. Such a conceptualization would suggest various types of inputs which bear logical relationships to components of institutional development. So, for example, construction of buildings may be expected to relate to the number of students served, but it will not have much direct connection with the quality of students. In this way,

Figure 5.5: Input — process — output framework combined with framework of university development

Component of University Development	Inputs	Processes	Outputs
Development of University Management Capacities	Financial Expert for 6 months	Technical Assistance	Operating financial Management System
	2 personal computers	Training	3 trained computer operators on a financial accounting program
Development of Curriculum	Expert Consultant for 2 years	Technical Assistance	Revised Master's program in Engineering
		Training	6 professors with in-service training and experience in curriculum development
Enhancement of Teaching	Audio-visual Center and equipment	Provision of equipment	Equipped AC Center
	AV Assistant	Technical Assistant	Equipment functioning in classes
Enhancement of Research	Research library	Provision of books	Functioning library
	10 Researh grants of $10,000	Support for individual research	10 completed research projects research
Enhancement of Accessibility	TV Studios	Distance education through TV	500 Distance education course graduates after 3 years
	$500,000	10 Scholarships for minority students	10 Minority students graduate after 4 years
Enhancement of Ability to Deal with Environment	1 Planner for 2 years	Development of strategic plan	University strategic decisions according to plan
Development of Physical Plant	Dormitory for 100 students	Construction	100 Additional students in residence
	10 Classrooms serving 300 students	Construction	Increased teaching capacity by 300

various types of inputs can be analyzed in a logical fashion allowing the researcher to deduce and test hypotheses about relationships.

As these illustrations show, two dimensional frameworks enable us to have a more precise understanding of the dynamics of the situation than obtainable with overall global descriptions alone. There is no limited to the possible configurations which can easily be tailored to the particular purpose at hand.

The Logical Framework Analysis (LFA)

Some frameworks are highly conceptual and these can be the most useful. One of the most powerful frameworks for investigating educational processes is the logical framework analysis designed by the United States Agency for International Development. The LFA is not just a research framework, but it provides a structure for project planning and evaluation research. It is essentially a planning and evaluation model which contains sixteen cells arranged in two dimensions as described in Figure 5.6. Unlike most other frameworks, the LFA helps systematize and apply a rational approach to knowledge with a research base. The rational part of the model is its logic. The various cells are interrelated in the vertical dimension and also interrelated horizontally. Turning first to the vertical logic, it is assumed that if we contribute certain inputs we expect certain outputs. Thus, there is a necessary and sufficient relationship between inputs and their corresponding outputs. At the next level of vertical logic we again assume a causal inference. If we achieve those outputs, then it is assumed that we have achieved the purpose. Continuing the final step, it is assumed that if we achieve the purpose, we are expected to achieve the goal. As we move from the lower level (inputs) to the highest level (goal) the relationship tends to become more loose, less causal. For the relationship to hold we rely on certain assumptions which are outlined on the far right for each level. These assumptions are the factors not controlled by the project but which influence its implementation and chances for success. The horizontal dimension is an explanation of how we measure the various inputs and outputs. The second column includes what are called objectively verifiable indicators. These are predetermined reliable and valid measures which indicate the status of input or output delivery, the achievement of the purpose or the attainment of the goal. The third column explains how they will be measured.

Figure 5.7 illustrates the LFA in a practical example. The Eastern Townships region in Quebec is becoming increasingly French-speaking and the English community, once in the majority, has been experiencing difficulty in assimilating and preserving its access to jobs and opportunities. To help address the problem of a lack of French competence among English school graduates, the Lennoxville District School System introduced a program of bilingual education which it was hoped would encourage school graduates to stay in the Eastern Townships and become gainfully employed (Anderson, 1985). The adopted program provided a bilingual full-day kindergarten followed,

Figure 5.6: Logical framework matrix

Narrative Summary	Objectively verifiable Indicators	Means of Verification	Important Assumptions
Program Goal: The reason for the project, the desired end toward which the efforts are directed (program or sector goal), and for which the project is a logical precondition.	**Measures of Goal Achievement:** Conditions which will indicate that the goal has been achieved.	The way that the indicators can be objectively verified.	**Concerning Long term value of program/project:**
Project Purpose: That which is expected to be achieved if the project is completed successfully and on time. The 'real' or essential motivation for producing outputs.	**Conditions that will indicate purpose has been achieved: End of project status.** The objectively verifiable condition which is expected to exist if the project achieves its purpose. The signs which will indicate that the project is a success'.	The way that the indicators can be objectively verified.	**Aff ecting purpose to goal link:** An event or action, over which the project team has little control; a condition which must be assumed to exist if Goal is to be achieved.
Outputs: The specific kind of results that can be expected from good management of the project inputs.	**Magnitude of Outputs necessary and sufficient to achieve purpose:** The magnitude of the results and the projected completion dates.	The way that the indicators can be objectively verified.	**Affecting output-to-purpose link:** An event or action, over which the project team has little control; a condition which must be assumed to exist if Purpose is to be achieved.
Inputs: Activities and resources necessary to produce the outputs.	**Resources and Expenditures for each activity:** The types and cost of resources for each activity with target dates.	The way that the indicators can be objectively verified.	**Aff ecting input-to-output link:** An event or action, over which the project team has little control; a condition which must be assumed to exist if Outputs are to be achieved.

Figure 5.7: Logical framework analysis for Eastern Townships French second language program

Narrative Summary	Objectively Verifiable Indicators	Means of Verification	Important Assumptions
Program Goal: To maintain English school system in Eastern Townships	**Measures of Goal Achievement:** 1 Schools stay open with sufficient numbers 2 Parents positive to FSL	1 Enrollments 2 Attitude Tests	**For achieving goal targets:** 1 Lack of in-school French learning is a constraint to graduates staying in the Townships. 2 People will support an English system that teaches French. 3 Parents will stay in region. 4 Jobs will exist for grads. 5 Sec. school will carry on language training.
Project Purpose: To significantly increase French language competence of LDSB graduates.	**Conditions that will indicate that purpose has been achieved: End of Project Status** 1 Grade 6 grads. functionally bilingual	1 Standardized tests 2 School records 3 Success in secondary school French	**For achieving purpose:** 1 English rural schools will continue to exist in Quebec. 2 Program will be effective in teaching French.
Outputs: To produce elementary school graduate competent in French.	**Magnitude of Output:** 1 120 children graduate per year from 9 schools begining in 1986	1 Enrollment statistics	**For achieving outputs:** 1 Program will be accepted by government
Inputs: 1 FSL Coordinator 2 Program development resources 3 Teacher training and selection 4 Full day bilingual kindergarten	**Implementation Target** 1 Bilingual kindergarten by 1980 2 New program developed on following schedule: 1 – 1981 2 – 1982 3 – 1983 4 – 1984 5 – 1985 6 – 1986	1 Reports of coord. 2 Teacher and principal report 3 External evalution reports	**For providing inputs:** 1 Extra teachers can be funded 2 Government will allow program to be offered.

in the later grades, by one hour each day of intensive French. The expectation was that this treatment would lead to school graduates competent in French who would remain in the region able to find employment. Figure 5.7 illustrates the logic of the LFA approach for this experiment. Note how the LFA is logically organized so that the inputs are assumed to lead to the outputs, purpose and goal. Note also how the effectiveness of schooling is to be measured. The measurement constitutes an agreed-upon definition of what the parents considered successful bilingual education. The purpose, of course, goes beyond the final examination and becomes an interesting research question which is observable and measurable. One should pay particular attention to the fundamental assumptions listed on the right hand side. The logic of the Lennoxville experiment relied on these assumptions and they were fundamental to the research program which evaluated it.

Conclusion

In conclusion, a successful research strategy is facilitated if structured into some type of framework which relates previous research and present understanding to new questions which can then be adequately explored. The development of a new framework or the application of an existing framework to a new group or setting often constitutes the basis of significant research which extends understanding and knowledge. If the ultimate purpose of research is generalization and prediction, conceptual frameworks greatly facilitate its achievement. They presume more complex patterns of interaction than a simple A causing B. Rather they infer that various dimensions of A have various types of relationships to the multi-dimensions of B and, furthermore, that the relationship may vary with other conditions which can be viewed as multi-dimensions of C.

References

ANDERSON, G.J. (1966) 'A Statistical Analysis of Input-Output Differences Among Quebec Protestant Secondary Schools.' Unpublished MA Thesis, McGill University, Montréal.
ANDERSON, G.J. (1970a) 'Effects of classroom social climate on individual learning', *American Educational Research Journal*, 7, pp. 135–52.
ANDERSON, G.J. (1970b) 'Effects of course content and teacher sex on the social

climate of learning', *American Educational Research Journal*, 7, pp. 135–52.

ANDERSON, G. (Ed.) (1985) *Lessons in Policy Evaluation: A Report on the Lennoxville District French Second Language Program* 1979–1984 (Monograph), McGill University, Faculty of Education, Montréal.

ANDERSON, G.J. and WALBERG, H.J. (1968) 'Classroom climate and group learning', *International Journal of Educational Research*, 18, pp. 277–86.

ANDERSON, G.J. and WALBERG, H.J. (1972) 'Class size and the social environment of learning: A mixed replication and extension', *Alberta Journal of Educational Research*, 18, pp. 277–86.

ANDERSON, G.J. and WALBERG, H.J. (1974) 'Learning environments', in WALBERG, H.J. (Ed.) *Evaluating Educational Performance: A Sourcebook of Methods, Instruments, and Examples*, Berkeley, California, McCutchan.

FRASER, B.J., ANDERSON, G.J. and WALBERG, H.J. (1982) *Assessment of Learning Environment: Manual for Learning Environment Inventory (LEI) and My Class Inventory (MCI)*, (Third Version), Western Australia Institute of Technology, Perth Australia.

LUSTHAUS, C., ANDERSON, G. and ADRIEN, M.H. (1989) 'Changing trends in the role of Canadian University in development assistance', *Changing Trends in Canadian International Development Assistance*, Montreal, McGill-Queens. In Press.

WALBERG, H.J. and ANDERSON, G.J. (1968). 'Classroom climate and individual learning', *Journal of Educational Psychology*, 59, pp. 414–9.

WALBERG, H.J. and ANDERSON, G.J. (1972) 'Properties of the achieving urban classes', *Journal of Educational Psychology*, 63, pp. 381–5.

Chapter 6

Planning a Research Study

All large projects can be facilitated through planning; research studies are no exception. This chapter outlines the various steps required to plan and conduct an effective research study. It reviews the essential elements in conducting a study and is intended to provide an overview to place in context the details which are reviewed more completely in subsequent chapters.

Many studies are jeopardized by failing to recognize all the various steps required and by not allocating time and resources to accommodate these requirements. Research activities also can be exceedingly time-consuming, particularly for the inexperienced researcher. It is hoped that acquaintance with the basic process of planning and conducting a research study will conserve effort and facilitate production of a competent piece of work.

Some people claim not to plan. While this may be correct at one level, they probably do plan, though they may not verbalize it or write it down. The approach used in this chapter is that of a fully planned attack on the task. It is an approach used successfully by empirical researchers, particularly those who engage in experimental work. It is also used by researchers on contract who must analyze costs and bill for the research services provided. While such an explicit model might be overly specific for many needs, elements of the model should be useful to all those anticipating research. It should be emphasized as well that planning does not necessitate a linear work sequence. Indeed, to avoid tedium, the nature of the research process is such that a mix of activities is recommended. While in theory, the scientific method is explicit, in practice most scientists tend to conduct their research in round-about ways and put it together in linear form only when they write it up.

Figure 6.1 lists a generic set of steps in the research process together with space to record the time allocated and time frame in which to conduct them. The table has been filled in for a typical dissertation assumed to last a year. The checklist can be used to plan the research study in advance and allocate time accordingly. The novice researcher may be shocked at the number of things to do and more so at the total time it will require to do them all. Bear in mind that a dissertation may represent a year's work or more, so considerable time is expected.

One might well ask whether all these steps are required. The following section adds a few observations on the major activities.

1 *Administration*
   This is recorded merely so it will not be forgotten. Conducting a study is similar to other aspects of life such as looking after personal finances. It requires organization or it may cause problems later on.

2 *Defining and redefining the research problem*
   Chapter 3 dealt with problem definition. The only information to add is the necessity for redefinition as the research unfolds. Often the initial problem will be recast as data are collected and analyzed. This is an important step in research and often makes the difference between an excellent study and one which did not capture the full potential of what could have been discovered. The process continues throughout the period of research and is a constant struggle both conceptually and in terms of its written form.

3 *Thinking about the research*
   This element has not been made explicit on the chart. It is included because it takes a great deal of time and energy and relates clearly to problem redefinition. It is important to think about all aspects of a study and to view it from different angles at different points in time. This clarifies the study, improves it, and enables the researcher to see a logical path to its conclusion.

4 *Conducting the library search*
   The researcher has to conduct a thorough search of previous theory and research related to the problem. Two interrelated approaches are suggested. First, it is useful to conduct an electronic data search using a system such as ERIC. This does two things. First, it helps in defining the problem for it forces the researcher to specify the key descriptors which

Figure 6.1: Planning framework for one year research study

Task/Activity	Month 1	2	3	4	5	6	7	8	9	10	11	12	Total (Hours)	Key dates/ Milestones
Aministration														
– buying supplies	3	1	1	1	1			2					15	
– organizing to do work	4	4	4	4	4	4	4	4	4	4	4	4	48	
– developing systems to store and retrieve information	10		5		5			5					25	
– other														
Defining problem														
– general reading	20	10	10	10	10	10	10	10	10	10	10	10	130	General problem area decided month 1
– discussion with colleagues	8	8	8	8	8	8	8	8	8	8	8	8	96	
– preparing statement (draft 1)	12		4										12	Draft problem statement month 2
– feedback from colleagues on statements	4		4										8	
– revising statement (draft 2)	6												6	
– discussion with supervisors(s)	2	2	2										6	Submission of complete proposal month 4
– initial consideration of methodology	12		20										32	
– revision of idea			5			5							10	
– other														
Review of Research														
– time in library	20	20	20	10	10	10	10			10			100	
– ERIC search	10	5	5								5		25	
– journal search	20	10	10								5		45	
– other sources (experts, personal etc.)	5	5	10	5	5	5							35	
– reading material	40	40	20	20	20	5							145	
– writing paragraphs			40	30	50								120	
– developing outline	5	5	5										15	
– preparing tables			10	10									20	Draft lit. review month 4
– drafting review # 1			20	20									40	
– feedback from colleagues on review			5										5	
– revising review # 2				20									20	
– feedback from supervisor			2										2	
– revising review # 3								10					10	Penultimate lit. review month 8
– revision of problem statement (draft # 3)					5								5	
– other														

Methodology	Hours	Milestone
— defining sources of data	10	
— searching for published instruments	15	
— developing instruments	10	Instruments selected/developed month 4
— pilot-testing instruments	10	
— revising instruments	10	
— layout and design of instruments	5	
— preparation for printing	5	
— definition of sample	5	Methodology decided by month 5
— selecting sample	5	
— writing methodology #1	25	Methodology section first draft month 6
— revising methodology #2	20	
— revising methodology #3	15	Methodology revised month 10
— other		

Conducting Research	Hours	Milestone
— data collection	120	Data collected months 6–8
— data coding/processing	80	
— data analysis	240	Data analysis complete month 9
— computer interface	40	
— preparing tables	40	
— preparing figures	40	
— writing results #1	60	Preliminary results drafted month 10
— revising results #2	40	Final results section month 11
— revising results #3	20	
— obtaining feedback/criticism	40	

Report Preparation	Hours	Milestone
— editing of manuscript	70	
— arranging typing	25	
— proofreading	25	
— format/layout	15	
— references	35	Dissertation submitted month 12
— abstract	20	
— translation of abstract	5	
— preliminaries (title pages, etc.)	5	
— appendices	30	
— administration	25	

Totals:	151	189	217	191	68	177	212	209	211	147	147	161	2090

define the problem and enables a search of what has been done previously on the specified themes. Secondly, it provides a general map of the type, quantity and location of previous research on the subject. Particularly relevant studies can, of course, be accessed through these electronic search systems.

The other approach is the browsing approach, whereby the researcher goes to the library and searches through various sources of information in order to find relevant material related to the topic. In practice, many topic areas are addressed most thoroughly in two or three key journals. In this way, the researcher can conduct a search by journal and examine all these issues of a given journal from the present backwards in time. This will provide a good indication of the scope of the field and how it is evolving.

In both approaches, the researcher is obliged to record the information found. Today, photocopying is the most effective means of compiling a library of research articles on a given theme. Underlining and highlighting enables easy access to the relevant parts of the manuscript. Care should be taken that explicit reference information is available on the title page of each article. If not there, it must be written in as this will be essential later for the reference section of the study. In practice, most researchers scan such articles in the library, obtain copies and only later do a thorough analysis of what the articles say.

5   *Conducting the literature review*

The accumulated research articles must then be reviewed. This is a time-consuming but creative process which in itself is a vital research activity. Various steps may be mixed to produce the finished product. Key studies can be reviewed in paragraph form extracting the vital questions, findings and conclusions. Overall, the research review needs to be organized and it is such organization which distinguishes an excellent review from one that merely covers the base. Organization of the review should evolve from theoretical conceptualizations or from a conceptual framework which evolves from the theory or the research questions. In this way, the various studies can be organized and the prose can be knitted into an overall picture of what the literature concludes.

As well as the review in prose, modern literature reviews tend to present the findings in some graphic form, generally through tables and figures. These summarize the various studies and articulate their findings so that an overall summary can be obtained in tabular form. This again is a difficult procedure since there are few blueprints and models for literature in a given field (see Chapter 8).

6 *Methodology*

The methodology section of a research study describes what was done and its particular methodological components. The methodology section can take a variety of forms depending on the type of thesis and the tradition out of which it emerges. In general, it will define the sources of data including the sample if a sampling approach is used. If an experimental study, the experimental design will be described. Most methodology sections also describe the steps and procedures used, report on the data collection instruments and indicate the limitations of the study (see Chapter 9).

7 *Instruments*

All good research includes some type of instruments. These may range from empirically validated questionnaires or psychological tests to a general framework for field notes in qualitative research or general means of classifying information in historical research. The point is that instruments must be obtained or developed. If developed, the procedure can be time consuming but its quality is instrumental to the overall success of the project. Later chapters describe methods of constructing questionnaires and interview protocols.

8 *Data collection*

Research involves the collection of primary source data which is obtained through reading, observation, interviews, the administration of tests or questionnaires. Whichever methods are used, the data must be collected. In the case of an experimental study, the experimental treatment or procedure must also be introduced.

9 *Data analysis and presentation*

Once the data are collected, they must be analyzed and the analysis may range from statistical work using computers to hand tabulations and classifications as in qualitative or historical research. Data analysis is one of the more interesting aspects of the study for it includes the possibilities of discovery and reconceptualization of the research questions. Rarely can analysis be prescribed and conducted in an entirely routine fashion. More typically analyses must be done and redone in order to capitalize on the particularities of the data which have been collected. Thus, cross tabulations will require changes in break points, factor analyses will reveal varying numbers of factors and multivariate analysis will entail different approaches to the data which lead to the most parsimonious solution.

As the data are analyzed, they must be displayed in ways that will convey to the reader what has been discovered. Since raw data are rarely presented, the data must be classified and grouped into tables and figures. This, too, is an important if time-consuming task.

10   *Writing the study*

One of the most difficult challenges is the actual writing of the research report. In the physical sciences, researchers often conduct the study completely before writing it up. In the humanities and social sciences, however, the written presentation of the study has a much greater importance and it occupies most of the researcher's time. In practice, it is best to write early and to keep abreast of the progress of the research through the writing. So, for example, the problem statement and introduction should be fully written before the data are collected. It helps to have a draft of the literature review as well, so that the actual data collection and analysis fits in well with the prior research.

Such writing generally necessitates rewriting and thesis research is a major case in point. Work with colleagues and supervisors will provide feedback and require continual rewriting until the words begin to convey accurately and completely the intended message. The planning framework makes provision for three drafts of each section. This is the minimum number that should be planned for and three drafts are standard for many experienced writers. Those with less experience may require more.

Conclusion

The main advantage of planning is that you know where you are going and how to get there. If you do a good job of planning in advance, you may realize that you have insufficient means or resources to reach your goal in the available time. Thus, the plan is useful in helping you redefine your problem. It also, of course, allows you to monitor progress and make needed corrections as you proceed. Finally, if you record significant milestones such as submission deadlines you can help ensure that you meet your obligations.

Chapter 7

Scholarly Communication

Educational research has been portrayed as an activity whereby society accumulates knowledge. Knowledge is accumulated through the written word and researchers have an obligation to record and communicate their findings. There are various ways by which researchers spread their results. Their own teaching is an obvious method. There are also scholarly conferences at which academics in each discipline gather annually to hear the latest results and findings of leading researchers. Researchers also publish research papers, reports and books which convey research literature. While some communication about research is in oral form, by far the most prevalent communication medium is the written word, whether in print form or through electronic or optical retrieval systems. For this reason, the researcher must know how to communicate. There are two aspects to the task, scholarly conventions and literary excellence. There are established scholarly conventions for making references, constructing tables and organizing results which prescribe how one conveys research information. These conventions are followed by all researchers and have been developed over the years. The new researcher is obliged to learn and follow them. Mastering these conventions is part of the socialization of researchers and denotes attainment of professional status as a researcher. There are also the literary conventions of the language which also need to be mastered if one is to convey information concisely, yet completely and clearly.

The purpose of this chapter is to give new researchers a quick introduction to the task of research writing. It is in no way considered a replacement for some of the contemporary definitive works on these matters (see Strunk and White, 1979; Gowers, 1954; Williams, 1981; Zinsser, 1980), but it does attempt to provide a few quick principles which will get people started and pointed in the right direction. There is a great deal to learn and many beginners become discouraged because every time they put the pen to paper, they seem to be violating some rule of scholarly style or writing protocol. The chapter first deals with the process of scholarly publication. It then goes on to describe the mechanical aspects of scholarly editorial style, giving a brief synopsis of some of the main conventions. It then discusses writing style and offers some tips on how to write and improve your writing. Finally, it goes into the conceptual area of organizing research writing so that it suits the medium and the needs of its audience.

Scholarly Publication

The graduate student who prepares fellowship and research grant applications begins to know some of the substance of the life of an academic. Most scholarly publication processes involve similar steps. Let me begin by describing the procedure for submitting a paper to an academic conference. Generally, such conferences send out announcements to the members of the professional association to which they relate. Someone interested in preparing a paper then submits a proposal which in some cases is merely a title but more frequently is a page or two describing the research and its contribution. These submissions are made about six months before the meeting is held. A review panel then goes over the submissions and selects those that it considers most worthy of presentation. Very often such proposals relate to research which is in progress but not yet complete. Acceptance of this submission implies a commitment to complete the research prior to the conference. The presenter is then scheduled a slot in the conference program and arrives generally with copies of the paper in hand. A short presentation, generally about twenty minutes, is made and sometimes there is an appointed discussant or questions from the audience are received. Copies of the paper are normally available for distribution and for those who request them, by mail. Too often such papers are read aloud, the researcher failing to recognize the important difference between an effective oral presentation and the reading of written words. Such papers should always be talked through or depicted visually without reading lengthy prose, but that is not the subject of this chapter.

The submission of papers to a journal follows a similar procedure. In this case, there is no special invitation and anyone can submit a manuscript at any time. One submits the paper and it is generally given a quick review by the journal editor who, on deciding of its general interest, sends it to a panel of reviewers. Most often there are two or three reviewers who are themselves academics and who undertake a blind review; that is, they evaluate the paper without knowledge of its author's name. Papers recommended for publication sometimes are sent back to the author for further revisions but once accepted, the paper is scheduled for publication. This might take a year after the paper was submitted and in leading journals, the rejection rate is over 95 per cent. Research scholars are not paid for their papers but publish for their general commitment to an academic career, the advancement of knowledge, and the enhancement of their personal prestige and reputation. In short, its high on ego, low on cash.

Books are developed by the author and submitted to a publisher, generally first in proposal form and then sample chapters may be developed. Increasingly, publishers are using the process of external review to assess the quality of manuscripts. Once they undertake to publish, then the author works diligently with the editor of the publishing house to revise the manuscript in every detail. In this case, the author is paid a royalty, generally about 10 per cent of the retail price of the book. It is not a route to riches, however, as press runs for academic books are generally only a couple of thousand copies.

Scholarly Editorial Style

With all these various outlets for publication, authors are obliged to follow established stylistic conventions in their writing. Of all such systems of conventions, the one which has probably had more research and development than any other and the one I recommend is that of the American Psychological Association (APA) as summarized in its *Publication Manual* (1983). This Style Manual began in 1928 and has been revised periodically over the last half century. It provides a straightforward method for citing references and is generally amenable to the requirements of modern word processing. A few other style manuals are also highly developed and some are preferred by people in historical research, but the APA Manual should be learned thoroughly by every social scientist. Most authoritative journals will not accept manuscripts in any other style. It is the author's obligation to write things according to convention and a manuscript failing to do so will be returned. The same applies for theses and dissertations which are sometimes subject to criticism because they have violated these editorial rules. In extreme cases, theses have been graded unsatisfactory largely because the student was sloppy in dealing with these

Figure 7.1:   Examples of general referencing in textual material

1   Quasi-experimental approaches (Campbell and Stanley, 1963) are an alternative ...
2   The problem of validity has concerned many researchers (Campbell and Stanley, 1963; Gaye, 1987; Fisher, 1923).
3   Smith's study (cited in Jones, 1975) reveals ...

conventions. While conventions may seem unimportant to the new researcher, violations of conventions indicates that one is a novice. If the treatment is inconsistent and sloppy, it further suggests the possibility of sloppiness in the research itself. Serious researchers should, therefore, obtain and become familiar with the Manual. You can also receive valuable tips by picking up journals which follow APA style and examining the way the various articles are written, organized and referenced. If even that fails, there is now a software program that sets up the references for you.

The Use of References

Practically all research relies on, and refers to, previous research in its particular field. Reference to previous research establishes one's familiarity with the general field and places a research study in context. There are two general methods by which previous work can be referenced. First, one can make general reference to a previous work by citing the author, followed by the date in parenthesis, e.g., Smith (1986). This is used to back-up general assertions or to acknowledge that someone else has done a study in a similar area. In one sense it is simply a genuflection to other respected researchers, but it is important in showing the links your study has with previous research. Often several studies are referred to when making an assertion. Examples of this type of referencing are shown in Figure 7.1.

The second method for references incorporates direct quotes. Short quotations of fewer than forty words can be run into a sentence in the text with quotation marks around the quoted passage, followed by parenthesis, the author, date and page number, e.g., (Smith, 1986, p. 245). Sometimes the sentence structure is varied and the page number is separated from the author. When longer passages are quoted, they should be indented in total. There are no quotation marks used and the same conventions follow for the author, date and page number. These conventions are shown in Figure 7.2. Where an author wrote more than one article in a given year, these are

Figure 7.2:   Examples of methods for referring to direct quotes in textual material

---

1   Smith (1988) found that 'participants with higher motivation scores performed consistently higher in final tests' (p. 93).
2   'Participants with higher motivation scores performed consistently higher in final tests' (Smith, 1988, p. 93).

Notes: These quotes, being short, are included in the normal format of the text. Quotes of more than forty words are indented in a free-standing block concluding with the reference in one of the above forms.

---

designated by placing the suffixes a, b, c, after the year of publication, e.g., (Smith, 1986a; 1986b).

The Reference List

In APA style, each reference cited in the text must be accompanied at the end of the publication by a full citation in a list of references. Note that this is not a bibliography as it contains only those things specifically cited. It is arranged alphabetically and multiple works of each author are listed chronologically. The accuracy and punctuation of these references is of critical importance. Furthermore, there are detailed conventions for how works with various types of author in various sources are to be cited. It is beyond the scope of this chapter to provide all the variations but the reference section at the end of chapters illustrate several common types of reference. For more elaborate examples, see the APA Manual (1983), Table 17, pp. 118–33.

Tables and Figures

Empirical research generally incorporates tables which convey a great deal of direct information more simply and understandably than prose alone. There are several examples of tables in this book which can be referred to for sample formats. In APA style, all tables have a number; they have a title which describes their content; they have only horizontal lines; and they have headings on top of columns and often notes following the table. The format for these is also prescribed by convention.

Figures are similar to tables except that they contain pictures and sometimes prose. I follow the convention of using tables when there are numerical values and calling everything else a figure.

Other Conventions

A number of other conventions are often done incorrectly by the novice. Numbers less than 10 and those beginning a sentence are written in words. Numbers 10 and greater are written numerically. Abbreviations of titles are put in parenthesis following the first mention of the title. Underlining is used to designate italics. Words can be combined with numbers, e.g., 3 million.

Today, sexist terms of any sort are not considered good form, so one must take great pains to exclude the use of sexist words in writing. The APA Manual includes a guide to non-sexist terms. It sometimes takes considerable pains to avoid what has become cliched conventions but once you have learned to do this, it comes easily. Avoid such terms as she/he.

In academic writing, only use 'we' when there are two authors. The royal 'we' is not acceptable. Some people use 'I' but I prefer to avoid it.

Writing

Academic writing is not only one of the most difficult aspects of conducting research, but it is the most anxiety provoking. Even experienced researchers are afraid to write and virtually everyone organizes a myriad of ways to avoid or ritualize their writing behavior. The written word is public, and if you don't say it right, your thoughts are confused, or worse, you will be judged to have nothing important to say and everyone will know. People fear that others will scoff at their ideas leaving them vulnerable and defenceless. To make it worse, writing tends to be done in private so there are no role models. The novice does not realize that the experienced author or the graduate student's mentor goes through the same anxiety, the same process of drafting, redrafting and redrafting once more. Believe me, the apprehension is natural and if you learn to treat your early drafts as what they are, and seek assistance from your peers and those more experienced than you, then you learn much and produce prose which to the reader seems like no effort at all.

The problem in all types of writing, and especially academic writing, is to convey the precise meaning that is intended. You know your topic intimately but the reader doesn't, and the challenge is to put together the words in such a way that you convey to the reader exactly what you intend. Unlike journalistic writing, academic writing is clear and orderly. There are no surprises. There is no climax. The reader should know what the paper is about from the first sentence and be able to follow the storyline clearly at every stage. Research intends to be objective so you are not interested in creating a mood or in colouring the phraseology to transmit a value. There are no irrelevancies or asides. Academic writing must conserve words because publications cannot afford to print all but the most necessary.

Outlines

Clear expository writing relates to an outline. However, the task of developing the outline before you write often becomes a more onerous task than the writing itself. My view is that you must have an outline, but not necessarily before you begin your writing. It can be helpful to write a stream of consciousness which is essentially a predraft. In fact, research now shows that the process of writing is a form of thinking and writing your thoughts helps to develop them. It gets you writing without any formality or risk because much of such a predraft will be read only by yourself. The mistake many students make is that they hand in this pre-draft. Instead, use it as a way of organizing your thoughts and from it create a coherent outline. Remember, too, that there is no one right outline. Any writing problem has many solutions and it may take many tries before you find one that works for you and your problem. Thus, don't be dismayed when your supervisor has you reorganize your work several times. Like you, your supervisor is grappling with the problem of how to help you say it clearly and you are both struggling with a task that has no pre-determined solution. Even before you revise a submitted draft it might be desirable to submit a revised outline first. The outline organizes what is to be said clearly, develops it logically, and brings it to an obvious conclusion. Outlines can be made at various levels of detail and often they are revised many times before the finished work is complete. It is often useful to make an outline for a single paragraph as that will improve what the paragraph says. The failure to develop outlines is often the cause of sloppy and incomprehensible writing.

Paragraphs and Sentences

Paragraphs are the building blocks of prose and sentences are the substance of paragraphs. I have found that paragraphs can be used to construct a story in the same way that bricks can be used to build a house. What you need, however, is good paragraphs or you won't be able to hold up the structure. Each paragraph requires three essential ingredients: a beginning, a middle and an end. In academic writing, this almost always implies a minimum of three sentences in every paragraph. The first introduces the paragraph and its purpose. There is then one or more sentences developing the substance of the paragraph, and finally a sentence which concludes it. Remember this is not creative writing where you might use a single word in place of a paragraph for a certain effect. In academic writing, you want to paint a clear and accurate picture and to do so you need fully rounded paragraphs.

The sentence is the substance of the paragraph and sentences come in a great variety of types and sizes. Each sentence must express a complete thought and be grammatically correct. Two aspects of sentences bear emphasis: the form and the substance. The substance is formed by the words and words should be chosen which are short and simple, yet which convey a precise meaning. Use technical words only for their intended technical meanings. Many sentences can be improved merely by crossing out all redundant and unnecessary words. This tightens and sharpens them. Also, don't be afraid to throw away sentences which after several drafts no longer advance your argument. If they are overly general or too full of qualifiers, they tend to suck the energy from your prose and should be deleted.

With respect to form, the form of sentences and the variation in form develops a particular style. The soul of a sentence is its verb and this determines its form. Verbs should be in the active voice and often in academic writing the past tense is used because you are describing what happened in the past. Use the active voice by saying 'The students completed the questionnaire' rather than 'The questionnaires were completed by the students'. Use adjectives sparingly and rely on your verbs to convey the meaning. One helpful tip in writing is to examine writing by an expert and use the sentence structures there as containers into which you pour your own words. This will give you a variety of sentence structure patterns which can be used and varied in order to make your writing more interesting, readable and clear.

How to Write

Writing is a complex activity and like any such chore, it is often difficult to get started. In my experience, the worst starting point is the beginning; for the beginning, particularly the first sentence, is the most difficult of all in the whole piece. It is best, therefore, to begin with the easiest writing: the descriptive prose which tells about the data collection, the instruments, the sample, the procedures used and things which have taken place which you know well and can talk easily about. The secret of beginning to write is to begin and if you can find any starting point, this will be a great help. Remember to write in paragraphs and even if they do not fit where you initially put them, they can be rearranged later and used as a contribution to the whole.

Photography teaches a valuable lesson to the writer: you are judged not for the pictures you throw away, but on the few you don't. Poor photographers bore their friends by forcing them to sit through long evenings of unselected and unsorted slides. Pleasurable slide presentations show only the best, and the surviving shots are organized by theme and carefully sequenced. Remember this when writing. If you draft volumes and then edit it down, preserving the best paragraphs and sentences and organizing them in different ways from the way in which they were written, you will make major improvements in the finished product and the readers of your work will appreciate the difference. Twenty years ago, Herbert Walberg taught me this approach to scholarly writing. Herb was a master at producing a draft and could do so in one evening. Furthermore, he was not afraid to circulate it widely for criticism and often sent our papers to distinguished scholars considerably more senior than we were. When the reactions came in we would tear apart the pages, stack all the page ones in a pile and then go through the various comments, editing and re-writing a page at a time. The revised paper would then be submitted to a journal and their comments would lead to final revisions before publication.

I know of no author who can write his or her best prose at the first try. I equate writing to plastering a joint in a gyprock wall. It takes three coats to do it right and the best expert might be able to do it in two but three is always more secure. Thus, the secret of writing is to rewrite. Bear in mind that the text you are reading right now, as all finished products, had a long life before you saw it. In fact, this point was only inserted into the text on the last of many drafts. It is often helpful to get it all down and then to go over it smoothing and contouring so that the exact intent can be conveyed. Personally, I find it best to use a word processor and after writing each sentence, I go back to the one before and ultimately smooth out the whole paragraph.

A second way of improving your writing is to re-read it after leaving it aside for a period of time. It is also helpful to re-read it aloud as this readily shows up obvious mistakes (what Becker, 1986, refers to as editing by ear).

Finally, there is nothing better than a good critic. Certain people are endowed with the gift of being able to criticize writing in a useful and constructive way. Many cannot do this at all and will merely return your work saying it is good. Regardless of whether they have knowledge of your research field, critics who can take the pains of thoroughly revising your work are invaluable. In searching for writing exemplars, scholarly journals are typically not the best sources. They rarely employ professional editors, but rely on academics to conduct the editing and most academics are themselves poor writers and ineffectual editors. Books and popular magazines do utilize skilled editors and most manuscripts are painstakingly reviewed, often to the amazement of first-time book and magazine authors who in scholarly journal publications may not ever have had to make any substantial changes.

Organization of Research Writing

Sample Outline

In developing an outline, the various sections and sub-sections relate to one another in hierarchical ways. Thus, there are both titles and sub-titles. Generally in academic writing three or four levels of headings are suitable to convey any meaning. The convention should be set up and followed throughout the research report. In this way, the reader knows what is a part of which larger section. In my writing, I have found that a decimal system of numbers is helpful in organizing thoughts and keeping track of headings. Figure 7.3 gives an example of an outline or Table of Contents for a thesis. The headings are typed exactly the same way in the text as in the Table of Contents. Here there are three levels of headings. A few parts bear special reference.

Fundamentals of Educational Research

Figure 7.3: Sample table of contents from a thesis on transfer of training (Algranti, 1988, pp. iii–v)

Table of Contents

The Title

The title of a report must convey its content but must not be so elaborate as to obscure the message. There is a delicate balance between a title which is too long and one which is too short. A good critic is sometimes helpful in deciding what is an appropriate title.

Abstract

The abstract is one of the most important parts of a research report. It conveys in 100–200 words the substance of the study and the abstract is all that most readers will come in contact with. It is unfortunate that the abstract is often written last and in haste. In 1987, I spent six months developing an abstract system for the Canadian International Development Agency which provided a format for two-page abstracts of evaluation reports. Each abstract took an average of two full days to write and most were revised many times after the initial draft. This illustrates the difficulty of conveying in a few words the substance of a study. Interestingly, that system has been helpful in assessing the quality of evaluation reports, many of which do not contain information essential to the production of the abstract.

Appendices

Appendices include long technical descriptions or other material which would break up the flow of the text if included there. Each appendix is self-contained with its own title and story. Typically, appendices include data collection instruments and such things as lists of people interviewed.

Conclusion

Writing of all types is a highly creative activity. The work you produce is unique to you and did not exist before you wrote it down. In this sense, it is a good indication of your thinking, your experience and training and your attention to convention and detail. Good writing is a pleasure to produce and a pleasure to read. Poor writing is a great chore and the obligation of university professors to read so much of it is one of the more distasteful parts of the role. Hopefully, this chapter will spare you and your professors from at least some avoidable grief.

For Further Study

AMERICAN PSYCHOLOGICAL ASSOCIATION (1983) *Publication Manual* (Third Edition), Washington, DC, Author.

BECKER, H.S. (1986) *Writing for Social Scientists*, Chicago, University of Chicago Press.

STRUNK, W. and WHITE, E.B. (1979) *The Elements of Style* (Third Edition), New York, MacMillan.

WILLIAMS, J.M. (1981) *Style: Ten Lessons in Clarity and Grace*, Glenview, Scott, Foresman.

ZINSSER, W. (1980) *On Writing Well: An Informed Guide to Writing Non-fiction*, New York, Harper and Row.

References

ALGRANTI, C. (1988) 'The Effects of Training on Job Performance: A Study of the Factors Effecting the Learning Transfer Process.' Unpublished MA Thesis, McGill University, Montreal.

GOWERS, SIR E. (1954) *The Complete Plain Words*, Baltimore, Penguin Books.

Chapter 8

Reviewing the Literature

Successful research is based on all the knowledge, thinking and research that preceded it, and for this reason a review of the literature is an essential step in the process of undertaking a research study. A review of literature is a summary, analysis and interpretation of the theoretical, conceptual and research literature related to a topic or theme. It is broader than a review of the research which reviews research literature only, and it generally provides the framework for and bridge between a piece of original research and the work which preceded it. One major exception is the historical study where the research review is essentially data collection for the research because there is not a body of related literature in the same sense as for most other types of research. Thus, the historical research review looks at new sources or combines old sources in new ways. It differs considerably from the type of review described here. This chapter considers the purposes of a review of literature, it outlines the essential steps in conducting a review and it suggests ways of presenting it.

Reviewing the literature is not something that is done, completed, put aside and forgotten. Review of the literature is a process which for the experienced researcher is ongoing and life long. In the beginning, one should become familiar with the basic works related to a field of research. This is generally the position of a graduating masters student. At a PhD level, one should have more depth of understanding and will have interacted with some of the researchers, issues, debates and criticisms. The PhD graduate will typically have a deeper knowledge of these specific fields so that in some cases at the point of completing the dissertation the PhD graduate will be a world expert in that particular sub-field which was the subject of the dissertation. The ongoing researcher has the perspective of time. He or she will follow the literature through its six types of knowledge (see Chapter 4) and will gain the wisdom of experience. Thus, such a researcher will have an intimate appreciation for how the field has evolved, what research studies have been published that re-directed the field, the critical debates and criticisms of that type of research. Furthermore, such researchers will have contributed to the evolution of the field and, therefore, will have interacted with its evolving directions. It is typical for graduate students to review the literature early in their studies and then to direct their attention to the collection and analysis of data. It is always wise, however, to continue reviewing the literature as your study unfolds. The study itself might take a year or more to complete, and during that time some significant literature may be published.

The Purpose of the Review

Reviews of literature are becoming increasingly important as the number of studies and amount of knowledge in each field has escalated. In fact, research reviews are no longer required formalities; they have become research activities in their own right. They involve many of the same steps as doing original research. If done well, they collect data, analyze and interpret it, and write it up with conclusions which will benefit other researchers. In research journals, the main purpose of the review is to convey the background that a professional who is not an expert in the specific field needs to know in order to comprehend the subsequent study.

In a thesis or dissertation, the review has other important dimensions. It provides an example of your work and indicates to the reader your general level of scholarship. The quality of your work, its accuracy, its inclusions and exclusions and its method of organization and presentation establishes your credibility as a researcher and provides a base of validity for your subsequent study. It ensures that your research is new and indicates its relation to the overall field. Without an adequate review there is a danger that you may be merely replicating unknowingly the work which went before. In this regard, the review provides an indication of whether a research study is warranted as well as an indication of its probability of finding something new and making a contribution. When successive studies have failed to produce positive findings it is likely that the area is sterile and does not justify further replication. A review can be very helpful because it indicates the methodologies which have been used by others in pursuit of knowledge in the discipline. It will describe the major experimental designs, the instruments used to collect the data, the populations with which the research was conducted and so forth. Finally, for graduate students especially, it is an excellent way to help in the overall process of sharpening the research question and limiting it so that it is do-able and relates to past research in the field.

Reviewing Secondary Sources

Secondary source materials are those written by an author who was not a direct observer or participant in the events described. Existing summaries and reviews are one example and these are a good starting point for students attempting to learn about a field prior to zeroing in on a specific research problem.

The *Review of Educational Research* is a quarterly journal containing critical, integrative reviews of research literature on significant topics. Its reviews often represent exemplary models of review and often pull together an area in ways which identify needed research directions.

The *Encyclopedia of Educational Research* and the *Handbook of Research on Teaching* are both excellent publications containing reviews by many of the world's leading scholars. They, too, suggest areas for future research.

Reference to these publications should be helpful in defining a topic and suggesting major researchers and studies conducted which relate to it. By grounding your study in previous reviews you will save yourself months of work.

Collecting the Primary Literature

The act of collecting the literature involves browsing, skimming, reading and photocopying relevant works. Two types of literature need to be distinguished: the conceptual literature and the research literature. The conceptual literature and indicates the variables and areas in which research is to be pursued. Good research generally has a theoretical or conceptual basis, so you need to be familiar with these aspects of the discipline if you are to assess other research studies and design your own. Those who have taken a graduate course in a specialty will have this background; those pursuing new areas will need to do considerably more work.

As well as an understanding of the theoretical and conceptual literature, a review of the literature considers previous research. That is, it reviews studies done in the field and summarizes their major conclusions. The latter are found in journals and in dissertations and research reports.

In the beginning, one tends to read generally and extensively all materials related to the field. Graduate students will have to read much more than people experienced in a discipline who are familiar with the basic works. An excellent beginning is to obtain a bibliography from a professor or other knowledgeable expert who has compiled a listing of the major works in a given field. This is especially helpful for the theoretical foundations. The *Bibliographic Index* provides the source of bibliographies published as part of articles and books. If you can locate a recent bibliography on your topic it will save immeasurable time.

Research studies present somewhat different problems. In some instances, a great number of research studies appear to bear on the problem under investigation. Generally, this occurs when the research problem is not sufficiently focused. In such instances, it is helpful to pick out studies which are most specific and which might help cast the problem in a new frame. The other extreme occurs when there are almost no studies in the problem area. In some cases, this is a result of a lack of research with the descripters indicated: in other cases it implies that the research problem is too narrow in focus. In the latter situation, the net can be broadened and research can be sought without some of the narrower restrictions descriptive of your problem. You might still be able to preserve these restrictions in your problem statement but within the context of a broader literature on the subject.

The process of collecting literature is an ongoing process. As it unfolds it will be advisable to begin classifying studies into the theoretical and conceptual articles; those which bear generally on the topic, and those which have a specific and direct relationship to the problem under study.

Because the review of literature is a research process it becomes important to describe the methods employed in conducting it and its limits and limitations. A good research problem is grounded in one or more disciplines and these should be acknowledged. Within disciplines, there may be different theoretical perspectives with which you should be familiar, but generally one emerges as the basis for your study. Among the research literature you ideally want studies with a similar focus. The major factors in the design of studies, the instruments used, the populations involved and the recency of studies are all taken into consideration. For this reason, it becomes important to record and report on the conventions and rules used to exclude various sources of literature. In general, you will report the steps taken to define the boundaries of the literature you include. It is easy to be faulted for excluding important things but not so if you have limited the scope of your review and have thereby excluded them on rational grounds.

Analyzing the Literature

The conceptual and theoretical literature is reported on in order to demonstrate your understanding of the evolution and state of the field. It is exceedingly helpful if you can derive or borrow from the literature a conceptual framework which can form the basis of the research review and of your study (see Chapter 5). Such a framework will outline the critical factors and variables and indicate some interaction among them. It will probably then serve as a useful way of organizing the review of research. The various research studies selected for inclusion are then organized in some fashion either using the conceptual framework or at least by categorizing them under distinct headings.

The best and most salient works will be selected for review. Thorough studies of the quality of educational research (see Persell, 1976) indicate that 30–40 per cent of published studies are of poor quality with poor designs, inappropriate designs and conclusions not supported by the evidence. Major categories of problems with internal and external validity have been noted by Campbell and Stanley (1963), but in addition, the reviewer should be sensitive to deliberate bias, sampling problems, the use of poor or untested instruments, non-equivalent control groups and poor conceptualization. It is important to assess the quality of the studies reviewed so that the best can be given the most weight and so that obvious mistakes can be avoided.

The review itself will weave together the studies into an interesting and informative story line, out of which come useful conclusions. Reference to a given study will range from a genuflection to its importance in the evolution of research in the field to a major description and critique of the study and its methodology. You are attempting here to summarize the state of the art of research in the field. To do so, you will pay attention to **what**, **when**, **where**, **who** and **how** it was done. The research review indicates **what** research has already been undertaken in the field and the results achieved. This is the typical purpose of research reviews but it is not the only one. The reviewer should be sensitive to **when** the research was conducted.

Research in the social sciences is contextual and often follows cycles so that a flurry of activities for a couple of years may be followed by a period of relative inactivity. It is important to know whether the research contemplated is in vogue at the moment or whether it has been exhausted only later to be rediscovered when different approaches and issues come to the fore. The question of **where** refers to the geographic base of the study and for Canadian researchers much of the literature refers to American studies, so there may be a need for further research in the Canadian setting. **Who** was studied becomes important because a lot of research attempts to extend the work of previous researchers to new populations — different age groups, genders and so forth. Finally, the question of **how** the study was conducted is particulary important for one contemplating research. Not only should you be generally familiar with the methods employed previously, but they often provide a route which your study can follow. Instruments can sometimes be used from previous studies and you can often identify methodological weaknesses which justify a new more sophisticated piece of analysis.

Analyses of previous research used to be strictly in narrative form. Today, there is an increasing justification for tabular presentation since there are so many studies on a given topic. A carefully designed table including the author, date, subjects, methodology and conclusions can be exceedingly helpful in cutting through a great mass of literature. Such tables also serve as an excellent way of summarizing the verbal narrative. In their most elaborate form these tables include statistical estimations of the size of the effects enabling different studies to be compared in a valid way.

The summation of all this analysis should be the formulation of general conclusions about the state of the art of research related to the topic. Future directions should be relatively self-evident and this should set the stage for the proposed study. At the same time, the review can serve to clarify definitions, assumptions and limitations which are useful for the contemplated research. Very often, the review is concluded with a set of new research questions or hypotheses which emanate from the conceptual framework and research that has been studied. These become organizers for the problem to be investigated.

Presenting the Review

Presentation of a review of literature differs in the journal article or short research proposal from that found in a dissertation or thesis. In the former case, other researchers who are knowledgeable in the field constitute the audience and they do not require extensive narrative. They do require reference to several salient studies which set the stage for the subsequent research. Of course, some journals specialize in publishing extensive literature reviews and these help shape the field in their own right. For that purpose, and for most student thesis work, a review of literature should be treated in some respects, at least, like any other piece of research. It normally has an introduction which lays the basis for the review. Here some of the theory and conceptual work might be included setting the framework for the review of research studies that follows. This section might also refer to previous reviews in the area and set the stage for what is to come. Another section should outline the major methods and procedures used. This will include the sources of data and its limitations. In some cases, the criteria for relevance of studies is reported here. Finally, it might go on and describe how the studies are to be grouped in the results which follow. A section on findings will outline the major studies, what they found and will weave them together into an integrated picture of the state of the art. The review would normally conclude with a summarization which summarizes and brings together what was discovered. This section might reiterate the research problem to be investigated and outline the various research questions to be explored. As with any research paper, the review refers to a list of references. This must be scrupulously accurate and presented in acceptable publication style. Any sloppiness here will reflect the possibility of sloppiness in the study which follows. Only the references cited in the review are listed and the list of references is placed at the end of the proposal or study, but before the appendices.

Conclusion

A good literature review is a pleasure to produce and a joy to read. It gives you something concrete to do early in the study and builds your confidence that the definition and design of your study extends what has been done before. It is a good test of you and your problem as it requires diligence, care and thoroughness. It spans the range from strictly mechanical work to highly conceptual thinking. It sets the context for your research and foreshadows your probable contribution.

References

CAMPBELL, D.T. and STANLEY, J.C. (1963) 'Experimental and quasi-experimental designs for research', *Handbook of Research on Teaching*, Chicago, Rand McNally.

PERSELL, C.H. (1976) *Quality, Careers and Training in Educational and Social Research*, Bayside, NY, General Hall.

Part III
Research Methods

Chapter 9

Introduction to Research Methods

What is a research method? A research method is an approach to addressing a research question or problem. Methodology can be compared to fine cooking in that there are many approaches to each product. The French certainly don't make their bread like the Greeks or Italians make theirs, and the taste and texture of the product differs considerably one from to the other. Which product you prefer is a matter of personal taste and perhaps relates, as well, to what you intend to do with the bread. No matter how you process your bread, all approaches require essential ingredients: flour, yeast and water. In the same way, research methods all need data, though its precise nature varies from one approach to another as does the method by which it is processed. What you achieve as your product depends both on the quality of the data and on the way in which it is processed.

To conclude the cooking analogy, many of the best cooks are masters of one particular approach. The same holds true of research methods, but as in the case of cooks, some people are able to combine approaches and improvise depending on the particular challenge at hand. It is useful to observe that the best cooks are often well-grounded in one approach even though they may later go beyond it. For the beginner, it makes considerable sense to learn one approach thoroughly before straying too far into the unknown. Many beginning researchers mix their methods without a good understanding of any one of them. For example, graduate theses often contain some empirical results followed by one or two case studies. In many instances, neither approach is particularly well-handled and the result is merely a learning experience of no general use to anyone but the person who did it.

Any good research proposal or report should include a section on methodology. It provides a separate explanation of what was done and how it was done. The next section describes what the methodology section should contain.

Essential Ingredients

Whatever approach one follows, there should be a thorough description of the key ingredients, enabling any other researcher to understand what was done and replicate it if he or she so desires. The precise nature of the information varies according to the method chosen and what follows is a generalized schema with qualifications noted when appropriate. The methodology section of a research proposal or report of a completed study should include reference to appropriate elements from those that follow.

General Approach

I like to begin the methodology section with a short description of the general approach followed. This may only be a paragraph or two but is important as a way of grounding the methodology in one or more of the traditional approaches used (e.g., experiment, case study, correlational study).

Procedure

In general, all studies should include a section on procedure. The procedure consists of a general statement of how the study was undertaken, who was contacted, when and by whom, what forms the data collection took, ethical issues, and all other matters which would permit another competent researcher to replicate the study. In essence, the procedure section gives a clear and straightforward account of what was done. In a sense, it provides a general overview of the methodology section and portrays the context for specific details which are described more fully in separate sections which follow.

Framework

In some studies there is a need to describe the framework followed (see Chapter 5). This framework often results from the review of literature and is described in that section of the research proposal or report, but there are instances where it fits more logically in the methodology section. Wherever it fits, when a framework is used, it needs to be described fully.

Research Questions

In the same way, the research questions and sub-questions need to be included. In my preferred approach these emerge from the literature review and are included as the conclusion to that section. In this way they set the stage for the methodology section which follows.

Sources of Data

The sources of data should be fully described whether they be documents, settings that were observed, people interviewed or people who completed scales, tests or questionnaires. When the study involves a sample, that, too, needs to be described as well as the sampling procedure used in selection of the sample. The sample is normally described in terms of the numbers of people with the various characteristics called for in the framework of the study. These are often reported in numerical and tabular form. The sampling procedure must also be carefully articulated in order for the reader to understand the relationship of the sample to the group or target population from which it was drawn (see Chapter 18).

Instruments

The data collection instruments also need to be described. Instruments include tests and questionnaires, observation schedules and any other tool used in the collection of data. Ideally, the reliability and validity of the instruments should be reported. If any of the instruments were used in previous studies, that should be noted as well as a clear description of any alterations or modifications which may have been made. In general, the methodology section describes each instrument in two or three paragraphs and a copy of the actual instrument is included as an appendix.

Analysis

A brief description of the particular type of analysis followed should be included. It provides another level of detail to that described in the introductory section on general approach. If there are new or adapted methods of analysis used, they may require considerable technical detail to convey clearly what was done. If standard approaches were used, these are described in shorthand. For example, if it is a statistical study, there are generally technical terms which describe statistical procedures used (e.g., analysis of variance). Sometimes this section also outlines the particular decision conventions used in the statistical analysis such as the adopted level of significance.

Limitations

Finally, all good studies should indicate the limitations of the research. These are the factors which might threaten the objectivity or validity of the study and its generalizability. This section includes both error resulting from inherent design limitations and those which occur as the study progresses. In the game of conducting and reporting research, there is no harm in having limitations but it is bad form not to admit them.

Choice of Method

As one goes about choosing a research area, one must also consider the general method to follow. Often these decisions are interrelated. You are advised to choose a method which builds on your orientation and is supported by your training, but you must also be sensitive to the relationship of the central research question to the method for addressing it. The subsequent eight chapters describe eight different methods which span various levels and research approaches. Each chapter identifies the essential elements of the method, describes it and suggests how it works.

As an orientation to those methods Figure 9.1 describes how the various methods relate to different sorts of research questions and concerns. The research concern here is the integration of disabled children into regular classrooms. As illustrated in the example, each of the eight research methods leads to different sorts of questions.

The **historical** concern might be of interest to historians studying views of the disabled child and approaches to social justice. It

Figure 9.1: *Example of varied concerns of eight different research methods in response to the integration of disabled children into regular classrooms*

Method	Major Concerns/Research Questions
Historical	How have disabled children been treated in the past?
Descriptive	What proportion of children are classified as disabled and in what ways are they schooled?
Experimental/ Quasi Experimental	How does the performance and attitudes of disabled children who are integrated compare to that of children educated in a separate school?
Correlational	What are the best predictors of success for disabled children integrated into a regular classroom?
Ethnographic	What happens to the culture of a regular classroom when disabled children are introduced?
Program Evaluation	How successful was the school system's program of integrating disabled children?
Case Study	What happened to John Smith when he was integrated into a regular classroom?
Policy Research	In what ways can the school system deal effectively with its disabled pupils?

might also be useful for the contemporary researcher to understand better the present state of evolution in our treatment of disabled children.

In many cases, such as particular school districts or settings, we do not have good descriptive data on how children are classified and assigned to schools. That becomes the focus of **descriptive methodology.**

Experimentalists are most concerned with differences in performances and attitudes of children under different sets of educational conditions. Their concern would lead to an experimental study whereby children under different treatment conditions would be observed and the effects monitored.

The **correlational** researcher would be concerned with such things as predictors of success for the integration of disabled children. They would attempt to determine the personal and environmental conditions which led to success.

The **ethnographic** researcher is concerned with the culture of the learning setting and would focus on the effects of this intervention on the whole classroom social environment.

The **program evaluation** mode would focus on a more practical type of research. Its concern is to understand the effectiveness of such an innovation and to determine whether the school system's objectives were achieved through such an intervention.

Case study methodologies might focus on what happens to an individual or perhaps to an individual classroom setting. Case study methodologies are typically eclectic and combine some of the elements of ethnographic research, program evaluation and descriptive methods.

The **policy researcher**, on the other hand, is concerned with more abstract and generalizable considerations. Policy research goes beyond the individual situation or setting and attempts to look at the overall social problem of disabled pupils and how they can be effectively educated.

Through this example, you should begin to understand the differences inherent in the various methods and realize that they focus on different sorts of concerns. Obviously, historical research is concerned with the past, differentiating it from all other methods, but every method has a particular focus and concern. If your research questions suggest one of these concerns then they also suggest which method is appropriate for pursuing them. Thus, if you want to predict, you need to use a correlational type of method; if you want to evaluate, use a program evaluation model; and, if your concern is policy, you are advised to draw from a policy research base. Once you become familiar with each approach, you should be in a position to identify how questions link logically to approaches. Bear in mind also, that these methods are not pure and researchers often combine approaches. For example, you might do historical or descriptive work to identify an issue or problem and then follow it up using predictive approaches. Success at prediction might suggest applications in the realm of educational policy.

Conclusion

Research method is an approach to examining a research question. There are a number of approaches to do so and this text reviews eight such approaches. As you attempt to define and refine your particular research problem, you should consider its methodological implications. Make sure that the problem you wish to pursue is suited to the method you intend to apply. Make sure also that you have the background and strengths required in that method to be able to apply it successfully to your chosen problem.

Chapter 10

Historical Research

Most of us are interested in the past and curious about the way things were in former eras. Those whose curiosity reaches the stage of commitment to do something about it will be interested in historical research. Historical research is past oriented research which seeks to illuminate a question of current interest by an intensive study of material that already exists. Historiography refers to the systematic collection and objective evaluation of data related to past occurrences in order to explore research questions or test hypotheses concerning causes, effects or trends of those events that may help explain present events and anticipate future events. Since history deals with the past, the purpose of historical research cannot be to control phenomenon. Instead, the research is intended to help understand or explain what went on and perhaps to predict into the future. Such journals as the *History of Education Quarterly*, published by the History of Education Society and the School of Education of New York University provide good examples of the types of historical studies that are currently under way.

Description

Historical research shares a great deal with qualitative research in education even though it may make use of quantitative material. Like other forms of qualitative research, the concern is with natural behavior in a real situation and the focus is on interpretation of what it means in the context. Unlike other forms of educational research, the historical researcher does not create data. Rather, the historian attempts to discover data that exists already in some form.

Problem Definition

Historical research problems arise from personal interests which are often kindled by exposure to a person, event or logical source of unused original data. In a review of historical topics, Beach (1969) identified five generic types of topic common in the history of education.

Biographies, institutional histories and histories of particular educational movements are prevalent. In such works the historian seeks to describe what happened. There need not be elaborate hypotheses or startling new issues; the motivation is to describe something that has not been fully described before. There are countless local opportunities for such research and these make good problems for the beginner. Note that with institutional history, the historian tends to approach the task from a social and historical point of view, whereas the same subject can be studied by researchers in institutional development or organizational analysis.

Current social issues form another generic topic type. Such issues as the privatization of schooling, the accountability movement, gender and civil rights beg the question of how such issues were viewed in previous eras. These topics are also descriptive, though explanation typically follows. For example, Bayley (1987), in an analytic study, examined why modern languages were introduced into the curriculum in England a century ago. Her study addressed the issue of resistance to the teaching of practical subjects in secondary schools and related as well to important gender differences which suggest new perspectives on historical inequality.

A third type of historical inquiry involves attempts to interpret ideas or events that had previously seemed unrelated. For example, the relationship of educational opportunities for youth aged 16–20 and problems of youth unemployment.

A related type is the synthesis of old data or the combination of such data with new historical facts or interpretations.

The fifth type of historical problem is called revisionist history. It is an attempt to reinterpret events that other historians have already studied. As might be expected, this is the most advanced type of historical research and is the one requiring most experience.

These five types of issues provide a good starting point for the problem definition process. You must go on, however, to determine whether a sufficient data base exists to permit a successful study. If there are reams of data you may need to confine the topic by limiting the time span of a personal or institutional history. In doing so, there are often definable eras which suggest logical breakpoints. As with all types of research problem, the definition process should continue as you begin collecting and analyzing the data. In doing so, you may uncover unthought-of issues or possibilities which may raise the conceptual level of the study. For example, in studying an educator you could find evidence of the introduction of an educational innovation or method years earlier than previously believed.

Procedure

Basic Steps

Unlike most research procedures, historical research tends to be idiosyncratic depending both on the individual doing the research and on the nature of the topic. In general, however, historians tend to go through the following six steps:

1   Specification of the universe of data required to address the problem adequately.
2   Initial determination that sufficient data are available.
3   Data collection through
    a)   consideration of known data
    b)   seeking known data from primary and secondary sources
    c)   seeking new and previously unknown data.
4   Initial writing of report and descriptive phase of research.
5   Interaction of writing and additional data search and examination.
6   Completion of interpretative phase.

Sources of Data

Educational historians typically make use of four types of historical data sources: documents, oral records, quantitative records and artifacts. Documents are by far the most common data source, but there are many categories of documents ranging from print materials like newspapers, committee reports and yearbooks to informal handwritten documents such as letters, diaries and memoirs. Historians distinguish between intentional documents, produced for public consumption, and unpremeditated documents written for personal use. The intended purpose of the different sorts is different which affects the validity of the information they contain. For example, oral records include not only oral histories recorded to illuminate the past, but also songs, tales and ballads passed from one generation to another. Quantitative records are also important sources of historical data. Tax roles, class lists, birth registries, school report results and other quantitative records can give useful information about participation in education, performance and so forth. Artifacts and relics include objects and sometimes documents which have antiquarian significance. Old school texts, report card forms, corporal punishment devices and old photographs are examples.

It is important to distinguish between primary and secondary data sources. Primary sources refer to documents written by a witness to the events, whereas secondary sources render a second-hand version of what happened.

Data Collection

One difference between historical research and most other types is that the researcher has no ability to create new data. He or she must work with what already exists. Occasionally, it is possible to incorporate interviews and other such techniques as part of historical research. Much of it, to be sure, is conducted in detective-like fashion whereby information is traced to source and those knowledgeable about the event or situation are contacted and used as informants and also sources of written data. In general, quality historical research relies on primary data sources and one should ensure that sufficient sources of this type exist in order to address the problem.

The particular research topic or problem will suggest the logical types of data that may possibly exist. So, for example, a study of a person will attempt to locate biographies, photographs, letters, diaries and newspaper references whereas a study of attendance patterns in a school will focus on other types of historical records. The researcher brainstorms a universe of possibilities and then develops a search plan. Three types of sources need to be identified. Preliminary sources such as bibliographies, atlases and other such standard references will need to be consulted merely to see what general descriptive information exists about the people, places or events of the research. These general references should lead to secondary sources such as books, theses, articles about the thing being research. Thirdly, one needs to identify potential primary sources and their probable location. These may be found in archives, museums or personal collections. A search plan should proceed from the general secondary sources to the specific primary sources and should be explicit if it is to aid the process. The researcher can then pursue the plan and be sure that relevant sources of data are covered.

As the data collection process begins, the researcher has to record the information gathered. Previously, this had to be painstakenly copied by hand on cards for later analysis, but today, photocopying is the norm. One difficulty, however, is the nature of historical material. Much of it is fragile and must be handled with extreme care. Sometimes it cannot be copied either because people won't give permission, it cannot be removed from a location without copying facilities, or it is in faded condition and can only be copied by using elaborate photographic techniques.

Occasionally, historians collect data using sampling or other statistical techniques. In this case, the standard quantitative procedures would be used.

Be sure that you accurately label and classify the data. If voluminous, historical data can be overwhelming and useable classification systems are a big help. Systems from file folders to computer data bases can be used for the purpose.

Data Analysis

An important issue in the analysis of historical data is to realize that data in historical research were not developed in the first place for use in research. The data had a life of their own and were recorded and filed to fulfill someone else's purpose. For this reason, much information is distorted, or biased, or otherwise invalid. The researcher must evaluate the data, a process generally referred to as historical criticism. Two aspects need to be considered: the source and the content. Thus, historical criticism includes external criticism, establishment of the authenticity of the source including its date, author and legitimacy, and internal criticism, evaluating the accuracy and worth of the statements contained in an historical document. This implies evaluating and weighing data according to the extent to which the primary source observer was a credible witness. Information recorded at the time of an event is given more credibility than that reported a long time afterwards.

The central role of the historian is the interpretation of the data in the light of historical criticism. Each fact and supposition must be carefully weighed and added to the case leading to the research conclusion. One challenge for the researcher is the development of a framework for organizing and interpreting the data. Many can be used, but two are worth noting here: organization by date and according to concept. The latter implies identifying key issues or themes then organizing and interpreting the data on that basis.

The historian must carefully weigh the extent to which causality can be inferred and generalization is justified. Historical evidence, like a one-shot case study, cannot be repeated. Furthermore, there is no control group so one can never be sure if one event caused another. The best that can be done is to establish a plausible connection between the presumed cause and effect. Similarly, historians must assess the extent to which the situation of one educator or school was reflective of the general pattern at that point in time.

Writing the Report

As the data collection and analysis procedure progresses, the historical researcher synthesizes the data and writes it up. This is quite analogous to the creation of a review of research as there are no set formulas nor are there prescriptions for how to do it. It is a case of constantly revising and reflecting, and obtaining criticism and advice from others in order to develop the most defensible resolution of the problem. If a framework can be developed, that may suggest a logical organization, but that, too, is idiosyncratic.

In historical research, the review of literature tends not to be a separate section nor is it done independently from the research itself. Rather, it is integrated as part of the data collection, analysis and reporting. Furthermore, the literature tends to be much broader in historical study than in other forms of research. It may include all forms of written communication including primary sources like letters, minutes, legal documents as well as the typical secondary sources found in books and journals.

Thus, historical books and dissertations are of infinite variety. The development of a suitable outline goes a long way towards solving the research problem.

Limitations

A major limitation of historical research is that there is limited opportunity to test the conclusions in a new situation. It might be possible to validate a general conclusion, but much of it is specific to the situation researched, and unless new data are discovered it may not be profitably researched again.

A second limitation is that the data are always incomplete. You do not have the luxury of collecting more data since you presumably have all that exists. So, you are drawing conclusions from partial, if not fragmentary, evidence.

A third general limitation is the validity of the data themselves. Since they were not created to aid the research, they had another purpose and risk being biased. When there are divergent sources of data converging on a similar conclusion, this limitation is reduced.

All researchers bring their own perspective and personal baggage to the problem. The difference with qualitative researchers in general is that there are few conventions about the form of data collection and reporting requirements. The historian, therefore, like the novelist, can create a storyline and text which is only incidentally shaped by the available data. You or I might do it differently and we might relate a different history.

Conclusion

Historical research has its special rewards. People who own or control historical records are often keen to have researchers use them. It is fun to discover things about the past that give shape to present ideas and patterns of thought and it is rewarding to make a contribution to people and institutions which care about the past which affects them. Historical research is also something which can generally be pursued alone with no rigid timetables or artificial constraints. It is a labor of love limited only by your energy and imagination.

For Further Study

BEST, J. (Ed.) (1984) *Historical Inquiry in Education*, American Educational Research Association.

References

BAYLEY, S. (1987) 'Modern Languages as emerging curriculum subjects in England, 1864–1918.' Unpublished PhD Dissertation, McGill University, Montreal.

BEACH, M. (1969) 'History of education', *Review of Educational Research*, 39, pp. 561–76.

Chapter 11

Descriptive Methods

Descriptive methods are introduced here because accurate description is fundamental to all methods, although description is not really a method by itself. For this reason this chapter does not include all the elements normal for research methods.

Description is important because we often do not know the state of the thing being described. For example, we may be interested in the opinions of the population concerning some issue. In such cases a poll is typically taken by which the percentage for, against and undecided can be determined (note that the poll merely describes the result). Its interpretation is another matter. Sometimes researchers want to know the instance of some behavior such as the amount of time a teacher spends talking, the number of decisions a school principal makes in a day or the number of school windows broken in a year. Such descriptive data may be an end in themselves, or they might be necessary to formulate more detailed research questions or to structure a more precise data collection instrument.

Description may be quantitative or qualitative. Quantitative description is based on counts or measurements which are generally reduced to statistical indicators such as frequencies, means, standard deviations and ranges. Qualitative data can be presented in prose, or through audio tape, photographs or film.

Description

Any approach that attempts to describe data might be referred to as a descriptive method. There is a range of sophistication possible in any description whether quantitative or qualitative. The simplist quantitative description reports the data in raw form. As the description gets more sophisticated, the researcher groups the data and presents it in tables and figures. The use of descriptive statistics is merely a convenient way of description. Data are reported in tables organized to give a suitable overall picture at a glance. These simplify the description and lend meaning to data which in raw form is hard to interpret. The most complete and useful descriptions present data in matrices or frameworks (see Chapter 5) which convey data characteristics for sub-groups or different cells in the framework. Often summary statistics such as means, standard deviations, measures of normalcy and so forth are also provided. Qualitative description ranges from brief narrative passages to whole books devoted to the description of a phenomena or setting. In their most complete form qualitative descriptions lead to interpretations which are the basis of ethnography as a method. In general, most studies include such description to some degree, though it may be a minor part of the whole.

There are several uses of descriptive methods which are sufficiently common to be methods in their own right.

Content Analysis

Content analysis is applied to the analysis of data in documents and refers to the systematic description of the contents of documents. Four common uses for content analysis are:

1   to describe the relative frequency and importance of certain topics;
2   to evaluate bias, prejudice or propaganda in print materials;
3   to assess the level of difficulty in reading materials;
4   to analyze types of errors in students' work.

At its simplest level, content analysis involves counting concepts, words or occurrences in documents and reporting them in tabular form. One generally structures a measure which lists the topics to be counted. In this way, one can analyze bias in materials. The treatment of women in text books, for example, can be assessed by counting the number of positive references, the number of negative or gender stereotypical responses, and so forth.

This example illustrates one major limitation of content analysis: it counts as data only what is there and rarely what is missing! In such applications, one must guard against the fallacy of unbiased omissions. Often, the problem is that the target group of interest is not mentioned in the text at all, rather than being mentioned in negative terms. Thus, if one were considering the stereotyping of women, it might be advisable to compare the references to men to those implicating women and to assess the extent of equal treatment.

The other approach to content analysis involves the development or use of a formula or scale with which to analyze such things as the reading level of materials. A number of standard scales for this purpose are based on such variables as the numbers of words per sentence, the occurrence of selected words from a standard list and so forth. These scales can be applied to any text and will indicate its reading level, which is most commonly expressed as a grade level equivalent. In the same way researchers can develop scales to measure the occurrence of concepts, types of arithmetic problems or anything else of interest.

Tracer Studies

Tracer studies involve the tracking down of people who were participants in prior educational experiences (World Bank, 1983). In this sense, tracer studies are longitudinal methods which involve tracking people from one point in time to another. Some people erroneously use such methods to attempt to show that the educational experience caused the present state of former participants. The assumption is that by finding out where people are and what they are doing, we can attribute what they have done to their prior training and experience. Chapter 10 describes the fallacy of attributing cause-and-effect in such studies. If inappropriately used, tracer studies are invalid, but they are effective for studying such phenomena as attrition or brain-drain. In one study (Universalia, 1982), my colleagues and I were able to trace 93 per cent of Caribbean trainees previously supported by the Canadian International Development Agency and found that 76 per cent were residing in their country of origin, with 70 per cent in jobs directly related to their training (p. 51). This study provided considerable support for the cost-effectiveness of a program which was suspected of encouraging a substantial brain-drain. Tracer studies incorporate the use of telephone directories, mailing lists and personal networks to track people whose whereabouts may have been lost.

Sociometry

Sociometry attempts to assess the social structure within a group of individuals by ascertaining the status of each individual in the group.

Various tools are used for this purpose but they generally share a common procedure. They ask people to identify those with whom they have most affinity. This is generally done by asking members to indicate persons with whom they would most like to do an assignment or share other responsibilities. The whole group may thus pick first and second choices and these are analyzed to find the patterns of interpersonal relationships in the group. Persons who are most popular are called stars, and those who no-one selects are referred to as isolates. Sociograms are special types of figures which report the findings of sociometry.

Problem Definition

The challenge in problem definition with descriptive methods is to be clear in advance what data are needed for the description. Indeed this is what separates the accomplished researcher from the casual observer. A trained researcher will define the data needs and the form of data before it is collected.

In some types of research **indicators** are defined. These are predetermined measures which are considered critical for the problem under study. For example, the number of students who drop out of school in a year would be an indicator. Another quantitative example would be the number of teachers who agree with a statement. Indicators might also be qualitative. For example, the extent to which a teacher is teaching the prescribed curriculum. Proper indicators provide a good index of what descriptive data are important. The major issue with indicators is to focus on the right issues. This is just a variation of defining the right research problem. Unless you can focus on exactly the right issue, the description may be of limited use.

One good way of focusing descriptive data is to plan the study in sufficient detail that blank charts and tables are prepared in advance. This effectively indicates how the data will be organized and presented and makes it perfectly clear what data needs to be collected. The data collection procedure then becomes filling up the empty tables. In qualitative research, techniques commonly used in making films can be applied. In that case, a story board is prepared indicating how the film flows from scene to scene and how the visuals match the narrative. In qualitative description the researcher can similarly define the problem by projecting forward to the particular perspectives and viewpoints that need to be portrayed.

Procedure

Instruments

The most commonly used instruments for descriptive research are reports, texts, questionnaires, scales and observation schedules. Reports refer to all kinds of existing material from historical data to statistics. Sometimes people complete tests as part of their research permitting the researcher to describe performance of individuals or groups. Questionnaires may be used to collect self-report data on attitudes, preferences or background information. Research scales are instruments developed to measure attitudes, personality, preferences and so forth. Finally, observational schedules are often used by trained observers to observe a situation (Croll, 1986). Some of these can be highly detailed. For example, twenty-five years ago, one researcher (Flanders, 1970) developed a scale to record what a teacher did every three seconds. As with all good instruments, the researcher should determine the reliability and validity of observation scales. In the case of Flanders' interaction analysis, trained observers yielded highly reliable data on ten teacher activities, but despite many adherents the results never were shown to be related to the effectiveness of instruction, so the scale had no predictive validity.

Data Collection

Valid data collection requires clearly developed procedures and the involvement of researchers or data collection personnel who can follow the procedures consistently and who will not themselves influence the data collected. Most tests, questionnaires and scales contain explicit instructions on how they are to be administered. Observation schedules are often developed to collect systematic observation on educational settings. They are preferred by some to self-reports which tend to reflect socially acceptable responses rather than what might actually occur. For example, observations of classrooms suggests that many teachers talk 80 per cent of the available class time. If those teachers were asked, they would report talking much less, perhaps only 20 per cent (see Edwards and Westgate, 1987). Observation is necessary to collect valid data on this type of phenomenon. The difficulty with observational data is the relevance of what can be observed.

Often the underlying motivations may not be revealed through observation alone.

The question for the researcher is to determine the best data collection technique for what is being pursued. For example, if one were studying inter-race relations, you could give students a questionnaire to report their attitudes. Alternatively, you could observe the interactions among students of different races and have observational data on the extent of inter-racial contacts. In collecting observational data, four approaches can be used; the duration of behavior, frequency counting, interval sampling and continuous sampling. Duration recording examines the time that something occurs. For example, the time a student spends out of his or her seat. Frequency counts refer to the number of times the student would leave his or her seat. Interval sampling refers to what is happening to a particular individual at predetermined intervals. For example, what a teacher is doing every fifth minute. Continuous recording collects a narrative record of data in diary-type form. It reconstructs events as completely as possible. In some observational situations recording devices are used and the tapes are analyzed in order to have accurate measures of who was doing what when.

Writing the Report

Writing the results of qualitative description takes a great variety of forms. They range from elaborate verbal descriptions including actual quotations of speech to a wide variety of tabular and statistical summaries of what is being described. With quantitative data, one generally arranges the results in tables. These should be arranged in conventional format with appropriate title, headings, labels and footnotes. In most research reporting, the tables are an integral part of the text. If they are factual and totally descriptive they often stand on their own merits, such as a table describing the sample. More typically, explanation or interpretation is provided in the text and one refers in prose to the general results in the accompanying table. In a sense you direct the reader to the significant features shown in the descriptive table. For example, you might say: 'As shown in Table 1, 90 per cent of the male respondents agreed or strongly agreed with the statement'. This type of prose complements the tabular display and provides continuity in the text. This convention applies to all data reporting and analysis, whether descriptive or more complex.

Limitations

Descriptive data is subject to two general types of limitations, those related to reliability and validity. To maximize reliability, one needs to use procedures and measures which will lead to consistent results no matter who is involved in collecting the data. The issue in quantitative description is to define indicators precisely and to structure data collection instruments which lead to reliable results. In qualitative methods, the problem is largely in the training and experience of the researcher who records and reports the data.

A more common problem is that of validity, having the data relate to what you think you are describing. One problem is choosing inappropriate indicators and focusing on the description of things which are not relevant to your intention. You may focus for example on behaviors as an indicator of attitudes but might not uncover important attitudes that do not manifest themselves in overt behavior. There are a wide variety of limitations caused by intentional or unintended biases in the researcher. In using quantitative data, the researcher must be careful to present results in a fair and unbiased way. It is easy to group and present statistics in ways which emphasize a particular point of view. Similarly, descriptive data can easily be presented to mislead. The researcher therefore must constantly struggle to eliminate these tendencies. A fourth problem is the sampling problem and the generalizability of results, or external validity. The problem is that the descriptive data reported refer to a specific sample or set of observations which may not relate to the general pattern. This limitation is often a limitation of reporting and is caused by the tendency of some researchers to talk about their observations in ways which suggest that they apply in general rather than to a specific sample or set of circumstances. It is all right to have limitations, but only if they are acknowledged openly and taken seriously in data interpretation.

References

CROLL, P. (1986) *Systematic Classroom Observation*, Lewes, Falmer Press.

EDWARDS, A.D. and WESTGATE, D.P.G. (1987) *Investigating Classroom Talk*, Lewes, Falmer Press.

FLANDERS, N. (1970) *Analyzing Teacher Behaviours*, Reading, MA, Addision-Wesley.

UNIVERSALIA MANAGEMENT GROUP LTD. (1982) *Canada Training Awards: Mid-Project Evaluation*, Montreal, Author.

WORLD BANK (1983) *Tracer Study Guidelines*, Washington, DC, Author.

Chapter 12

Experimental and Quasi-Experimental Methods

The dominant influence of psychology and the behavioral sciences on the field of educational research is felt most strongly in the applications of experimental designs to educational problems. These disciplines use experimental methods in which the researcher manipulates some cause and observes the effects which are assumed to relate to the cause. Typically, there are two groups: the experimental group and the control group. The experimental group is the one receiving the experimental treatment, and the control group, used for comparative purposes, does not receive the treatment. The nature of this method is such that many researchers use hypothesis testing as a way of framing their research questions. Some tentative hypothesis is established, and the experimental treatment is used to test the validity of the hypothesis. Experimental methods are inherently quantitative, so the field of experimental design is closely linked with statistical methods and procedures. Experimental design is a highly sophisticated and technical field which can hardly be represented in one chapter. The purpose of this chapter, therefore, is to provide an overview of the principles and differences between experimental and quasi-experimental methods.

Description

The Experimental Method

The experimental method is the only method of research that can truly test for cause and effect relationships. In an experimental study, the researcher manipulates at least one variable, controls some variables and observes the effects. The experimental variable that is manipulated is called the **treatment** and is the thing presumed to be making the difference. Treatments include such things as the method of instruction, the types of reinforcement or the arrangement of the learning environment. The experimental method has its roots in the work of Fisher (1925) who conducted controlled agricultural experiments. When different types and amounts of fertilizer were applied to different plots of land, it was possible to monitor the growth of crops and determine which treatment was preferable. As applied to education, the method involves experimentation that, for example, randomly forces students into different types of courses and measures the results. This randomized assignment of student into educational programs is the essence of the classical experimental design.

In graphic terms, one form of true experiment can be depicted as follows:

$$R \quad\quad O \quad\quad X \quad\quad O$$
$$R \quad\quad O \quad\quad\quad\quad\quad O$$

The top line is the experimental group which receives a treatment X. Subjects are randomly assigned to this experimental group or to the control group on the bottom line (randomization denoted by R). The Os indicate observations, generally referred to as pre-tests and post-tests. Thus, both groups are pre-tested, one gets the treatment and both are later post-tested. Comparisons between the test scores of the groups theoretically indicate the effect of the treatment.

A fundamental principle of experimental design is that the participants be randomly assigned to experimental and control groups. When such random assignment is done, there is every reason to believe that the two groups are equivalent. No other method is as effective in making groups equivalent. There is a temptation to believe that matching of individuals in pairs is an effective way but this belief is fallacious. The only approach using matching that can be justified is when matched pairs are then randomly assigned to one group or another.

Such an experiment rests on the fundamental assumption that the effect is related to the cause. This is not necessarily so, as there can be many other factors which influence the results. For example, it has been observed that sometimes the control group, feeling that they are being deprived, deliberately work harder to compete with the experimental group. This is termed the 'John Henry Effect', after the folk hero who, on learning that he was to be replaced by a stream drill, challenged the machine to a contest and outperformed his technological rival, only then to fall dead! To compensate for such effects, researchers sometimes give a **placebo** to the control group, that is some treatment which is intended to make the group feel that it is receiving something special, when in reality, the placebo has no effect on the outcome. A sugar pill in medical research is the best example.

Another example of problems with the experimental method is the 'Hawthorne Effect', which is named after the experiments of the Hawthorne plant of the Western Electric Company in Chicago, where fifty years ago employees were found to perform better no matter what the researchers did to alter the working environment. They reacted to the special attention they received, and that was the real cause of their performance change. These are just two examples of problems with the validity of even carefully designed experiments. Additional validity problems are described later.

Quasi-Experimental Methods

The ex-post-facto, or causal-comparative method examines differences between groups which differ on some natural characteristic. In true experimental designs, the researcher not only manipulates the cause or treatment, but also randomly assigns people to one group or another. Quasi-experimental designs are those where there is also an artificially manipulated treatment, but where randomization is not possible. A typical quasi-experimental design, called the 'non-equivalent control group design' is depicted in the following diagram:

$$O \qquad X \qquad O$$
$$O \qquad \qquad \quad O$$

This is precisely the configuration of the true experiment previously described, except in this case, the participants have not been randomly assigned to receive the treatment or not. On the surface it would appear that if we looked at the changes between pre-test and post-test scores, we can make comparisons of experimental and control groups. In quasi-experimental designs, this is precisely what is done. However, it is fallacious to assume that the treatment is necessarily the cause of observed differences. Since the groups were not randomly formed, the participants must be assumed to be different. For example, children who attend French immersion programs can be compared to those who attend a different type of French instruction. Although such measures as IQ may be similar for both groups, they cannot be assumed to be identical. The parents of children in French immersion may have higher educational aspirations for their children, or for some other reason, might encourage them to take the immersion route. In this case, their higher achievement may be strictly a result of their home environment and have less to do with the nature of their educational experience. As this example illustrates, quasi-experimental methods are often essential in educational research because of the ethical considerations which prevent researchers from assigning humans to different artificial treatments.

Single Group Designs

The previous designs incorporated more than one group, and relied on comparisons between groups. It is also common for researchers to study a single group. The one-shot case study (not to be confused with the case study approach described in Chapter 15) is depicted as follows:

$$X \qquad O$$

In this design, measurements are made after the treatment and the observations are presumed to relate to the treatment. As is readily apparent, this is a weak and insufficient design, though one which can be used in certain case study applications. A more typical design is depicted as follows:

$$O \qquad X \qquad O$$

In this case, measurements are made before and after the treatment, though just on the single group. Here, any changes are assumed to relate to the treatment. A somewhat stronger variation of this design is depicted as follows:

$$O \quad O \quad O \quad O \quad X \quad O \quad O \quad O \quad O$$

This is known as a 'time series design' in which multiple observations are followed by a treatment, after which a number of further observations are made. Obviously, in this approach there are more observations and a more reliable estimate of the pre- and post-experimental conditions.

Single Subject Designs

Occasionally, experimenters conduct research not on a single or multiple group, but on a single individual. These designs are used in clinical settings, where the primary purpose is therapeutic. They are most typically associated with behavior change and behavior modification. These designs rely on the principles of the time-series design, emphasizing repeated reliable measurements. It is important to establish the baseline behavior of the person as it occurs without treatment. For example, children who talk out repeatedly in class, get out of their seats, or undertake aggressive or abusive behavior can have their behavior modified through systematic reinforcement and ignoring of undesirable behaviors. Typically, the researcher takes great pains to establish the baseline of the disruptive behavior. This must be accurately measured and stable before any treatment can be introduced. Always in such one-person designs, a single variable is addressed at one time. So, for example, a child who both talks out and gets out of his seat, will be treated for one behavior problem only. The A-B design basically establishes a baseline in Phase A, and then introduces a treatment in Phase B, as depicted below:

O   O   O   O   X   O   X   O   X   O
Baseline Phase A   Treatment Phase B

In this case, multiple observations are made to establish the baseline, after which a treatment is introduced and observations are made during the treatment. For example, a child who gets out of his seat ten times per hour might then be systematically praised for remaining in his seat. That would be the treatment. One can then observe the effects of this treatment. Generally after a period of time, the treatment is withdrawn and, if successful, the improved behavior continues. This is termed an A-B-A design because the baseline and treatment phase are followed by another period of baseline observation. Other more complex variations are also used involving A-B-A-B designs. Questions of validity with such designs are interesting because they have inherent internal validity, since the subject involved serves as his own control. The external validity comes from repeated applications shown to have similar results.

Problem Definition

The definition of the problem relies on a clear proposition or hypothesis. In their strongest applications, experiments are formulated to test hypotheses derived from theory and prior research. For example, if a certain effect such as the tendency of people to learn when given positive reinforcement is known, then an experiment might be designed to test it under new circumstances. One school class might be praised daily by the principal while a control class is not and the experiment would measure the difference in performance between the two groups. The same approach to problem definition is used regardless of whether it is a true experiment, a quasi-experiment, a single group or a single subject design.

Procedure

Planning the Experiment

Most experimental designs rely on pre-testing so it is important to plan the experiment in advance. It is also necessary to design the experiment so that assignment to experimental and control groups follows the requirements of rigorous experimentation. An example is the Lennoxville French Second Language program I researched in nine schools (Anderson, 1985). There I was fortunate to become involved before a system-wide new French program was introduced and was able to test all the children in kindergarten the year before the new program was introduced. In that case, this group became the control to those who enrolled in kindergarten a year later and had the benefit of the new program. In such a situation, one could not withhold the new program from some children, so the children who were a year ahead were a superb control group. They were not alike as a result of randomization, but they were from the same environment as the others and in large numbers were indistinguishable. We also used as a comparison group, all other like-age children in Quebec who took province-wide French tests.

Sources of Data and Instruments

Experiments lend themselves to a wide range of data sources provided they are quantitative. Typical data includes counts of events, test scores, recorded observations and even physiological measurements. The instruments for recording such data are as varied as the data sources. They range from standardized, paper-and-pencil tests to attitude scales and timings of the 100 meter dash. Such instruments, however, have one thing in common. They must have required statistical characteristics and be reliable and valid. Experimental researchers invest considerable energies to develop reliable and valid instruments.

Data Collection

Because of their history and implicit preoccupations, experimental methods tend to emphasize standardized data collection. The testing conditions need to be the same, including the behavior of the experimenter, the environment and anything else that could affect the result. Often statistical differences rely on differences in test scores of only a few points, so it is important to take every precaution in data collection. The nature of the method implies no need for the major researcher actually to collect the data. Indeed, it is preferable to have someone who is expert at that specialized task do the job.

Data Analysis

Classic experimental design uses an analysis of variance approach and the experiment is designed to fulfill the conditions for valid statistical hypothesis testing. Thus, the various factors in the experiment (such as method of instruction or student gender) comprise a framework with a series of cells, each of which define experimental conditions (for example, method A for male students). The data collected are classified into cells and the statistical procedure indicates which, if any, effects are statistically significant.

It is beyond the scope of this book to describe all the intricacies of statistical analysis as applied to experiments, but an example may help. A simple example is the French second language comparison described earlier. Table 12.1 shows the means and standard deviations on a grade III standardized French test for the experimental group (with French kindergarten) and for the control group. The test-value for the difference between means is 5.25 which is statistically significant ($p < .001$). Thus, the experiment indicates that children in the experimental program would be unlikely to have scores this much higher by chance alone.

Table 12.1: Comparisons of grade III French test scores for groups with different educational programs

Group	N	Mean	SD
Experimental (French kindergarten and structured French program)	103	30.8	4.9
Control (Without French kindergarten)	111	26.4	7.2

Reprinted from Anderson (1985, p. 35).

Report Preparation

Experimental research is generally reported in scholarly papers and journal articles which follow a format prescribed by the conventions of the APA Manual. The study is introduced and briefly related to prior theory and research in the field. Next comes a section entitled method with sub-sections on procedure, sample, instruments, analysis. The results are presented in the third section (generally in tables) followed by a section entitled discussion. In their classic form, such articles separate the results from the discussion. The paper often has a con- clusion section followed by the list of references.

Limitations

Experiments and quasi-experiments do not always prove what the researcher thinks they prove. There are problems related to both internal and external validity. Experimental designers have identified eight major threats to the internal validity of experiments (Campbell and Stanley, 1963):

1 *History*
   History refers to the occurrence of any event in the environ- ment which is not part of the experimental treatment but which may have affected the dependant variable. For example, new adolescent romance might have more to do with school performance than a new curriculum.
2 *Maturation*
   The people involved may have changed or matured during the course of the experiment and this, rather than the treatment,

is causing observed results. For example, experiments in toilet training of your children often succeed because during the course of the experiment the child matures.

3 *Testing*

Testing refers to improved scores on a post-test because of the experience of taking a pre-test. In other words, the pre-test might sensitize people to particular questions and consequently increase their post-test scores because they have seen the questions earlier on the pre-test.

4 *Instrumentation*

Instrumentation refers to unreliability or lack of consistency in measuring instruments. Have the instruments used in the investigation been accurate and precise enough? For example, if an observer tires during a long day, the observations at the end of the day may be less astute than those in the morning.

5 *Statistical regression*

When people are selected because of their extreme scores, there is a tendency for them to score more like the average on subsequent testing. So, for example, if the children with the lowest IQ scores in a class are selected for some remedial program, they would be expected to improve their test scores on subsequent testing, whether or not they had the remedial program.

6 *Differential selection of participants*

The question here is whether the process of selecting subjects has influenced the findings. It often occurs when pre-formed groups are used and those groups were different before the study began.

7 *Attrition*

Have some of the participants left the experiment before the final results are in? It is possible that those finding most difficulty will leave the program, inflating the average scores of the remainder.

8 *Selection maturation interaction*

In this case, combinations of selection, maturation and so forth might affect one group differently from another.

External validity refers to the generalizability of results to the population at large. Major problems are:

1 *Pre-test treatment interaction*

Pre-test treatment interaction occurs when participants respond or react differently because they have been pre-tested. For example, if a pre-test is used, followed by an edu-cational experience, it could sensitize people to the important things to learn. Researchers sometimes use a blind experiment to eliminate this problem. That is, they give one group the treatment, the other a placebo and they do not reveal which group is which.

2 *Multiple treatment interference*

This occurs when the same participants receive more than one treatment in succession. It refers to carry-over effects which make it difficult to assess the effectiveness of a later experiment.

3 *Selection treatment interaction*

Selection treatment interaction refers to different rules per-taining to people being assigned to the experimental as op-posed to the control group.

4 *Experimenter effects*

Sometimes experimenters give unintentional cues which sen-sitize people to the desired result, sometimes referred to as the self-fulfilling prophecy. It can lead to artificial scores for people who are expected to do well.

The previous section on experiments noted several potential diffi-culties with those designs. Random assignment to treatment helps alleviate some internal validity problems, but such issues as attrition may still be factors. Quasi-experimental designs share many of the same problems with internal validity as characterized experimental designs. In addition, they are subject to the problem of statistical regression, differential selection of participants, and selection matu-ration interaction. With respect to external validity, the quasi-exper-imental approaches are more subject to problems because of the use of natural groups. Such groups might collectively be involved in other educational experiences which become third variables affecting the final results.

Conclusion

Generally speaking, experimental and quasi-experimental designs apply to the generalization and basic levels of educational research. The fact that they occur at the higher level opens the way to many more threats to internal and external validity. Experiments can be a useful tool in establishing generalization, but they can also be an inappropriate crutch when used without ample thought to their inherent weaknesses.

For Further Study

CAMPBELL, D.T. and STANLEY, J.C. (1963) *Experimental and Quasi-Experimental Designs for Research*, Chicago: Rand McNally.

References

ANDERSON, G. (Ed.) (1985) *Lessons in Policy Evaluation: A Report on the Lennoxville District French Second Language Program. 1979–1984*, Montreal, McGill University.
FISHER, R.A. (1925) *Statistical Methods for Research Workers*, Edinburgh, Oliver and Boyd.

Chapter 13

Correlational Research

Researchers often collect data on several variables and want to know about the relationships among them. In one sense this is a next level of description, an explanatory level that describes how one variable relates to another. Thus, description in educational research need not be limited to description using variables taken one at a time. Description gains added depth when it includes relationships among variables. In describing a group of teachers, for example, we could describe their leadership ability by listing scores they obtain on a leadership scale. We might also describe how well their pupils do on their final exams. We now have two different variables with scores on both pertaining to each teacher. The obvious question is whether these two variables are related. That is, do the pupils of teachers with high leadership scores perform any differently on final exams than those with low leadership scores? Research problems of this type are the subject of correlational research.

Description

Correlational research involves the calculation of a correlation coefficient which is a measure of the extent to which variables vary in the same way. Correlation coefficients range from −1.0 to +1.0 with 0 meaning no relationship between the variables, and 1.0 meaning a perfect relationship, one to the other. A positive correlation is one in which a higher score on one variable is related to a higher score on the other. This is expressed by a positive value for the correlation coefficient. When there is a negative sign, as one variable increases, scores on the other decrease.

There are a number of specific types of correlation coefficient such as the 'Rank Order' and 'Pearson Product-Moment' correlation. Each type is used for a specific purpose and type of data and it is beyond the present treatment to explain these differences. However, all types tend to work the same way conceptually, so if you understand the concept the rest is a matter of technical detail.

Correlation research is one way of describing in quantitative terms the degree to which variables are related. Typically, correlational studies investigate a number of variables believed to be related to an important variable such as academic achievement. The former are referred to as **independent variables** or **predictor variables** while the latter is known as the **dependent** or **criterion variable**. If two or more different predictors are both correlated with the same dependent variable, then in combination they can be made to correlate higher than either one by itself. This principle leads to a mathematical formulation known as Multiple Correlation. Multiple Correlation combines two or more independent variables to enhance the relationship to a dependent variable.

Without going into elaborate statistics, it is important to understand that the square of the correlation is more important than its absolute value. The square of the correlation indicates the proportion of variance held in common between the two variables. Thus, a correlation of .70 will imply .49 or 49 per cent common variance. Stated another way, 49 per cent of the value of one variable can be predicted from the value of the other. This is high for a research study. More typical correlations might be in the range of .5 which implies only 25 per cent common variance.

The correlation coefficient thus described refers to a linear relationship between variables. Beginning some twenty years ago, researchers have found curvilinear relationships (Anderson, 1968). For example, motivation level is related to performance in a curvilinear manner. If you have too little motivation or too much, you will receive lower performance scores than those with some optimum mid-level of motivation. If one wants to be sure what is going on it is a good idea to plot the scores on a graph and undertake a visual inspection of how the pairs of variables interrelate.

Problem Definition

There are two major approaches to addressing research questions using correlational methods: 'looking' and 'looking for'. Often one generates as many as fifty or more variables with corresponding scores on each variable for every person or element for which data has been collected. For example, a battery of tests might lead to a whole series of scores for the people taking it. In the 'looking' approach the researcher generates correlation coefficients among all variables and then examines them to see which ones are related. One then generally seeks explanations for why these relationships exist. This is an easy way to find significant relationships as the odds are stacked in favor of finding something and what is found can generally be explained. It is a sort of astrological approach to research in which natural and unnatural happenings add credence to a theory of generalities. Thus, this is a useful approach only for preliminary exploration which should be followed by more rigorous research approaches.

The 'looking for' approach is more rigorous as it involves making a prediction of significant correlations based on theory or prior research. The data are then examined to test the theory or principle in a new or applied situation. This is akin to the hypothesis-testing approach used by some researchers: If the theory is correct, then variable A should be related to variable B.

Another use of correlational research is for prediction. If two variables are correlated, then the scores on one can be used to predict the scores on the other. If one variable relates to a different point in time, then prediction may be useful. As one would expect, if many variables are correlated with another, then in combination better predictions can be obtained. As noted earlier, multiple correlation is the technique used for combining independent variables and relating them to a dependent variable. Multiple regression is the term used for predicting scores from such multiple correlations. Such multiple regressions can often lead to relatively accurate predictions and are important tools for the researcher interested in understanding how the predictors interrelate.

The researcher can analyze the multiple regression equation to see how the various predictors combine and interact to predict scores on the criterion variable. For example, a list of characteristics of teaching procedures and methods could be used to predict student success on final examinations and the equation would lead to understanding of how these teaching methods combine to relate to exam results. In this case the problem definition would be in terms of understanding how the various predictors lead to performance results.

A similar principle enables us to predict whether a person will exceed or fail to reach a given score. Thus, we can separate people into distinct groups in this way, such as those who pass and those who fail. The term for predicting group membership is discriminant analysis. It is a useful technique for predicting career success, the tendency to develop a given disease and so forth. It can also be a powerful tool often leading to upwards of 90 per cent success in accurate predictions. The statistical details are beyond the scope of this text.

Procedure

Sources of Data and Instruments

As the problem is defined so too are the sources of data and instruments. Data might already exist in a suitable form and may be able to be used for the purpose at hand. Alternatively, original data can be collected using any suitable test or data collection instrument. One caution pertaining to data is the need for a normal distribution in order to make appropriate use of the required statistics.

Table 13.1 provides an example of existing data which can be used to examine relationships among variables using correlation techniques. The table lists national statistics for the fifty countries with the highest under 5-year-old infant mortality rates together with data on the number of radio sets, school completion rates and male adult literacy. In this case the unit of analysis is the country and the statistics used are country averages on each of these variables. Note that in most developing countries, national statistics are not reliable or valid so one might question the overall utility of these indicators. This is one problem with correlational methods — they can capitalize on the errors and limitations in the data to produce statistically significant data which might be meaningless.

Researchers most often collect their own data using all sorts of instruments, such as attitude scales, results from surveys, statistics on file or measures of performance. Any instrument can be used as long as the data collected are approximately normally distributed. Of course, you also need paired data which is corresponding scores on different measures for each individual. In other words, if Mary Jane received 106 on an IQ test and 32 on a geometry test the scores 106 and 32 are paired as they both apply to the same individual, Mary Jane.

Data Collection

There is not much that is unique to data collection for correlational methods. The normal cautions and conventions apply. One useful rule

Table 13.1:   *Some basic indicators for the fifty countries with the highest under-5 mortality rate*

Country	Under-5 mortality rate 1987	No. of radio Sets per 1,000 population 1985	% of Grade 1 enrollment completing primary school 1980–86	Male Adult literacy rate 1985
1 Afghanistan	304	91	54	39
2 Mali	296	16	25	23
3 Mozambique	295	32	26	55
4 Angola	288	26	24	49
5 Sierra Leone	270	222	48	38
6 Malawi	267	245	28	52
7 Ethiopia	261	284	41	—
8 Guinea	252	30	37	40
9 Burkina Faso	237	21	75	21
10 Niger	232	49	67	19
11 Chad	227	219	29	40
12 Guinea-Bissau	227	34	18	46
13 Central African Rep.	226	58	53	53
14 Somalia	225	43	33	18
15 Mauritania	223	132	80	—
16 Senegal	220	109	86	37
17 Rwanda	209	58	47	61
18 Kampuchea	208	110	50	85
19 Yemen Dem.	202	70	40	59
20 Bhutan	200	14	25	—
21 Nepal	200	30	27	39
22 Yemen	195	22	15	27
23 Burundi	192	53	—	43
24 Bangladesh	191	40	20	43
25 Benin	188	74	15	37
26 Madagascar	187	—	30	74
27 Sudan	184	251	61	33
28 Tanzania, U. Rep. of	179	89	76	93
29 Nigeria	177	85	31	54
30 Bolivia	176	581	32	84
31 Haiti	174	21	45	40
32 Gabon	172	96	59	70
33 Uganda	172	22	58	70
34 Pakistan	169	90	34	40
35 Zaire	164	100	65	79
36 Lao People's Dem. Rep.	163	104	14	92
37 Togo	156	206	43	53
38 Cameroon	156	95	70	68
39 India	152	66	38	57
40 Liberia	150	228	—	47
41 Ghana	149	184	75	64
42 Oman	—	644	60	47
43 Côte d'Ivoire	145	133	89	53

Table 13.1: *(cont.)*

Country	Under-5 mortality rate 1987	No. of radio Sets per 1,000 population 1985	% of Grade 1 enrollment completing primary school 1980–86	Male Adult literacy rate 1985
44 Lesotho	139	28	27	62
45 Zambia	130	30	85	84
46 Egypt	129	256	64	59
47 Peru	126	203	51	91
48 Libyan Arab Jamahirya	123	222	82	81
49 Morocco	123	175	70	45
50 Indonesia	120	117	80	83
N of Cases	49	49	48	47
Mean, X̄	194.9	122.6	47.9	54.2
Std. Dev.	49.5	126.4	22.1	20.3

Note: Nations are listed in descending order of their 1987 under-5 mortality rates.
Source: UNICEF (1989)

of thumb, however, is that data collected from the same sources are more likely to correlate (and often spuriously) than are data sets from different sources. Thus, if you ask an individual different things on the same questionnaire you are likely to have them correlated. Validity of your findings are enhanced if you use different data sources. For example, if you were correlating student personality and performance it would be better to measure personality on one scale and perform-ance using another method such as how well the student performs in class.

Data Analysis

The data are analyzed using appropriate correlational techniques and the results are put into a correlation matrix. Table 13.2 provides an example for the fifty countries listed in Table 13.1. Correlation matrices have the same variables on the vertical and horizontal axes and each cell in the table indicates the correlation between the pair of variables corresponding to the cell. The diagonal always contains 1s since the diagonal cells represent the correlation of each variable with itself.

In the example, the correlation between variable 1 (under-5 mor-tality) and variable 3 (per cent primary school completion) is .397. This signifies that the higher the under-5 mortality, the lower the pri-mary school completion rate. Figure 13.1 shows the plot of paired data

Table 13.2: Correlation matrix for country indicators

Indicator	1	2	3	4
1 Under-5 mortality	1.0			
2 No. of radios per 1,000	−.236	1.0		
3 % Grade 1 completing pre-school	−.397	1.28	1.0	
4 Male adult literacy	−.542	.229	.265	1.0

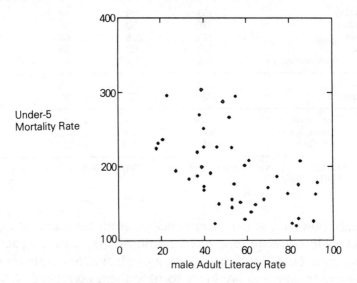

Figure 13.1: Scattergram of literacy correlates

points for the relationship between under-5 mortality and adult literacy. You can see a general but slight negative relationship. There is also a slight curvilinear tendency. It is not very strong when seen visually. Remember that the square of the correlation is the most important numerical data and the square of .542 is only .294 meaning that these two variables share only 29.4 per cent common variance. Thus, this result is not very useful for prediction.

The relationship does not imply that one variable is causing the other. They are related, but not necessarily in a causal way. What, then, does this result mean? In words, the higher a country's infant mortality, the lower its primary school completion rate. In reality, both variables are probably related to an important third variable such as poverty. It may be responsible for a causal relationship. This is called the third variable problem and is always a possibility with correlational research. It is always possible that some third underlying variable is responsible for the relationship between the first two.

Report Preparation

Reports based on correlational research generally follow a traditional research report format. The focus tends to be the correlation matrix and its interpretation. These days most published studies will go beyond a simple correlation matrix in interpreting the data. Computers make further analysis a straightforward matter and such techniques as multiple correlation offer possibilities for more complete understanding of the relationships among many variables, so they are now routine. For example, a multiple correlation approach to the data in Table 13.1 leads to the following regression equation:

Adult literacy = $-.196$ (under -5 mortality) $+.036$ (number of radios) $+.049$ (primary school completion) $+85.94$

Without going into detail, the equation shows that under -5 mortality (with its high coefficient of $-.196$) is the only significant predictor of adult literacy, when all predictors are considered together, even though the other variables also correlate with it. The resulting multiple correlation is .572, not much higher than the .542 of under-5 mortality alone. Thus, in this case, the battery of three predictors is little better than the best predictor by itself.

Limitations

The correlational approach has a number of important limitations.

1 Loose associations — Often variables are loosely associated and the correlational approach does little more then give evidence for these loose associations. Because the resulting correlations are low, they may not be helpful except in suggesting additional more rigorous forms of research.

2 Simplicity of linear model — Traditional correlation methods assume linear relationships between variables. The world doesn't always operate in such a simple fashion and application of correlational methods alone may miss important underlying relationships.

3 Unit of analysis problems — Researchers must be conscious of the true unit of analysis which is often the classroom or school rather than the number of students. Thus, one may in actuality have far fewer cases than presumed.

4 Significance problems — It is possible to obtain with large

numbers in the sample statistically significant correlations which are small in numerical terms. Such correlations may have little or no practical significance even though they represent more than a chance relationship.

5 Causality problems — Correlation does not establish cause-and-effect relationships and it is less rigorous than the experimental approach because variables are not controlled by the experimenter. There is also the ever-present possibility of third variables acting as underlying factors responsible for the relationships.

Conclusion

The correlational method is useful for initial exploration of relationships, particularly when there are a large number of variables. Another strength of the method is that it uses data obtained in naturalistic settings and it facilitates exploration of a large number of relationships simultaneously. Thus, correlational methods respond to the ambiguity and complexity of the real world. They uncover degrees of relationship rather than the all-or-nothing question posed by experimental designs which often focus on whether or not a relationship exists rather than its degree. The weaknesses have been largely noted. In conclusion, correlational methods are a useful starting point when new domains are being explored, but researchers need at some stage to go beyond correlational methods if they are to understand the world and accurately predict the future.

References

ANDERSON, G. (1968) 'Effects of Classroom Social Climate on Individual Learning.' Unpublished ED.D. Dissertation, Harvard University, Cambridge.
UNICEF (1989) *The State of the World's Children*, Oxford, Oxford University Press.

Chapter 14

Ethnographic Research

For much of this century, the field of psychology had a dominant influence on educational research. But it was the failure of the psychological approach to facilitate understanding of how classroom learning occurred that gave rise to an alternative methodology for educational research known as ethnography. Psychological research did an imperfect job predicting why some people learned and others did not, so researchers began to explore the setting and culture in which learning took place. This line of research was also much better adapted to some of the concerns of the 1960s. For example, when a bus-load of black children went, for the first time, to a previously all-white school, Robert Rist (1978), an ethnographer, was there to observe how they would relate to this new situation. This was an important political event and the researcher's concerns were for the whole context of this situation. It was clear that the approaches of behavioral sciences and psychology would not lend themselves to investigation of such sociological and anthropological phenomena.

While ethnography is relatively new in the field of education, it has a long and respected history in the fields of anthropology and sociology (see Bogdan and Biklen, 1982). The first Department of Sociology was founded at the University of Chicago in 1892. One of the leading early figures in the department was Robert Park who went there in 1916, after having worked as a newspaper reporter. He applied the techniques of journalism to the social issues of the day and encouraged students to go forth into society and observe how people lived, a revolutionary idea in education at the time. Out of that tradition emerged such classic studies as the *Sociology of Teaching* (Waller, 1932), *Street-Corner Society*, a study of life among poor Italian men in Boston (Whyte, 1955) and Becker's study of school teachers (Becker, 1951). Even the anthropologist Margaret Mead, after returning from Samoa, turned her attention to schools as organizations and the role of teachers in them (Mead, 1942). All these researchers used their previous background and training in qualitative methods and fieldwork to investigate educational phenomenon.

In the field of education *per se*, Elizabeth Eddy's study, *Becoming a Teacher* (1969), and Harry Wolcott's, *The Man in the Principal's Office* (1973), were early examples of ethnographic studies. Like all ethnographic research, these studies attempted to understand the culture in the setting under study. That is, the concern was with patterns of behavior and their meanings. Ethnographers generally study patterns as they relate to a natural setting. Thus, unlike experimental research, there is no treatment and phenomena are observed without any intervention other than the presence of the observer.

Ethnographic research must subscribe to all the typical ethical considerations of research in general. However, there are some particular issues with this method. While people enter the setting voluntarily and have allowed the researcher to enter, they soon forget why the researcher is there, and they tend to live their professional lives openly without particular regard to the consequences. For this reason researchers have to be particularly careful to protect confidentiality and the identities of the people they study. The other different issue is the possibility that the researcher's presence changes people's behavior in ways which are harmful. There are documented cases in the literature where the presence of researchers has led to overly strict classroom discipline, police brutality and other such evils, simply to impress the researcher. In analyzing the meaning of events, researchers should take particular care to ensure that the situation they observe is not merely a result of their presence and atypical of that culture.

Description

Rist (1975) defines ethnography as 'the research technique of direct observation of human activity and interaction in an ongoing and naturalistic setting' (p. 86). Also known as qualitative research, the main aim of ethnographic research is to discover and describe the culture in an educational setting. The approaches used emphasize inductive analysis, description and perception in the natural setting, rather than the concerns with measurement and manipulation characterized by the experimental method.

Ethnographic research involves participant observation,

description, a concern with process and meaning and inductive analysis. Participant observation is one of the distinctive characteristics of ethnographic research (Dobbert, 1982). Observation is not covert; it is open with the observer participating in the situation. Unlike a normal participant, the participant observer is there for a different purpose than other people in the setting. The participant observer participates but participation is secondary to the main purpose which is research. He or she collects systematic observations about the situation, and periodically withdraws from the setting to analyze the data. The participant observer tries to check his or her perceptions in order to be sure that understanding is valid. By the same token, the participant observer joins in as a learner in the naturalistic setting and becomes socialized to the ways and processes taking place. The concern in ethnographic research is the context, and therefore, the researcher goes there and participates in it. Contexts also include the full range of settings of interest to educators. Sociologists study prisons, families and groups; educational ethnographers study classrooms, schoolyards, buses and staffrooms.

Ethnographic research is inherently descriptive, and in its traditional forms, the description takes the form of words or pictures, rather than numbers. It is what one researcher has termed 'thick' description. Everything observed is recorded, studied and analyzed. This includes the setting, the participants, dialogue, events and the observer's behavior. The researcher guards against ignoring the obvious or trivial, because this may prove significant to understanding the situation.

Ethnographers are concerned with process: How do children tackle arithmetic problems? What is the pattern of interaction in a meeting of teachers? How do people acquire various labels and status within the setting? It is this concern with process that dictates a necessity to be there and participate. One part of process that occupies a good deal of the literature is the concern with entry, how the observer enters the setting. The researcher wants to enter naturally without causing alarm or worse, opposition to the whole idea, and the researcher does not want his or her presence to alter the situation. Entry also tends to set the pattern for the researcher's role in the group, so it is vital to think out possible problems and choose an appropriate entry strategy.

In ethnography, researchers are primarily concerned with what things mean. Interactions among people are analyzed for meaning. Nicknames that teachers acquire are similarly considered. The researcher constantly tries to put him or herself in the position of those being studied. What does a particular event or interaction mean to them?

Ethnographers tend to go looking, rather than go looking for something. Consequently, the detailed questions emerge after the researcher becomes immersed in the situation. This is totally different from the deductive approach of the experimental researcher.

The pieces of data are collected before the patterns are fully analyzed and conclusions drawn. In practice, inductive analysis leads to questions and hypotheses which may be tested deductively during subsequent data collection. The process is what some researchers have termed grounded theory, as the theory emerges from the grassroots and builds to an overall whole. The inherent danger is that the novice may go looking and not see what the more experienced researcher would identify as important. It is not easy to become a competent ethnographer, and universities with specialized shops in ethnography go to great pains to train graduate students in an apprenticeship fashion.

Problem Definition

There are two basic approaches to ethnographic research: open research and focused research. An open research design is used when little is known about the subject under consideration. It is used to develop conclusions and hypotheses and to create an overall picture of the situation. Focused research is used to study areas in which a great deal is already known and there exists an already identified problem, question or testable hypothesis. Focused studies consequently rely on built-in boundaries.

Ahola-Sidaway (1986) conducted a study of the transition of young children from elementary to secondary school. Nothing was known about the transition process, the concerns of students or how this affected them. Her study was a significant example of open research. Wolcott's study of school principals was another similar example. Naturally, the open approach will entail the collection of a broader spectrum of data than might be required when the study is focused.

Procedure

Gaining Entry

One of the major preoccupations of ethnographers is how to enter the field setting. You obviously need the permission of those who control access, but you also need more. You need the respect and trust of those in the setting and must establish a working relationship which gives you license to observe, to question and to participate, and all this must be done without appreciably altering the situation. In schools you must also be introduced to other participants such as children and their parents. It is generally sufficient to explain that you are a researcher studying how the school functions or how children learn or how decisions are made. You must avoid becoming too specific, however, or awareness of the exact focus of your study could change people's behavior in the setting. It is obvious that if you blow your entry you may jeopardize the whole program of research.

Sources of Data

The four major sources of data include archives, the physical setting, events and informants. Archival and written materials are usually used to establish the background or context of a situation, or to help in the analysis and interpretation of data obtained from other sources. As in historical research, one breaks these data into primary and secondary sources. Among the primary sources, calendars, diaries, notes about meetings, are often useful. Secondary material will include public documents and histories of all types.

Even experienced ethnographers record the physical patterns, such as seating patterns, arrangements of furniture, materials displayed on bulletin boards, pictures and so forth soon after they enter a setting. Sometimes photographs or video records are made to collect such data.

Much of the data in ethnographic research revolves around particular events which illustrate the socio-cultural patterns of the larger system of which they are a part. It is terribly important to record who said what, how people reacted, what led up to the event and the patterns which follow it. In some cases the actual dialogue is painstakingly reconstructed.

Finally, informants are used in most ethnographic research. These are people who are members of the group and participants in the situation, but who can shed particular light on the meaning of events or reactions. Most informants are approached informally and information is validated by asking them a specific question or two, which helps interpret what was observed. It gives the researcher an insider's view of the situation and clarifies value patterns, concepts and beliefs which cannot be directly observed. Informants also fill in a lot of gaps since the participant observer cannot be in all places at all times.

Instruments

In ethnographic research, the researcher is the major data collection instrument and the data are collected in field notes as described below.

Data Collection

Ethnographers collect their data in what are called field notes. These are a record of everything the researcher hears, sees, experiences and thinks. Typically, field notes are recorded in a stenographer's notebook. Two types of observations are recorded — descriptive and reflective. The descriptive portion has as its goal capturing a slice of life. Five things are normally written down: portraits of the subjects, a reconstruction of dialogue, a description of the setting, accounts of particular events, and the observer's behavior. The reflective part contains comments prefaced by 'o.c.', standing for 'observer comment'. It includes reflections on the analysis, including themes and lessons learned, reflections on method or procedures used in the study, reflections on ethical dilemmas and conflicts, reflections on the observer's frame of mind and points for further clarification.

Field notes should be written immediately after the researcher leaves the setting. The researcher should not talk about the events before the notes are recorded. The easiest method is to use a chronological account, and experience suggests that it takes three times as long to write good notes as it did to observe the situation. Field notes are often supplemented with interview transcripts, written materials and other data as described in the data sources.

Data Analysis

Since ethnographic research encompasses an inductive approach, data analysis takes place at every step of the research process. Much of it takes place in the field where the researcher develops analytic questions, plans further data collection out of leads and questions in previous notes. It also involves testing out ideas with informants, exploring relevant theoretical literature as you progress. The analysis in the field is also used to further define the problem and restrict the study. This prevents collecting an overwhelming amount of data.

After the data collection is complete, a period which may take many months, accepted wisdom suggests that you rest and distance yourself from the situation. Then you must develop some type of coding categories, using the techniques of content analysis. For some purposes it is useful to do this inductively and let the categories emerge. In other cases, you might use established categories to sort the material. Ten categories have been found to be particularly useful, as listed below:

1　The setting and context.
2　Definition of the situation.
3　Perspectives held by subjects.
4　Subjects' ways of thinking about people and objects.
5　Changes which take place in people or situations over time.
6　Regular activities, such as school recess.
7　Events.
8　Strategies used by people to accomplish things.
9　Relationships and social structures.
10　Methods and research procedures.

There are two ways to accomplish the task of sorting data. One is to do it manually by physically cutting up materials and sorting them into file folders, the other is to assign computer codes and to sort it electronically.

There are, of course, many other aspects to data analysis. Anthropologists use terms like event analysis, network analysis and pattern analysis for their work, but those topics will be left for further study.

Report Preparation

In this type of research the report is not attempted until the field notes have been collected, the data analyzed and the major conclusions have been formulated in the mind. In form, the report of an ethnographic study can be similar to that of other types of research. In the classic anthropological studies, the report begins with a statement of the study questions and explanation of how the questions were arrived at. This introduction is followed by the background research and theory which have led to the study design. The third section outlines the design and methodology in detail. Particular attention should be paid to entry into the field. The presentation of data attempts to describe the social situation from the inside, to tell the reader what it is like to be a member of the situation, and to provide a complete description of it for purposes of scientific understanding. There are many forms to the presentation of data. Some emphasize an insider's view, while others use a more detached, scientific view of the situation. Once the descriptive section of an ethnography has been completed, then higher levels of analysis aimed at achieving explanation are presented and conclusions drawn.

Limitations

Ethnographic research shares many of the limitations of historical research although at least the ethnographer has some control of access to data.

Will different observers get the same result? We all know that there is always more than one valid view of any social situation. People might agree on the facts of the situation but not on what they mean. The researchers' defence is that the work they do is much more scientific than that of teachers, artists or journalists. For them the research is primary. It involves rigorous record-keeping and they have no personal stake in the results. The reliability of informants' information can be another source of concern. The informants' social position in the group, his or her particular personality and the relationship of the informant to the researcher all tend to color the interpretation of data. In practice, researchers tend to triangulate their data and tend to develop levels of confidence in their informants and treat their information accordingly. The reliability of an ethnographic study is difficult to quantify and the results rely entirely on the astuteness of the observer. The observer is the only researcher there so the reliability of results depends as much as anything on the reliability of the observer, the primary data collection instrument.

The validity question begins at the internal level and that is the primary concern of qualitative researchers. The interest is in under-

Figure 14.1: Major differences between traditional ethnographic and formalized ethnographic research

Traditional Ethnographic Research	Formalized Ethnographic Research
Emphasizes in-depth description	Emphasizes explanation
Generally single researcher	Involves multi-person team
Emphasizes discovery of relevant questions and variables in the field	Emphasizes codification of questions and variables before beginning fieldwork
Emphasizes unstructured questioning and observation	Emphasizes standardization of data collection procedures through the use of semi-structured interview and observation protocols
Emphasizes extended presentation of verbal narrative	Emphasizes the systematic reduction of verbal narrative to codes and categories

standing the meaning of the particular culture being observed. Ethnographers argue that the existence of a natural setting enhances validity over that which might be found in some contrived experiment. They point to gorilla behavior which initially showed gorillas to be aggressive animals, but only because they had only been observed in captivity! In the wild, gorillas are inherently mild. Long periods of involvement and observation also help safeguard validity, so that the researcher comes to understand what the particular culture is all about.

External validity is much more problematic. Can the results be generalized to other social situations? More specifically, are the concerns of teachers similar in one school to those in another? In many cases, ethnographic research studies situations which have not been studied before. Perhaps it is fair to say that they give rise to tentative hypotheses and conclusions which, at best, can be investigated in other situations.

Conclusion

This chapter has described ethnography in classical terms. These days, as in other forms of research, ethnographers are beginning to use a variety of methodologies to achieve their aims. Figure 14.1 compares traditional, ethnographic research with what is known as formalized ethnographic research. The latter attempts to use the strengths of ethnography, while using approaches borrowed from other methodologies.

The design of any particular study will depend on the situation examined and the time and resources available to do the work.

For Further Study

BOGDAN, R.C. and BIKLEN, S.K. (1982) *Qualitative Research for Education: An Introduction to Theory and Methods*, Boston, Allyn and Bacon.
DOBBERT, M.L. (1982). *Ethnographic Research: Theory and Application for Modern Schools and Societies*, New York, Praeger.

References

AHOLA-SIDAWAY, J. (1986) 'Student Transition from Elementary School to High School.' Unpublished PhD Dissertation, McGill University, Montreal.
BECKER, H.S. (1951) *Role and Career Problems of the Chicago School Teacher*. PhD Dissertation, University of Chicago. Published in 1980, New York, Arno Press.
EDDY, E. (1969) *Becoming a Teacher*, New York, Teachers College Press.
MEAD, M. (1942) 'An anthropologist looks at the teacher's role', *Educational Method*, pp. 219–23.
RIST, R. (1978) *The Invisible Children*, Cambridge, Mass, Harvard University.
RIST R.C. (1975) 'Ethnographic techniques and the urban school', *Urban Education*, 10, pp. 86–108.
WALLER, W. (1932) *Sociology of Teaching*, New York, John Wiley.
WHYTE, W.F. (1955) *Street-Corner Society*, Chicago, University of Chicago Press.
WOLCOTT, H. (1973) *The Man in the Principal's Office*, New York, Holt, Rinehart and Winston.

Chapter 15

Case Study

Traditional methods of educational research which have emerged from the academic disciplines do not lend themselves well to a wide array of educational situations. The integration of disabled children into regular classrooms, the introduction of a new program or technique, the adoption of a new management strategy for an educational institution are just a few examples which don't readily allow tight control or experimental manipulation. Ethnography is one approach to some of these situations. Another class of research topics are specific situations or educational institutions which because of their individual histories or unique contributions are worthy of study as cases. Education is a process and there is need for research methods which themselves are process-oriented, flexible and adaptable to changes in circumstances and an evolving context. For such situations, the case-study method is often appropriate.

Case studies share something with evaluation studies in that they incorporate a wide range of separate methodologies. The major difference is that the case study does not necessarily evaluate or focus on the concerns of program evaluation. There are a class of case studies, known as evaluation case studies which do evaluate, but for our purposes we will examine the more generalized form of case studies. In general case studies, as in qualitative research, the emphasis is on understanding and no value stance is assumed. The case study method is not to be confused with case studies used as a teaching tool. In such fields as Law and Business, case studies are summarized and given to students to analyze and dissect. In this application, the data base is generally weak and the case is subject to various interpretations and various applications of theory. Case-study research, on the other hand, is highly data based and strives for the same degree of reliability and validity as any good research.

Followers of more traditional research methods sometimes look down on case study on the grounds that it lacks rigor. It incorporates no statistical tests and it does not readily permit generalization. None of these half truths need to apply to the case-study method, which, in its best form, is valid, rigorous and often generalizable. It is true to say, however, that the case study is one of the most difficult methods to do well and the poor examples sometimes reported do not enhance its reputation, but neither do they represent inherent characteristics of the method.

Description

Some people have confused historical research with case study. History deals with the past and case study deals with contemporary events. Others have confused evaluation and case study. The major concern of program evaluation is to find out what happened and its relationship to what was planned; whereas with general case studies, the concern is with how things happen and why. In this sense, case study shares a common concern with experimental research, but unlike the latter, case study does not attempt to control events. Evaluation case studies attempt to understand what is happening and link the contextual realities to the differences between what was planned and what actually occurred.

A technical definition of case study research has been developed by Yin (1981). A case study is an empirical inquiry that:

a) Investigates a contemporary phenomenon within its real life context when
b) the boundaries between phenomenon and context are not clearly evident and in which
c) multiple sources of evidence are used. (p. 23)

Problem Definition

One difficulty in case-study research is defining what the case is. While this might appear to be a trivial question, it can be profound. A case study might focus on a particular decision and how it was implemented. It might involve adoption of policy. It could involve the introduction of a new program or procedure. It might consider the deliberations of a committee or other group of people and their interaction. The famous Watergate case study by Bernstein and Woodword, for example, focused not on the Watergate burglary or Richard Nixon but on the cover-up which was the focus that lead to the unfolding case study. In any case study, the researcher should have a clear vision of what the case is and what unit of analysis the case examines.

The choice of a case implies a knowledge of some interesting issue or feature and that sets the general parameters for the important 'why' question. For example, one might ask why one developing nation prospered while its neighbors fell to ruin or why an individual with overwhelming physical disabilities is able to rise above great handicaps and excel in life. As soon as the case is selected and you begin to understand its dynamics, sub-questions will immediately become apparent. As in other case methods, they provide the general framework with which you explore the case.

The first major issue in case-study research is to focus on the problem — what is the issue that is being investigated? This, of course, relates clearly to the unit of analysis. In case-study research, the data are interpreted as they are collected. Inferences are made in detective-like fashion, so one must be clear on the issues being investigated. The issues give rise to critical questions and these can be summarized in an issues and questions matrix, as described in the following chapter on Program Evaluation. Typically, the questions occur at two levels. There are questions asked of specific individuals when they are interviewed or when they fill out questionnaires. There are also questions asked of the case itself. Remember to keep in mind that the major themes relate to how things are taking place and why. The emphasis in case study is on explanation and these types of questions help to do that.

Procedure

Planning a Case Study

A case study is difficult to do well so the researcher contemplating a case study should be experienced in all the requisite separate methods. He or she should have a deep understanding of the relevant literature, be a good question-asker, listener and observer, be adaptable, flexible and have an inquiring and unbiased mind. The beginner should be cautious, however, about using case-study methods prematurely. Case studies often lend themselves to team research and the complementary strengths of various team members can provide the necessary basis for a successful case study. In conducting a case study with a team the planning requirements for program evaluation will provide a useful guide.

Sources of Data

In conducting case studies, one typically uses six sources of evidence: documentation, file data, interviews, site visits, direct observation, physical artifacts. For most case-study topics, related **documentation** is generally available. This includes reports, letters, memoranda, agendas, previous studies and newspaper reports. **File data** is also important as it includes the records of service and performance, staffing rosters, other lists of names and, perhaps, internal reports and studies. **Interviews** are prime sources of case-study data. Not only does one typically interview a range of respondents, but the researcher attempts to identify key informants who are part of the case and have inside knowledge of what is going on. These individuals are critical to enhancing the validity of the conclusions drawn. Typically, case-study researchers engage in **site visits** and, therefore, participate in **direct observation**. Observational evidence can be very helpful for understanding why things are as suggested by other data sources. Occasionally, one assumes the role of a participant observer. This typically occurs when, because of the researcher's presence, he or she is invited to engage in work or community life. This is a typical approach of anthropological investigators. Finally, **physical artifacts** should not be overlooked. These can include student's art work, assignments or other such materials. With case studies, as with other methods, one should maintain meticulous notes and records of data. Be sure to record the source of documents and the identity of persons interviewed. In order to triangulate your data you will need to be able to retrace their sources.

An example of some typical data sources might be helpful. If you were compiling an institutional case study you should include a table of milestones, the dates and events which help in an understanding of the institution: changes in leadership, the introduction of new programs, construction activities. For an institution, an organigram and staff lists will be helpful as will be minutes of meetings, policy handbooks, regulations and perhaps even a diagram of the physical plant.

Instruments

Because of their multiple data sources, case studies incorporate the full range of formal and informal instruments, from questionnaires to observation schedules. In this respect, they are similar to program evaluation studies though they tend to be longer term and involve more time on–site and in that respect they have some common attributes with ethnographic studies.

Data Collection

As in any methodology, one should have a workplan, defining what will be done, when it will be done and how. Case-study methodology, like ethnography, tends to be a method of immersion. Therefore, the researcher cannot delegate the routine tasks to an assistant. In fact, there are typically no assistants in this type of research. The researcher must be involved in collecting virtually all the data and in interpreting, analyzing and recasting the issues and questions as the data collection unfolds.

Because the case study is part of a contemporary phenomenon, the data collection should ideally be phased so that the researcher is present as major events occur. While the detective can solve a murder after it is committed, it is far easier to be an observer of the events leading up to the killing. Of course, as in the detective example, one can reconstruct some of the past history in order to pick up the case and follow it from there. For this reason, you should be sure in advance that there is a sufficient data base obtainable to permit you to draw valid conclusions. It may be questionable to attempt a case study when key informants are no longer available.

An important aspect of data collection is creation of a case-study data base. Weak case studies generally confuse the data with its reporting, whereas the best case studies maintain a separate inventory of data with charts, tables and numbers which may not be reported in the case-study report but are included as appendices or can be retrieved by other interested researchers. When I conclude a case study, I generally finish with a full cardboard box of documents and other evidence which is archived for possible future reference.

Data Analysis

The masses of data potentially available in case studies can present insurmountable problems unless one knows what types of analysis are to be done. There are two general approaches to the problem. The preferred approach is to use an analytical strategy which takes the literature and theoretical background of the case and utilizes it as a framework for organizing the data. Thus, for example, if one were studying leadership in an organization it might be useful to use the 2×2 matrix in the Hershey and Blanchard (1979) situational leadership theory to classify data. The other approach is to utilize the techniques of the qualitative researcher and to organize the data into descriptive themes. The particular themes will emerge from a content analysis of the data and might well reflect the ten standard categorizations of data from qualitative research.

Researchers sometimes develop explanations which indicate causal links between events. As you explain phenomena, you begin to uncover ways of testing your explanation with other comparable data. One useful technique for doing so is called Pattern Matching, where the pattern of relationships observed in one instance are predicted in another. When the two patterns of interaction match, then validity is added to the conclusion. When I conduct case studies, I like to maintain a list of general conclusions learned about the data as it is collected. I then test these conclusions with informants and in my future data collection. They help direct the types of questions to be asked in interviews or the types of statistics to be located and checked and they keep me on track by helping prevent me from returning home without a crucial piece of information. In case-study research, the analysis phase takes place as the data are being collected. The opportunity to test them in the field is an advantage of this methodology.

Report Preparation

The form of the case-study report relates very much to the purpose for doing it and the intended audience. One typically publishes case studies as books and not often in the journal literature. Thus, researchers often take license and replace the dry deductive research style with lively narrative, sometimes incorporating suspense and intrigue. Typical formats can be linear, analytic, chronological, theory-building or suspenseful. I organized one case study into various themes suggested by the participants and in this way used the verbatim comments of parents, teachers and students to describe the complexities of an alternative school.

A case study is a teaching document generally incorporating a chain-of-evidence borrowing from the techniques used in criminological investigation. The chain-of-evidence notion is that you present the data in a tight and interconnected way so that the reader can follow the evidence and come to the same conclusion. Thus, the case-study report becomes a teaching document which takes the reader along a similar path to the one the researcher has followed in coming to his or her conclusions.

Limitations

Many critics of the case-study method argue that it lacks reliability and that another researcher might come to a differing conclusion. In defense of this charge, good case studies incorporate multiple sources of data. They create a case-study data base incorporating multiple data sources, as opposed to some other methodologies which base their whole conclusion on one particular test or questionnaire. Case studies, on the other hand, go beyond a single questionnaire or set of interviews. They incorporate all types of data and look for converging lines of inquiry. They use triangulation to interpret converging evidence, pointing to a clear conclusion. Conclusions suggested by different data sources are far stronger than those suggested by one alone.

With respect to internal validity, the strongest argument in favor of the case study is that it incorporates a chain of evidence. In doing so, the reader who was not present to observe the case, can follow the analysis, coming to the stated conclusion. Thus, the case study itself strives for internal validity, trying to understand what is going on in the studied situation.

External validity, or the extent to which generalization is possible, is not so easily addressed. It is very difficult to generalize on the basis of one case. Very often, however, there are multiple case studies in which various cases are studied and all of them are later analyzed. For example, in looking at case studies of university development in Third World countries, I have been able to observe a number of similarities and common occurrences. These have been turned into what are referred to as 'Lessons Learned'. A lesson is something derived from a given case but which has potential generalizability to other situations and settings. In this way, by analyzing a variety of evaluation and case-study reports, the Canadian International Development Agency (CIDA) has been able to develop a large corporate memory of lessons learned which can be retrieved from a computerized system and used in the planning of development projects. Every CIDA study now incorporates a section on lessons learned.

The extent to which generalizability is possible will relate to the extent to which a case is typical or involves typical phenomena. Multiple case studies sometime provide such a base and also often indicate exceptions within the cases. It is easy to identify an exception when there are multiple examples and it is also often possible to gain insight into the reasons such an exception exists.

Conclusion

Many situations and institutions suggest significant case studies and case studies are particularly fun to do. However, they are a difficult form of research in terms of theses, publication and academic kudos. They take a long time, often have scant theoretical underpinnings and are voluminous in their written form. Be sure if you set out on a case study that you know what you are getting into and be clear on why you are doing it.

For Further Study

YIN, R.K. (1981) *Case Study Research: Design and Methods*, Beverly Hills, Sage.

Reference

HERSHEY, P. and BLANCHARD, K.H. (1979) *Management of Organizational Behavior: Utilizing Human Resources*, (Third Ed.), NJ, Prentice-Hall.

Chapter 16

Program Evaluation

Evaluation is a prevalent activity in contemporary society. We evaluate people; we evaluate products; and increasingly, we evaluate educational programs and projects (Posavac and Carey, 1980). Evaluation is one good way of assessing whether or not what we are doing is achieving what it is intended to achieve. It also can be used to examine whether the approach being followed is the best way to achieve the desired result, and sometimes evaluation is intended to question whether what we are doing is appropriate to do at all. Sometimes the major purpose of evaluation is to improve a new program or activity. This is generally referred to as **formative evaluation** as its results are intended to feed back and improve ongoing practice. **Summative evaluation**, on the other hand, is directed at evaluating the consequences of a program and is often seen as the principal mechanism for making crucial resource allocation decisions about a program, including its continuance or termination.

While we refer to **Program Evaluation**, many of the same principles and arguments can be used in the evaluation of **projects**. A project is considered a well-defined activity or series of activities with one specific purpose. The time frame, inputs and results are known in advance as well as the costs of the project. Normally, a project is thought of as being self-contained. A program, on the other hand, consists of a group of related projects or activities undertaken in support of a strategic objective. Thus, while each project may have particular goals, the overall program should be the result of an institutional strategy and programming exercise.

People often raise the question of whether evaluation is indeed research. To be sure, there are a great many differences between the two activities. Ten of these are summarized in Figure 16.1. As noted in Figure 16.1, evaluation generally relates to practice and the specific

165

Figure 16.1:   *A comparison between academic research and program evaluation*

Academic Research	Evaluation
1 Relates to theory.	1 Relates to practice and technology.
2 Is built upon previous literature.	2 Literature reviews are often not pertinent to the evaluation issues, though lessons learned in previous activities are crucial.
3 Builds upon previous research activities.	3 Tends to be viewed as an isolated case study though the methodologies may be transferable.
4 Has methodological roots in experimental and quasi-experimental design.	4 Uses an eclectic assortment of methodologies which are more often of a case-study rather than an experimental nature.
5 Research is ongoing often in phases that relate to academic funding.	5 Conforms to time-frames of decision-makers and often occurs within a 3–4 month period.
6 Tries to be objective and value free.	6 Is rooted in values and politics.
7 Has limited concern with practical application.	7 The major concern is practical application
8 Prescription occurs when prediction becomes precise and/or theory becomes law.	8 Is immediately prescriptive based upon logic and experience.
9 Reports are written for other academic researchers.	9 Reports are written for implementors, users and other interested people.
10 Is intended to be published and publicly disseminated.	10 The extent of publicity is controlled by the sponsor of the evaluation.

project being examined. Rarely are circumstances which affect the outcomes being examined for the purpose of generalization. Thus, evaluation is not analogous with academic research, but it does incorporate many of the techniques of research, though for a much more limited purpose.

Much evaluation work comes out of a contract research tradition which differs considerably from the traditions of scholarly and academic research. One major difference is that contract research relies not on the researcher's agenda but on the concerns of an external sponsor. The sponsor is the client of the evaluation and the sponsor sets the major agenda, agrees to the methodology and effectively controls dissemination of the results. The major differences between academic and contract research have been summarized in Figure 16.2.

Whether a particular evaluation study is research or not will depend largely on whether it intends to shed light on general and generalizable concerns or whether it is for the specific purpose of the

Figure 16.2:   Ten differences between contract research and academic research

Contract Research	Academic Research
1 Is sponsored by an agency with a vested interest in the results.	1 Is funded by an agency committed to general advancement of knowledge.
2 Results become the property of the sponsor.	2 Results are the property of the researchers.
3 Studies follow explicit terms of reference developed by the sponsor to serve the sponsor's needs.	3 Studies rely on the established reputations of the researchers and are totally under their control.
4 Budget accountability is directly related to the sponsor and relates to agreed terms of reference, time-frames and methodologies.	4 Budget allocations are generally based on global proposals and accounting is left to the researchers.
5 The work is contractual between sponsor and researchers.	5 The conduct of research is based on 'good faith' between funder
6 The research includes applied recommendations for action.	6 The research produces findings and conclusions, but rarely recommendations except those related to further research needs.
7 By its nature, contract research tends to be interdisciplinary.	7 Academic research tends to extend an identifiable scholarly discipline.
8 Contract research frequently analyzes the consequences of alternative policy options.	8 Academic research is typically focused on a single set of testable hypotheses.
9 Decision-rules relate to predetermined conventions and agreements between the sponsor and the researcher.	9 Decision-rules relate to theoretically-based tests of statistical significance.
10 Research reports are intended to be read and understood by lay persons.	10 Research reports are targeted to other specialized researchers in the same field.

sponsor. In this chapter, we will assume a contract research model and examine evaluation using its assumptions. However, in the absence of a contractual sponsor, similar issues and methods can also be used.

Description

Experimental Approaches

Evaluation is a diverse field including models and traditions as varied as those in all of social science research. The early forms of evaluation came out of the experimental tradition, and good evaluations of a decade or two ago attempted to reflect sound experimental designs. As we all know, in education it is difficult to arrange the lives of people so that they conform to the essentials of experimental design. For this reason, new evaluation approaches have emerged which emphasize case-study and *ex-post-facto* models which do not build in the essential ingredients of an experiment. The experimental model shares with evaluation research a concern with comparisons among groups. I was involved in the late 1960s in a major North American curriculum evaluation project which is the only experiment with which I am familiar that used true experimental methods on a North American scale to evaluate a new secondary science curriculum (see Welch and Walberg, 1974). A sample of teachers were selected from all the known physics teachers (17,000 in all) and were randomly assigned to teach the new course or continue with their old one. All types of comparisons between the old and new courses were made. We evaluated knowledge and concept acquisition, attitudes towards science, the processes taking place in classrooms and a host of aptitudes of both teachers and students and their relationship to the teaching-learning process. At that time, evaluation had not developed as a separate discipline and we incorporated the classical procedures and approaches of experimental researchers. This was an unusually elaborate and rigorous evaluation model and I personally don't feel that the efforts required added much substance which newer more eclectic models would not have provided. In conclusion, in most educational applications, experimental models have limited utility and applicability. They impose design constraints which interfere with normal programming concerns and they emphasize comparisons between treatments rather than understanding of the dynamics at work.

Quasi-Experimental Approaches

Quasi-experimental research approaches, being much more flexible, have been used for years in evaluation projects (see Chapter 12). Since they do not require that individuals be randomly assigned to programs, they are easier to apply than true experimental methods. They have been used generally to address the question of what people learned or, more recently, what was learned by various types of individuals in various circumstances (aptitude–treatment interaction). Stated in that way, such evaluation becomes indistinguishable from academic research as it is intended to explore understanding of differences which might be generalizable. A good example of the quasi-experimental research approach to evaluation was the Lennoxville District French teaching program described in Chapter 12. In that example, a new teaching method was introduced and it was compared to alternative methods. In such experiments the line between evaluation and research is blurred.

Too often in the past, educational evaluation has been characterized by the use of elaborate methodologies to answer questions which should never have been asked in the first place. Unfortunately, most quasi-experimental methods have a track record of mixed or non-significant findings, educationally or statistically. Notwithstanding their research contributions, they, therefore, have not been particularly helpful in addressing broader evaluation issues or in guiding educational policies or practices.

Qualitative Approaches

In response to such limitations, in recent years the whole field of educational and public policy evaluation has blossomed. Many of the new approaches are not intended to emphasize comparisons but rather have as their central concern an emphasis on gaining in-depth understanding of the program and all its effects, both planned and unplanned. Such evaluation approaches combine the strengths of quantitative and qualitative methods and have much in common with case-study methodology. Like case study, their focus is on understanding, but they emphasize program effects rather than analysis of a case which is not necessarily a program.

The field has embraced various orthodoxies over the years. One approach was to examine the outcomes of projects in what was termed 'goal free evaluation' and to assess the program in terms of all its outcomes whether planned or unplanned. One trend even explored what is termed an 'adversary model'. This basically involves two sides of an evaluation — a pro and a con — and a case for each side is debated.

Logical Approaches

The most dominant Canadian model that has emerged is a logical approach developed by the Office of the Controller General (OCG, 1981) and it is used for mandatory evaluations of all Federal programs in Canada. The OCG approach, as adapted by the author and his

Figure 16.3: Summary of major issues of a logical approach to program evaluation

Major Issues	Essential Questions	Comments
Rationale	Does the program make sense? Are the objectives still relevant? Will achievement of the program's objectives ensure attainment of its goal?	The evaluator must understand the program and its environmental context.
Effectiveness	Has the program achieved its objectives?	The program must have explicit objectives on which everyone agrees.
Efficiency	How well has the program been managed?	In Canadian Government usage, the major concern with efficiency is project administration.
	Were there better ways of achieving the same results at less cost?	These issues must be examined within the cultural context.
	Were the most cost-effective alternatives used in managing the program?	
Effects and Impacts	What has happened as a result of the program? What are the unplanned effects? What are the probable long-term program consequences?	The evaluator must be sensitive to both planned and unplanned program effects.

Note: Adapted from Office of the Controller General Canada (1981).

colleagues, suggests four major issues to be addressed in program and project evaluations. These are summarized in Figure 16.3. The major contributions of this model are its emphasis of project rationale and project effects and impacts. I consider these essential areas for exploration in any evaluation.

Program **rationale** is the type of fundamental issue which typically remains overlooked. However, it is often the crux of whether or not a program makes sense. For example, in the mid-1980s soon after the government of Robert Mugabe assumed power, I participated in an evaluation of a project to support rural secondary schools in Zimbabwe. The project was indeed effective in producing school graduates, but I had trouble with what they were learning. The schools taught British O-levels and A-levels and some subjects were full of references to the culture, history and geography of Britain but had little to do with the needs of Zimbabwe after independence. This is a classic rationale question in that one questions what is being done or why.

Program **effectiveness** is the extent to which the program has achieved its objectives. That is, the extent to which planned outputs were achieved. For example, if the objective is to obtain 100 school graduates, the evaluator counts the number who actually graduated. Graduation may be the objective, but it is not the whole story. It is possible that though the participants graduate, they become introverted or resort to a life of crime, or leave the profession for which they were trained, a common problem with teachers. That raises the issue of effects and impact discussed later.

Program **efficiency** is another issue which few evaluations consider. The program may be achieving appropriate things, but not in the most efficient way. In practice, the whole program management function is assessed as part of the study of efficiency. Thus, in a noncomparative way the evaluator examines the various management functions such as coordination, control, planning and decision-making and assesses how well these functions are performed.

Program **effects** and **impacts** refer to the totality of what the program is doing. Effects are short term while impact is the lasting contribution of the program. For example, programs which train teachers in developing countries generally produce the teachers, but often fail to improve education in the country. Largely because of their low status and poor wages, many teachers leave the profession once they have sufficient qualifications to find a better job. The evaluation question is that of finding out what the program is doing to the education system. Such effects go beyond the project or program outputs and concerns of effectiveness. Naturally, both planned and unplanned consequences should be studied.

Problem Definition

The first question that needs to be asked is why the evaluation is being undertaken. There are a number of general reasons for evaluating programs and projects, the most important of which are:

1 To determine whether to continue or discontinue a project or program.
2 To improve the program's practices and procedures.
3 To adjust specific program strategies and techniques.
4 To obtain data for use when instituting similar programs elsewhere.
5 To help decide how to allocate resources among competing programs.

6   To validate program results to outside funders.
7   To determine if the program is meeting its stated objectives.
8   To measure a program's effects and impact.

These general reasons give some guidance as to the purpose of an evaluation. In practice, the purpose must be worked out much more specifically. The first step is for the person sponsoring the evaluation to develop **Terms of Reference** (TORs). Terms of Reference are the specific issues and concerns which the evaluation is to address. In most Federal programs, the TORs reflect the OCG guidelines, however, they normally also provide much more detailed descriptions of what the evaluation is to include. Appendix I shows a sample of such terms of reference for an evaluation of a Canada–Thailand university linkage program (Universalia, 1988). Typically, the major questions in the TORs derive from the project or program management plan or the logical framework analysis (see Chapter 5). Terms of reference usually include the evaluation objective, evaluation issues and questions, a definition of who the evaluation is for, the evaluation schedule and available resources for it.

One of the first jobs of the evaluator is to go over the TORs to clarify the meaning of the questions, to make sure that the specifics are well understood, that any hidden agendas are uncovered and to find out who is to use the evaluation results.

The objectives for the evaluation help in defining the problem. They foreshadow some of the important questions, but in themselves they do not adequately define the problem. For this purpose, one must understand the program and its functioning. Then the TORs can be translated into more specific questions and sub-questions as described later. These form the real problem definition.

Procedure

Preliminary Decisions

By its nature, evaluation is a political activity and in conducting any evaluation one needs to be fully aware of what one is getting into. Increasingly, the Federal government and other sponsors are incorporating mandatory evaluation for all programs. In such cases, evaluation is expected and the political problems are minimized. In public education, on the other hand, evaluation tends to be the exception, reserved for new programs or those about which questions have been raised. Too frequently, evaluations are commissioned merely to get rid of program managers who have fallen out of favor. One must constantly ask why the evaluation is really being commissioned, whether there is commitment to follow through with the results, and whether the evaluation is a genuine activity or the evaluator is merely being used to fulfill someone else's agenda. Be sure you can live within these parameters before you agree to proceed.

Some evaluations are done by an individual, others involve a whole team. It is important that whoever does the evaluation has the background of knowledge, experience and credibility to be in a position to do the job. Occasionally, participatory evaluation is undertaken in which people who have been involved with the project or program participate directly as members of the evaluation team. This is particularly valuable in formative evaluations, where the purpose is to gain understanding of what is going on and how to improve it. One major advantage of participatory evaluation is that it is easier to communicate and implement its results than when the evaluation is done externally. However, such participatory evaluation sacrifices credibility as it is generally not perceived as independent. Whenever there is a team of evaluators, the management of the team raises additional complications. There should always be a team leader and the roles and responsibilities of each team member should be clearly specified in advance. Invariably, the leader is responsible for preparation of the final report which can be difficult to prepare when it involves integrating work of several team members.

The Workplan

One of the first tasks of the evaluators is to develop a workplan which is a document describing in detail the methodology to be used in conducting the evaluation. The advantage of the workplan is that once approved by the client it constitutes agreement on how the evaluation will take place. Evaluations offer unlimited opportunities for misunderstanding and the workplan helps clarify things in advance. Typically, the workplan will include a statement of the objectives and purposes, of the major issues and questions together with a description of how each issue is to be addressed, any instruments to be used in data collection, a breakdown of the tasks and activities to be completed, the responsibilities of team members for the various tasks, the time each task will take and an indication of the format of the evaluation report. The next four sections outline some of the elements of the workplan.

Sources of Data

Evaluations generally include numerous sources of data. People are one of the most important sources. The evaluator must obtain information from those most knowledgeable and involved in the program. These will include staff as well as senior managers who may have initiated the program and, in the case of many education programs, the evaluation may also include students. A second source of information are the documents which describe the program. The program proposal and any progress reports will be exceedingly helpful in the evaluation analysis. Most Federal projects involve a logical framework analysis or equivalent, an inception report or management plan and often quarterly and annual reports. All these are essential project documents. Project files also contain important information for evaluations. Finally, visits to the site of the project are often indispensible as they show the dynamic and often provide incidental data available in no other way.

Evaluation Framework

In my experience, in conducting numerous project and program evaluations, one of the most useful tools is that of an evaluation framework. The framework is a concrete translation of the terms of reference into key issues of the evaluation, the questions that must be addressed and the data sources and methods used to collect the data. Figure 16.4 indicates a reduced version of such an evaluation framework for the Thailand university evaluation described in Appendix I. Typically, I develop such a framework from the terms of reference and then go over it in great depth with those sponsoring the evaluation. We agree not only on the issues and questions but also on the method and data sources to be used to address them. The framework is also very useful in allocating responsibility for activities and in planning the exercise so that sufficient time is allocated to each issue and question. Sometimes there is a column added between questions and data sources. It is entitled **Indicators** and it lists the objectively verifiable indicators for each evaluation sub-question.

Instruments

Once the preferred methods of data collection and the source of data for each sub-question have been decided, data collection instruments need to be developed. One of the most common instruments used in evaluations is the interview protocol. In practice evaluators develop a series of protocols for various categories of respondents. Generally, the most significant and politically important respondents are interviewed while more routinized data is collected with questionnaires. The importance of well-planned interviews cannot be over-stressed since they provide a means of building trust and confidence in the process of those who will be called upon to implement any recommendations. Besides interview protocols and questionnaires, evaluations should normally include such instruments as blank tables into which quantative data can be recorded. This is particularly useful for effectiveness questions where planned and actual outputs can be listed. Observation schedules, frameworks for content analysis and diagrams are also often useful. In the latter category, it is sometimes useful to construct from documents a planned or presumed organization chart which is modified and updated during the data collection.

Data Collection

Many program evaluations involve case-study methodologies and incorporate all types of quantitative and qualitative data. Major methodologies include: observation, interviewing, questionnaires, unobtrusive measures and sometimes diaries, meetings and the use of knowledgeable informants. One of the major concerns of the evaluator is the validity of the data obtained. The major safeguard on validity is to obtain confirmation from as many data sources as possible. The method is referred to as **triangulation**, whereby various sources of data point in the same direction relative to a given conclusion. It is important throughout the study, but particularly during the data collection, that one be sensitive to the personal and ethical issues involved in evaluation research. The evaluator naturally has a position of power over those being evaluated and, therefore, he or she must be sensitive to the concerns and real lives of people who might be affected by the results.

In practice, the collection of data begins when the evaluation is first proposed. The first step involves a review of all program documentation. This precedes development of the workplan and is indispensible in developing the right questions, the best procedures and methods of data collection. As soon as the evaluator is on board, he or she begins receiving reactions and information from those involved. However, the public and formal data collection begins after the

Figure 16.4:   *Specimen Evaluation Framework Matrix: Thailand Institutional Linkages Project (ILP) Evaluation*

Issues/Questions	Sub-Questions	Data Sources
1 Project Context and Rationale		
1.1 What is the relationship of Thai universities to national development?	1.1.1 What are the key policy features of the National Development Plan that relate to Thai universities?	1.1.1 National Dev. Plans University Dev. Plans Government Documents Ministry of University Affairs
	1.1.2 What is the institutional development status (stage of development) of Thai universities? a) program development? b) staffing? c) finance? d) projected growth?	1.1.2 National Dev. Plans University Dev. Plans Government Documents Ministry of University Affairs University Presidents, Deans
	1.1.3 What involvements do other donors have with Thai universities?	1.1.3 Donor Interviews Donor Reports
1.2 Describe project evolution.	1.2.1 What were key project development milestones?	1.2.1 ILP Status Reports (May/86) CIDA/AUCC Interviews
	1.2.2 What was the Canadian context for LFA assumptions?	1.2.2 Project Team Interviews Thailand Country Program (1985–90) University Interviews
1.3 Assess the validity of project rationale.	1.3.1 What were project assumptions?	1.3.1 LFA CIDA Interviews Project Design Consultant Interviews

1.3.2 What extent are they valid?	1.3.2 Project Team Thai universities Reports
1.3.3 What assumptions to were overlooked?	1.3.3 Project Team Thai universities Reports
1.4 Assess the appropriateness of overall project design.	
1.4.1 Did CIDA have an adequate understanding of the context of Thai universities and their links to national development?	1.4.1 CIDA/Thai Documents CIDA/AUCC interviews Ministry fo University Affairs
1.4.2 Was there an adequate understanding of the interconnectedness of the education system of Thailand?	1.4.2 CIDA/AUCC/Thai Interviews Education Sector Reports Thai University Informant
1.4.3 Was there adequate understanding of the policy environment for the project in Canada and Thailand?	1.4.3 CIDA/AUCC/Thai Interviews Documents
1.4.4 Were alternative methodologies for managing the ILP explored?	1.4.4 CIDA/AUCC Interviews CIDA Files Project Design Consultant Interview
1.5 What do we know about institutional development and linkages in developing countries?	
1.5.1 What are key development agencies doing?	1.5.1 IDRC Interviews/Documents UNDP Interviews/Documents Ford Foundation Interviews/Documents USAID Interviews/ Documents
1.5.2 What has been learned?	1.5.2 IDRC Interviews/Documents UNDP Interviews/Documents Ford Foundation Interviews/Documents Swedish Int'l. Dev. Agency

Figure 16.4: *(Cont.)*

Issues/Questions	Sub-Questions	Data Sources
2 Project Efficiency		
2.1 Has the organizational structure developed by AUCC/STIC led to effective processes for the achievement of the project purpose?	2.1.1 Is the project organigram clear and does it provide an adequate understanding of authority relationships and channels of communication?	2.1.1 Plan of Operation Interviews RTG/CIDA/AUCC/STIC/MUA/Canadian Embassy
	2.1.2 Does the organigram identify the relevant groups?	2.1.2 Plan of Operation Interviews RTG/CIDA/AUCC/STIC/MUA/Canadian Embassy
	2.1.3 Are the roles of involved groups clear, appropriate, able to be carried out?	2.1.3 Plan of Operation Interviews RTG/CIDA/AUCC/STIC/MUA/Canadian Embassy
2.2 Are there appropriate policies and procedures in place to manage the ILP Project activities?	2.2.1 Are there appropriate policies and procedures for generating linkage proposals?	2.2.1 Guidelines for the institutional ICDS Proposal format. Other Policy/Procedure Documents
	2.2.2 Are there appropriate policies and procedures for selecting proposals for funding?	2.2.2 Canadian University Interviews Thailand University Interviews CIDA interviews, STIC Interviews
	2.2.3 Are there appropriate policies and procedures for monitoring project activities?	2.2.3 CIDA Interviews Project Team Interviews AUCC, STIC Interviews
	2.2.4 Are there appropriate policies and procedures for reporting on project activities?	2.2.4 CIDA Interviews Thai Government Interviews Project Team Interviews AUCC Interviews

2.3 Overall, are ILP Project activities appropriately managed?

2.3.1 Have sufficient numbers of proposals been generated to permit choices being made?

2.3.1 Files and records
AUCC/STIC Interviews
Canadian and Thailand University Interviews

2.3.2 Is the selection/review process fair?

2.3.2 Files and records
AUCC/STIC Interviews
Canadian and Thailand University Interviews

2.3.3 Are adequate, systematic data developed for controlling project activities?

2.3.3 Project Reports
Files and records

2.3.4 Is the management team appropriately participative?

2.3.4 Management Team Interviews (IDO, STIC)

2.3.5 Are project participants appropriately informed?

2.3.5 Management Team Interviews Can./Thai Universities

2.3.6 Are there adequate operational plans?

2.3.6 Management Team Interviews Files and records

2.3.7 Are there adequate decision-making mechanisms?

2.3.7 Management Team Interviews Files and records

2.4 Are financial management and controls adequate?

2.4.1 Are budget guidelines and procedures realistic?

2.4.1 AUCC/CIDA Documents Interviews

2.4.2 Were adequate budgets developed?

2.4.2 Budgets/Interviews

2.4.3 Were budget reports timely, adequate, to enable CIDA to control the project?

2.4.3 CIDA Interviews
CIDA/AUCC/University Files

Figure 16.4: (Cont.)

Issues/Questions	Sub-Questions	Data Sources
	2.4.4 Was management by exception utilized?	2.4.4 Reports AUCC Interviews
	2.4.5 Were disbursements made in a timely manner?	2.4.5 Reports AUCC Interviews
	2.4.6 Are there adequate audit provisions?	2.4.6 AUCC/University Interviews Audit Reports
	2.4.7 Was CIDA appropriately involved in the development and revision of financial reporting procedures?	2.4.7 CIDA/AUCC/Canadian University Interviews
3 Project Effectiveness		
3.1 What are the planned vs. actual outputs with respect to strengthening Thai universities for Thai development?	3.1.1 To what extent was leadership strengthened?	3.1.1 Thai and Canadian University Interviews
	3.1.2 To what extent were administrative systems developed?	3.1.2 Thai/Can. University Interviews Documents, On-Site Observations
	3.1.3 To what extent was academic programming developed?	3.1.3 Thai/Can. University Interviews Documents, On-Site Observations
	3.1.4 To what extent were staff and students developed?	3.1.4 Thai/Can. University Interviews Documents, On-Site Observations
	3.1.5 To what extent was a supportive culture developed?	3.1.5 Thai/Can. University Interviews Documents, On-Site Observations
	3.1.6 To what extent was a more adaptable institution, more able to cope with change, developed?	3.1.6 Thai/Can. University Interviews Documents, On-Site Observations

3.2 What are the planned vs. actual outputs with respect to an increase in the capability of Thai universities in Energy and Natural resources and other development priorities?	3.1.7 To what extent were systems developed to access resources?	3.1.7 Thai/Can. University Interviews Documents, On-Site Observations
	3.1.8 Are the inputs and/or outputs able to be sustained?	3.1.8 Thai/Can. University Interviews Documents, On-Site Observations
	3.2.1 What linkages were developed in what sectors?	3.2.1 Can. University Documents, Interviews, Reports and On-Site Visits
	3.2.2 What linkages are planned in what sectors?	3.2.2 Plan of Operation, Can. University Documents, Interviews, Reports and On-Site Visits Ministry of University Affairs
	3.2.3 What is the relationship between linkages and government development priorities?	3.2.3 Thailand National Development Plan, Can. Univ. Documents, Interviews, Reports and On-Site Visits Thai Univ. Development Plan/Documents
3.3 What unplanned effects have occurred as a result?	3.3.1 What unplanned effects have occurred in Canada and Thailand?	3.3.1 Project Reports, Interviews, On-Site Visits
3.4 What is the likelihood that outputs pertaining to the project goals and purposes will be achieved by 1988–90?	3.4.1 What has been the experience to date of implementing linkages?	3.4.1 Synthesis of Data
3.5 What factors are hindering achievement of project outputs and how can they be overcome?	3.5.1 Can hindrances to project objectives be overcome?	3.5.1 Interviews with Key Participants

Figure 16.4: (Cont.)

Issues/Questions	Sub-Questions	Data Sources
4 Sustainability		
4.1 What lessons have been learned from the ILP?	4.1.1 What are the development lessons?	4.1.1 Synthesis of all Previous Data
	4.1.2 What are the operational lessons?	4.1.2 Synthesis of all Previous Data
4.2 Under what conditions should a Phase II be supported?	4.2.1 What are necessary and sufficient conditions for Phase II?	4.2.1 Synthesis of all Previous Data
4.3 What would be the nature of a Phase II?	4.3.1 Describe key management features of Phase II?	4.3.1 Synthesis of all Previous Data
	4.3.2 Describe key program features of Phase II.	4.3.2 Synthesis of all Previous Data

Notes: 1 In this example, it was premature to examine impact so the concern was sustainability, the extent to which the project is likely to be maintained.

2 Many detailed sub-questions have been omitted from the example.

3 Source: Universalia (1988, pp. 34–40).

workplan is developed. Though there are generally many phases to the data collection reflecting the various instruments and sources of data, formal visits to the project site are of particular importance. Meetings should be pre-arranged and one must be sure to give all stakeholders an opportunity to express their views fully and privately. It is generally poor on ethical grounds to report who said what about others, but it is acceptable to provide generalized perceptions or quantify them by indicating the number of respondents holding a particular view. In my work, data collection is not complete until the whole evaluation is put to rest. Reactions to a draft evaluation report are often insightful new perspectives and these are a crucial aspect of data collection.

Data Analysis

As with most forms of research, the analysis of data is seldom a linear didactic process but with evaluations it can be especially eclectic. Good evaluations will often involve all types of data and many forms of analysis and the challenge for the evaluator is to cut through any statistics or particular biases and personal points of view to come to the core of understanding about the project or program being evaluated. In objective terms, is it effective? What unplanned effects is it having? Does it make sense to continue such a project? Are the benefits sufficient to justify the costs incurred? In general, a compatible evaluation team is most helpful in going through this stage of the analysis. Once consensus is reached, the challenge becomes to write the report.

Writing the Report

An evaluation report differs from most research in that it is an action oriented document and the users differ considerably from academic researchers. The readers have a stake in the results and, as with any human evaluation process, program leaders will take all comments personally. The final report should have no factual errors and there should always be a phase of report preparation in which program leaders can correct factual errors in the draft. Of course, there are also areas of judgment which may result in disagreement. These are areas where the evaluator's expertise takes precedence and for better or for worse, the evaluator's judgment will generally carry the most weight.

Most evaluation reports are overly long. The best reports cover the essence in not more than twenty to thirty pages, though they may have extensive appendices. The best evaluation reports have an executive summary which might be as little as two pages and should not be more than five or six. The question that needs to be asked is who are the major audiences for the report. Sometimes there are different audiences with different information needs yielding conflicting messages about the nature of the report. A typical report includes an executive summary, an introductory chapter describing the purpose and methodology followed. The results and finding are then organized according to the major issues of the evaluation. Generally, it should conclude with a summary of recommendations.

Limitations

A general limitation of program evaluation is that like many forms of research, it could be started much better after it is complete. That is, it is often not until the culmination of an evaluation that one fully understands the questions or best procedures to address them. One particular constraint that evaluations suffer is a timeline geared to the demands of decision-makers. They need information in time to make decisions and it is not always possible to have as thorough a piece of research as one would have liked. With academic research there are no decision-makers awaiting the results, so if necessary, one can begin again and re-analyze the problem and its solution.

It is easy to be critical of many evaluations as their validity is often suspect. The major reason is that few evaluations follow sound principles and research procedures. Perhaps the most common limitation is that they are not grounded in reliable and valid data. In fact, many reports use an expert posture which takes the form of a critique rather than a piece of research. We cannot escape our values, but we have an obligation to present data on which we base our conclusions. Then, in proper academic fashion, those who disagree with the conclusions will have all the data and the argument can be appropriately focused on interpretation.

Sometimes, of course, the data itself is suspect, often because the instruments were poorly developed, important sources of data were ignored in the workplan or the data were not collected with care. Validity is much improved through the use of multiple sources of data for each question. With proper triangulation it will be difficult to refute conclusions which follow logically from multiple data sources.

Unlike other forms of research, the true test of the validity of an evaluation is its application and effects on the program being evaluated. A good evaluation will address the objectives of its sponsor and will lead to positive changes in the program under study.

Conclusion

Many evaluation reports sit on shelves and nothing much happens as a result. Good evaluation reports are only one step in the overall evaluation process which involves people and probes them to action. Sometimes the results are implemented because of the power and authority of the evaluator and the terms of reference calling for a program audit or a concrete decision on continuance. More often, the results of the evaluation will filter down to the project in a variety of ways. Research on the effects of evaluations indicate that they are often most effective when there is someone within the project who is convinced of the merits of the evaluation and champions its dissemination.

For Further Study

OFFICE OF THE CONTROLLER GENERAL CANADA (1981) *Principles for the Evaluation of Programs by Federal Departments and Agencies*, Ottawa, Minister of Supply and Services.
POSAVAC, E.J. and CAREY, R.G. (1980) *Program Evaluation: Methods and Case Studies*, New Jersey, Prentice-Hall, Inc.

References

WELCH, W.W. and WALBERG, H.J. (1974) 'A course evaluation', in WALBERG, H.J. (Ed.) *Evaluating Educational Performance: A Sourcebook of Methods, Instruments and Examples*, Berkeley, Calif, McCutchan.
UNIVERSALIA (1988) *Mid-Project Evaluation of the Thailand Institutional Linkages Project Program*, Montreal, Author.

Chapter 17

Policy Research

People beginning an involvement in educational or social science research often think of research in terms of solutions to important social problems. This is a worthy aspiration, but unfortunately not generally within the realm of competence of the beginner. This is the arena of policy research and it involves more than technical competence alone. Policy research is a human activity which explores social issues and problems within their real-life context, attempting to account for the political and practical dimensions of a problem as well as exploration of the technical dimensions of possible solutions. Often policy research assumes a 'what if' stance: What if we integrated physically disabled pupils in our schools? What if we jailed all drinking drivers? What if we doubled the pupil-teacher ratio? These are the types of issues which extend beyond simple experiments, which are broader than evaluations of existing programs and which are the only common form of research which acknowledges and explicitly incorporates values. Thus, policy research extends technical analyses to existing contexts which the researcher must understand sufficiently to be able to forecast the effects of possible strategies and decision alternatives. Policy research is firmly grounded in the policy-making arena and is best tackled by those familiar with that arena.

Description

Policy research is defined as the process of conducting research on, or analysis of, a fundamental social problem in order to provide policy-makers with pragmatic action-oriented recommendations for alleviating the problem. (Majchrzak, 1984, p. 12).

Policy research is distinguished from policy analysis which is the study of the policy-making process. That tends to be of theoretical interest whereas policy research is clearly practically oriented. Only policy research and program evaluation include consideration of the context into which the study results are to be applied. While evaluation research examines an existing program, policy research may explore a course of action not yet put into practice. In both types of research, the researcher must be sensitive to the types of study recommendations that are feasible given the existing socio-political environment (House, 1982; Yeakey, 1982).

Policy research tends not to be bound up in a particular discipline. In fact, it is best pursued when the varying strengths and perspectives of several disciplines can be brought to bear on a problem. For example, in attempting to determine the consequences of developing universities in a Third World country, a labor economist might focus on the effects of a supply of graduates on labor and wage structures; the sociologist might assess the effects on social class and tribal patterns; the educator might explore the effects on retention rates in elementary and secondary schools; the expert in population studies might anticipate changes in fertility patterns; the political scientist might predict a change in the balance of power. Thus, it is the combination of these diverse perspectives which provide the information required by the decision-maker who has ultimate responsibility for a course of action.

Because of its grounding in the context and the many approaches that can be valid in pursuit of decision alternatives, policy research is less prescriptive in method than are most other forms of research. Similarly, its formats and reports vary greatly and are often dependent on what the consumer needs.

Policy research is often conducted by think-tanks or institutes set up to consider social issues. Sometimes these bodies receive funds specifically to explore a defined issue. At other times they receive core funding to analyze fundamental issues of their own choosing. University researchers, consultants and occasionally in-house researchers also may undertake policy research.

Policy research holds some things in common with strategic planning which can use an environmental scan in much the same way that policy research attempts to incorporate environmental data into its predictions.

Problem Definition

A problem poorly defined can not easily be solved and one legitimate function of policy research is to explore the definition of the problem. For example, the famous Coleman Report, *Equality of Educational Opportunity* (1966) which examined educational equality for black children in American schools made its major contribution in clarifying the definition of equality. To be separate was to make black schools inherently unequal and Coleman focused attention on the outputs of schooling rather than on the inputs allocated to schools. This shift in argument gave a new and more important meaning to equality. It was a lot different for the policy-makers when challenged to equalize outputs than merely to equalize inputs. Similar examples relate to family planning which has dimensions of meaning to target groups which go far beyond the technical requirements. Thus, understanding the problem in its context is a legitimate purpose of policy research.

Most studies attempt to go beyond definition to the development of decision-alternatives and recommendations based on probable consequences of a potential decision. The definitional issue with policy research often concerns the boundaries of the problem. In analyzing the possible ban of all smoking in public places, for example, one could restrict the analysis to health costs and benefits, or it could also include such aspects as the political costs and benefits, the effects on employment, and so on. The scope of the problem is often a function of its sponsor since sponsors have vested interests in their particular concern. The researcher, of course, must decide whether the scope prescribed is sufficient to permit an honest intellectual exploration of the problem.

Procedure

Planning

Often in policy research a senior researcher takes a first kick at the problem in order to clarify its definition and determine the types of research competencies required to conduct a thorough analysis. Only then can a research team be formed. Generally speaking, policy research is undertaken by teams as it thrives on diverse backgrounds and points of view. The particular problems will generally dictate the specific skill requirements. One study may require an economist while another has most need of an expert in statistical modeling.

Research Framework

In policy research, one often develops a conceptual model of the social problem. The first step in conceptualizing a study might be the development of a preliminary model. Such a model would generally delineate the definition, assumptions, values and presumed causes of the social problem. This, in itself, is a complex task and there are no set prescriptions for how it is to be done. Researchers often build graphical models or computer simulations of the problem. These indicate presumed relationships between variables which can later be quantified.

Once the preliminary model is developed, specific questions can be formulated. The nature of the questions will depend on what is possible in the context, the type of impact desired for the study and the particular variables which are considered to be malleable. Malleable variables are variables that can be changed to improve the social problem such as the provision of lunches to school children or changes related to racial segregation in schools. The particular research questions formulated should be do-able, timely and important.

Sources of Data

In policy research the data sources can be highly varied ranging from government statistics and census data to survey data collected to obtain reactions to a particular question or scenario. In one study in which I was involved, the problem was to develop a policy for the future development of the independent Jewish schools of Montreal. The central question related to the potential and possibilities for schools serving the different branches of Judaism to combine their physical facilities and become more efficient and effective. In this case, accurate enrollment figures and demographic data were essential for forecasting enrollment trends in the various schools. In addition, the reactions of community leaders to various scenarios were required for the development of viable policy alternatives.

Data Analysis

It has been charged by some academics that policy researchers are at the fringes of existing social science methodology, as they need to adapt, combine and improvise methods as they go. Be that as it may, policy researchers do borrow the methods of all other researchers and use surveys, case studies, qualitative and quantitative methods. Often, these methods are applied as sub-studies which investigate a particular aspect of the policy phenomenon. Based on all the evidence available, the policy researchers hammer out their results and draw their conclusions.

The technical analysis will suggest recommendations which are formulated for discussion. The recommendations are then analyzed with respect to implementation and effects. This generally involves the prediction of potential consequences of recommendations, the estimation of the probability of implementation and, in many cases, the recommendations are revised accordingly. For example, in the study of Jewish schools, it was necessary to propose the construction of new facilities. Several different combinations of existing school clientele and various locations for new buildings were considered and tested with key informants before they were rejected or taken to the next stage.

Report Preparation

Because policy-makers are busy people, studies may need to be communicated in diverse ways, from oral presentations to informal conversations to formalized reports. The policy researcher must be sensitive to the fact that the policy-maker is constantly weighing the political and social consequences of the recommendations advanced, and this often dictates the nature and use of a written report. In some cases, a written report is a good trial balloon which provokes a public reaction, itself an additional piece of vital data for the policy-maker. If the reaction is favorable, that generally adds to the political viability of the recommendations.

Limitations

It is not difficult to criticize any approach to research which is eclectic, as the strength of the method will be only as sound as the particular researcher and instance. In fact, critics may dismiss policy research in general as it does not follow a generalizable method whose limitations can be identified in advance. Remember, however, that policy research is an attempt to provide information to decision-makers. Decisions made with the benefit of information are logically better than those made in ignorance. This is perhaps the true test of the validity of policy research, and its validity, therefore, is a function of its effects on social progress. This may require the full passage of time before its true effects are known.

Conclusion

In conclusion, the policy researcher must be concerned with four major issues: the policy making context of the social problem; the range of definitions of and values held about it; the types of recommendations that would be feasible; and the form of report that would be helpful to the policy-makers.

For Further Study

MAJCHRZAK, A. (1984) *Methods for Policy Research*, Beverly Hills, Sage.

References

COLEMAN, J.S. (1966) *Equality of Educational Opportunity*, US Department of Health Education and Welfare Office of Education.
HOUSE, P.W. (1982) *The Art of Public Policy Analysis*, Beverly Hills, Sage.
YEAKEY, C.C. (1982) 'Emerging policy research in educational research and decision-making', *Review of Research in Education*, 10, pp. 255–301.

Part IV
Research Tools and Techniques

Chapter 18

Survey Research

Many studies in education and the social sciences use surveys to describe the characteristics of groups of people called populations. Characteristics range from attitudes, opinions and measures of performance to basic descriptive characteristics, such as age and gender. So, for example, we might be interested in the educational backgrounds of school principals or in the attitudes of parents who choose to send their children to private schools. Such information is not available from any other existing source, so the survey provides a means of obtaining it.

While at first glance it would appear desirable to collect data from all members of the group, a procedure called a census, this is often not practical and, in fact, it might not be desirable. Consequently, we conduct a survey where we attempt to reach a sample of the desired group or population and collect detailed information from them. Thus, a survey is intended to study a population by selecting and studying a sample of people who belong to it. After selecting the sample, we can then collect our information, using mailed questionnaires, telephone or face-to-face interviews.

Sample surveys are attractive as a means of probing research questions for two major reasons. First, they are much more efficient in cost-benefit terms than would be a study of the whole population. Secondly, surveys are sometimes more effective in that it would take too long and require too many researchers to contact the whole population. It is better to do a thorough job with a representative sample than to do a poor job with everyone. Furthermore, in some cases, by the time so much data were collected, the population characteristics may have changed. On the disadvantage side, there are also two major issues. First is the problem of choosing a suitable sample and secondly, of actually collecting data on the people in the sample.

Restricting data collection to a sample need not be a serious limitation on external validity since with effective sampling techniques, one can generally obtain valid estimates of the characteristics in the whole population. This approach to research generally presumes an interest in statistical data on the population characteristics. Thus, statistics are involved and the challenge is to obtain statistical values which accurately reflect those in the population at large. It should be noted that valid sampling is necessary only when we want to generalize to the target population. When we conduct a pilot study we do so without incurring the cost of sampling and are interested in a quick test of instruments, procedures or research questions. The purpose of this chapter is to outline some of the basic principles of survey research and sampling which can be used in studies involving questionnaires, interviews or other types of tests and scales.

Defining the Sample

Target Population

The first challenge in this type of research is to define the universe or group of interest. This is called the **target population** and it is essential that it be clearly defined and its boundaries understood. The interest in sampling is to generalize to this target population and one cannot pick a suitable sample unless the target population is fully described. Most often, there are restrictions on membership in the target population and it is important to understand who belongs so that we know to whom the results can be generalized. If, for example, the interest is in parents who send their children to private schools we will need to define exactly what population we are interested in. How do we define a private school? Are parochial schools also included? Are we interested only in local private schools? Do we also include private schools far away? Thus, if we focus on the location of the schools we get one target population, whereas if we select parents by where they live we get another. Clearly, if we choose only local schools for our sample we cannot generalize to all parents living in the local area. We can only legitimately generalize to those parents who send their children to local schools. It is also true that the answers to these questions will dictate the ease with which one can find out who belongs to the target population. Thus, it would be easier to find out who sends their children to private schools in the immediate area than who sends them abroad.

Very often, we are also interested in some overlaid characteristics on the target population. For example, if we were studying school principals, we might have an interest in gender differences and, therefore, would like to direct our attention both to male and to female school principals. It is important to know something about the subdivisions within the target population if we are to choose an adequate sample to represent it. If, for example, there are few female principals we might make special efforts to over-represent them in our sample. Often, one has an overall conceptual framework in the study which divides the target population into such characteristics (see Chapter 5). This generally becomes the basis for drawing the sample.

There are many ways to define the target population. One common method is with the use of lists. The target population is defined as all those on the list. The difficulty is that there must be a list available for the group you intend to research and if it is to have utility, the list must be accurate and up-to-date. Very often people's names appear more than once on the same list. This is a common occurrence when membership lists of several organizations are merged, for example. Its result is that some people would have a higher chance of being picked for the sample and, furthermore, these people would be different from others in the population in that they would be members of more than one organization.

In the past, survey firms dealing with attitudes of the public at large often used telephone directories to identify members of the public, but even these lists have a number of serious limitations. They are incomplete since they exclude unlisted numbers and they are always out of date. In response to the problem, survey firms have developed a technique called Random Digit Dialing which uses a computer to generate random telephone numbers which then include new listings, unlisted numbers and any others not listed in the directories.

In conclusion, a fundamental principle in sampling is that one cannot generalize from the sample to anything other than the population from which the sample was drawn. If you don't define your target population clearly you may miss the point when you interpret the results found with the sample. A common, and serious, error among some researchers is to use a restricted group such as Montreal principals in the sample and then to generalize the findings to all school principals in Canada. This, of course, is a problem of external validity.

Drawing the Sample

The challenge in defining the best type of sample for one's needs is to make it **comprehensive**, to give every person a **known probability of selection** and to design it so that data collection will be **efficient**. On the first point, the greater the coverage permitted by a survey, the more valid the results will be. On the matter of selection probability, unless we know what chance for selection everyone in the target population has, we will not be able to generalize to the population and will have a problem with external validity. On the third point, efficiency is the major rationale for sampling in the first place so it is convenient to plan the sample in ways that make data collection most convenient.

Basically, there are two major categories of sampling, **probability sampling** and **non-probability sampling**. A probability sample is a miniature version of the population to which the survey findings are going to be applied. In non-probability sampling, for various reasons, one attempts to define the sample in ways which over-represent groups with certain characteristics. Thus, in non-probability sampling generalization to the population may be considerably more complex. Statistical theory makes it more direct to calculate statistical values based on probability samples and they will be the major focus of our attention in this chapter.

A **simple random sample** is the most common type of sample. It is one in which each person has an equal chance of being selected for participation and where each combination of participants is equally likely. For example, using a table of random numbers, one can select a hundred people from a given target population, yielding a simple random sample. In practice, if the target population is large a simple random sample may be difficult to draw using random numbers simply because everyone would have to be assigned a number. Alternatively, one can use a systematic approach to sampling by taking every nth person on a listing and including them. For example, if you wanted 200 out of a population of 2000, you would select every 10th name. One problem with this approach is the possibility of some periodicity within the list and that, consequently it could make the sample unrepresentative of the target population. For example, on a list of school system personnel, principals might head the listing for each school. One generally uses random numbers to pick the starting point of the list and you can start anew on each page in this way. This generally eliminates sampling problems resulting from a given type of individual appearing on the list at regular intervals. The other limitation of periodic sampling is that every combination of elements in the sample does not have an equal chance of occurring. For example, adjacent names on a list cannot both be included. While this violates one condition of randomness, researchers generally ignore the limitation and treat the data as strictly random.

In **stratified random sampling**, you first sub-divide the population into groups and then select a given number of respondents from each of the groups. For example, the groups could be schools within the school system and one would take a given number of people or proportion from each school. In practice, you might vary the number proportional to the total number of students or teachers in each school. This approach is particularly desirable when as part of your research framework you are interested in differences among the schools. It ensures that each school is represented and it enables school comparisons. Its disadvantages are that it often requires more effort than a simple random sample and it generally needs a larger sample size to produce statistically meaningful results because you should have at least thirty persons in each group or school to make comparisons meaningful.

Cluster sampling involves dividing the target population into groups and then choosing some of the groups on which to collect your data. So in the school example, if there were fifty-five schools, you might select ten of them and collect information from teachers only in those ten schools. A major advantage of cluster sampling is that once you have chosen the group, you can easily administer questionnaires in a group session, increasing the response rate because you have a captive audience. Thus, its advantage is its administrative convenience but its disadvantage is that it is not mathmatically efficient. You might also use two-stage sampling which involves a sample of clusters followed by a sample within each school. Generally you would use cluster sampling when the variations among groups are small and stratified sampling when the variations among groups are large.

Sample Size

The most perplexing question to both novice and experienced researchers is the question of sample size. How many people do you need in order to be able to generalize to the target population? I wish to emphasize that this is a highly complex topic and my attempt at simplifying it should not be considered the definitive word. Sampling is a topic worthy of a whole book in its own right. My assumption is that most graduate students and practitioners have neither the time nor resources to pursue the topic in depth, so I will give a few principles which should satisfy the casual user. Before addressing the size question, it is important to emphasize at the outset that the sample must be representative of the target population. If there are dropouts and problems with response rates, statistical estimates will no longer hold. This will be discussed further in a subsequent section. Because we are interested in statistical characteristics, the factors governing sample size are statistical in nature.

The major principles governing sample size are:

1 *Variability of characteristics being estimated*
   The greater the variability in the characteristics being estimated among units, the greater the number required to obtain a precise estimate of this characteristic. A trivial example illustrates the point. If you wanted to determine the gender of students in a single-sex school, a sample of one would suffice. If you wanted to estimate the average age of pupils in the school you would require more.

2 *Level of confidence*
   The laws of statistics deal in probabilities which means that although a sample will reflect the target population, different samples will vary one from the other. The larger the sample the more alike on average it will be to other such samples that could be drawn.

   For example, if you wanted to estimate the average age in a group, a sample of only ten people would give an average age which might vary considerably from sample to sample. With 100 people in the sample, the estimate would be more stable and the differences in average age for different groups of 100 would be minor. Researchers generally adopt a confidence level of .05 or .01. In other words, the sample characteristics will not differ from the population characteristics more than 5 per cent or 1 per cent of the time (see Chapter 1). The greater the tolerance here, the smaller the sample will need to be.

3 *Tolerance for sampling error*
   How precise do we want the estimate to be? In a close

election a few percentage points can make a great difference in the outcome. This is one reason pollsters cannot call a close election early in the evening — they don't yet have a large enough sample. In most studies, we are content to be able to estimate population characteristics within 3–5 per cent of their true or population values. Here, too, the more precision we want, the greater will be the sample size requirements.

4 *Sample size versus proportion*

A somewhat surprising statistical fact is that it is the absolute size of the sample and not the proportion of the population which is the major determinant of precision. Thus, one can have a relatively small sample with an infinitely large population such as the population of a country and still get acceptable results. A smaller target population will need a sample size which, while generally slightly smaller, is for all practical purposes similar. In general, the major gains in precision are made steadily as sample sizes increase to 150 or 200 after which the gains in precision are much more modest.

5 *Sub-divisions or cells*

The number of sub-divisions for statistical analysis is critical. If you intend to apply a framework and divide the sample characteristics into cells, then as a rule of thumb you should try and have no fewer than thirty in each cell. Thus, if you are splitting the sample by gender, you would need at least sixty. If it is gender by three levels of education, that would require six cells and you would need 180 in the sample.

Table 18.1 illustrates clearly the possibility of accurate forecasts with modest samples when the population is large and the sample is drawn at random.

In summary, the major concern in choosing a sample is that it be large enough to be representative of the population from which it comes. No significant differences should exist between the sample and population on any important characteristic. Thus, the sample should not be older or more experienced or from a different social class or anything else different than the overall population. It is the overall population which is of interest and the sample is just a convenient way of getting at the population characteristics. Sample size is one possible source of error. It is generally of much less importance than the sources described below.

Table 18.1: *Theoretical sample sizes for different sizes of population and a 95 per cent level of certainty*

Population	Required Sample for Tolerable Error of			
	5%	4%	3%	2%
100	79	85	91	96
500	217	272	340	413
1,000	277	375	516	705
5,000	356	535	879	1,622
50,000	381	593	1,044	2,290
100,000	382	596	1,055	2,344
1,000,000	384	599	1,065	2,344
25,000,000	384	600	1,067	2,400

Maintaining Representativeness

The Problem of Low Response

No matter how well the sample is designed and selected, if people drop out for whatever reason, the remaining respondents will not be representative of the population. Refusers are different because they refused. Those who don't mail back the form may be busier, more apathetic or whatever and their omission will bias the results. Hence, once the sample has been defined, the important consideration then becomes to get people to respond in the data collection. Any drop-off in this regard will make the sample unrepresentative of the population and will jeopardize the external validity of all the values obtained.

There are basically three problems: non-contact, refusals and inability to respond. First there is **non-contact** with or lack of accessibility to respondents. The fact that they are in your sample and you can't contact them indicates a problem. The possibility that they have moved or don't answer their telephone or respond to their mail indicates that they demonstrate characteristics which make them different from those who do respond. Since the sample has to be representative, any self-selection in this regard becomes a problem.

The second problem is that of **refusing to respond**. It has been estimated by recent researchers that refusal rates for telephone surveys have stabilized at about 24 per cent; with care they are as little as 7 per cent. In most educational research, we are not concerned with the public in general, and instead focus our research on sub-groups such as teachers, selected parents or pupils. These audiences have a personal and professional interest in educational research and will be more supportive providing our research makes sense to them.

The major problem is not that people refuse, but that they do not take the time to return mailed questionnaires.

A sub-problem is when questionnaires are returned and individual items are left blank. One never knows whether to include the other question responses or to throw out that respondent entirely. Generally, researchers make individual judgment calls when this occurs. This leads to the third problem, **inability to respond**. The most common reason in educational research is that people don't understand the questions because they are poorly phrased or formatted. The solution is to pilot test the questionnaire and use question forms which have been proven to work (see Chapter 19).

In conclusion, the importance of a complete response cannot be over-emphasized. Any fall-off will jeopardize the generalizability of sample statistics to the population. Every effort should therefore be taken to help ensure as complete a response as possible. Recent experiences indicate that response rates of about 65 per cent can be obtained relatively easily if the respondents are at all interested in the study. Special efforts can increase this level appreciably and if 65 per cent is not possible, there could be something fundamentally wrong with the study design. You are better off with 90 per cent response from a sample of 100 than with 70 per cent response from a sample of 200.

Methods of Enhancing Response Rate

Research has shown that response rate is very much a function of how the respondent is approached. A pre-letter can be a valuable means of enhancing response to interview studies. Such a letter should never be more than one page. It should be printed on letter-head stationary with a personalized salutation and individually signed. The contents should include an introductory statement informing the respondents that they will be called for an interview, why they were selected and how subsequent contact will be made.

With mailed questionnaires, the package that arrives is of great importance. It should contain a cover letter, together with a professionally prepared questionnaire, a self-addressed stamped envelope and the envelope should have an actual postage stamp rather than a metered sticker. This is because a stamp is less impersonal and to throw it away or peel it off is inconsistent with most people's sense of propriety. As noted later on the design of questionnaires, design features such as format and length will determine response success.

Figure 18.1: *Typical response rates over time for a mailed questionnaire*

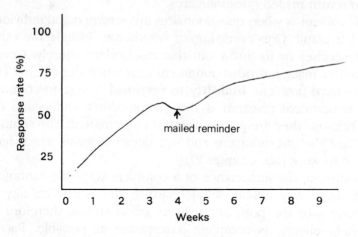

A follow-up mailing will further enhance returns and where possible telephone contact can be most helpful. Figure 18.1 indicates a typical pattern of responses for a mailed questionnaire. The times shown are reasonably representative of what one can expect in this type of survey. The time it takes to respond or the number of reminders required divide the sample into sub-groups whose responses can sometimes be used to predict how non-respondents may have answered. Tables 18.2 and 18.3 indicate actual rates of response for two different types of survey conducted by the author. The first survey was targetted to people who had completed a particular training program during the past 18 months. Questionnaires were individually addressed and were sent in a bilingual (French and English) format. The responses in Table 18.2 came from a survey of agricultural extension workers in Africa. There the questionnaires were distributed by government departments and returned directly. The extended length of response time reflects the remoteness of many respondents and presumed inefficiencies in the postal system. These two surveys, on two different continents and in two widely different situations, resulted in a high overall rate of response. This was due in part to the use of well-developed and professionally printed questionnaires, personalized cover letters and a general commitment of those involved to the purpose of the survey. This is the type of situation one hopes for. Response rates in the neighborhood of 80 per cent are excellent; 60–65 per cent is more typical.

I have experienced considerable success using a follow-up phone call. Personal contact of this nature generally ensures a response, and people who are reluctant to fill out forms are often willing to answer

Table 18.2: *Actual response to a national survey of 395 Government of Canada employment counselors*

Number of Weeks Since Mailing	Response by Week Completed	Unopened	Total Returns N	%
1	73		73	18
2	106		179	45
3	61	2	242	61
4	27	2	271	69
5	20	3	294	74
6	14	1	309	78
more than 6	11	2	322	82

Notes: 1 The questionnaire was mailed in the first week of March, 1989.
2 Unopened questionnaires were returned for individuals who were on leave or had resigned.
3 There were no significant variations in response by province.

Table 18.3: *Actual response to a national survey of 447 agriculture extension workers who graduated from the Malawi Natural Resources College, 1985–1988*

Number of Weeks Since Mailing	Response by Two-Week Period Completed	Unopened	Total Returns N	%
3	42	2	44	10
5	24	3	71	16
7	91	5	167	37
9	70	5	242	54
11	65	4	311	70
13	60	1	372	83

Notes: 1 The questionnaire was mailed during the first week of February, 1989.
2 Unopened questionnaires were returned for people who had resigned or moved.
3 The lengthy time required for responses to be returned relates in part to the slowness of the mail system in remote areas of the country.

questions on the telephone. With a well designed questionnaire, phone responses can be obtained and can be mixed with those gathered by mail.

Conclusion

Surveys are not a panacea in research; they are a necessary evil. they do enable the collection of data not otherwise available, but they introduce all kinds of problems and many potential new sources of error. The main pitfall with sample surveys is that many researchers forget what they are dealing with and consequently begin to assume that the data they have is actual data pertaining to the target population rather than a pale reflection of it. Use sample surveys, but treat your results with appropriate skepticism. The next two chapters will provide further design and implementation information about the two data collection instruments most often used in educational research: the questionnaire and the interview.

Chapter 19

Questionnaire Construction

The questionnaire has become one of the most used, useful but also abused means of collecting information. If well constructed, a questionnaire permits the collection of reliable and reasonably valid data relatively simply, cheaply and in a short space of time. However, there are many sloppy questionnaires and these yield unreliable data of limited validity and utility. The decision to use a questionnaire is generally motivated by a need to collect relatively routine data from a large number of respondents. They may be in one or several locations such as schools, in which case a questionnaire can be administered in a group setting, or they may be widely dispersed and the questionnaire is most efficiently sent by mail.

A good questionnaire is difficult to construct, and to do the job well will probably take ten to fifty hours, including pilot testing, revision and formatting. While time consuming, questionnaire construction is a good way to sharpen what you really need to know, and if done thoroughly, it will greatly facilitate the data analysis phase of the research. The task of questionnaire construction can be facilitated through six essential steps as outlined in this chapter.

Determine Your General Research Questions

To develop valid questionnaires, you must first identify clearly your general information needs. Your needs will relate to the general types of information you require and from whom. Different target groups may be the source of different types of information and the questionnaire will be used only to obtain information which cannot be found more efficiently or more validly another way. The more specific your information needs, the easier it will be to design questions that will achieve your goals. A clear understanding of your needs will help you limit your questions to the information you need and no more. In a busy world there is no place for questions which might be interesting to ask but aren't related to the central theme.

The development of sharp general research questions (see Chapter 3) is an essential step in developing a questionnaire to collect data pertaining to those questions. As noted in Chapter 16, and illustrated in Figure 16.4, the general questions or issues can be turned into an evaluation or research framework which provides the overall topic categories for the questionnaire. An example of a general research question is 'Who are the program participants?' Such a specific but broad question immediately gives rise to sub-questions.

List All the Required Sub-Questions

Each of the broad research questions asked should generate a number of sub-questions (see Figure 16.4 for an example). If your research relates to a research framework, it will be relatively easy to list many sub-questions which are necessary to fill out your understanding of each main issue. Of course, not all the sub-questions will be addressed through the questionnaire as the questionnaire questions will be limited to those best answered by the questionnaire respondents. Other sub-questions may be better answered using other techniques such as study of files and documents, or may be better directed to someone other than the questionnaire respondent.

Following the example of step 1, sub-questions could include: What is the age distribution of program participants? What level of education have participants attained? What is their gender? Such questions are not themselves questions on a questionnaire. They indicate what you want to know, but may not yet be in a form suitable for the questionnaire itself.

As a final task before drafting the questionnaire items, you should highlight, underline or place a checkmark beside each sub-question that will be addressed through the questionnaire. Before moving to the next step you will save yourself time later if you ask yourself whether each sub-question is absolutely necessary. It is easy to have a lot of questions and much harder to restrict yourself to a manageable number of important questions.

Figure 19.1:   Sample fill-in-the-blank item

How many management courses have you completed
in the past two years? _____

Draft the Items

Once you have written your research questions and sub-questions, questionnaire items will immediately become apparent. Working from each sub-question, you should brainstorm as many items as may be needed to gain full understanding of the sub-question. There is an infinite range of question types and many beginners waste time trying to generate creative approaches to questionnaire wording and format. My advice is to master six basic question formats before you attempt alternatives which may get you into trouble. Years of experience have taught me that these types will serve most needs and that if presented as shown here, respondents will understand the items and you will get reliable responses which are as valid as any obtained with a questionnaire. Thus, these six common question formats should serve as models for your work:

Fill-in-the-blank

This common format asks a question and leaves a blank for the response. The stem should be a complete sentence rather than just a phrase. Normally, the answer should not be more than a word, number or phrase (see Figure 19. 1). Note that the answer blank should follow the question. I prefer it to be on the same print line as the last phrase of the question and of a length appropriate to the length of response expected.

Multiple choice

These questions are similar to the fill-in-the-blank type except that the respondent is given a choice of answers and must check one. Sometimes there are discrete response options (e.g., sex: male or female) in other instances a range of values is presented (e.g., annual income: $10,000–$20,000).

It is generally preferable to provide the respondent with choices than to present a blank to be filled in; however, this requires you to have an idea of the range of possible responses. Many people put a line instead of a box, but this confuses some respondents as it is not

Figure 19.2: Sample multiple choice item

How many days of training have you completed during the past 12 months?

none	☐
1–5	☐
6–10	☐
11–15	☐
16 or more	☐

---

readily apparent in a long list of answers which line corresponds to which choice. The box should follow the answer choice rather than precede it. Whenever possible, answer choices should be listed in a single column, but in practice this often consumes too much space, so two columns are common. The danger with more than one column is that people will miss the second column and choose only from the first. The problem is not serious when the choices are in numerical sequence or refer to a defined and inclusive set of options such as the district of residence.

Distinct choices may make analysis easier than is the case with completely open-ended questions, which may have to be reduced to groups later. Furthermore, they provide natural groupings for comparing respondents of various types (see Figure 19.2).

Comment on

Similar in format to the fill-in-the-blank question, this type of question attempts to elicit extensive comments. It poses a question and leaves adequate space for a short paragraph. While this format is essential for in-depth understanding, such questions should not be over-used. They tend to bias the results by giving a greater weight to those who are verbally expressive and tend to evoke responses only from those with extreme views. Furthermore, the information is difficult to analyze and can often be obtained in other ways. Extensive use of these items is a sign that the questionnaire writer has taken an easy route. More thought in planning will pay dividends later on. The example in Figure 19.3 illustrates this type of question:

Figure 19.3: Sample comment on item

To what extent did the training session relate to your job needs?

_____

_____

_____

Figure 19.4:   Sample list item

List three weaknesses of the training session:

1 _____

2 _____

3 _____

As with all question-types which require a narrative response, the amount of space you provide will generally indicate the degree of detail you expect. Sometimes a parenthetical note is added instructing the respondent to add extra sheets as necessary.

List

Asking the respondent to list things is a good way to find out views in an unbiased way. This open format forces the respondent to think up answers without having a list of 'acceptable' options from which to choose. In my experience it is best to force the respondent to list a specified number of views, say three or five. Otherwise, the responses of a few vocal individuals may outweigh the majority who list very little. If each respondent lists three, then it is easy to conduct a content analysis by counting the number of times each theme is mentioned. The example in Figure 19.4 illustrates such an approach. A useful variation on this item is to ask for the list **in order of importance**. This provides additional information on the potency of each suggestion and it enables you to weight the order when making your analysis. For example, the most important weakness can be assigned a weighting of 3, the second 2, and the third, 1. Thus, in this example, first choices are three times as potent as third choices. A variation on this form is to ask the respondent in a subsequent question to pick the one from the list which is most important.

Likert scales

The Likert Scale is one of the most useful question forms. The scale is named after Rensis Likert, who developed this format in 1932. In its most popular format the respondent is presented a sentence and is asked to agree or disagree on a three, five or seven-point scale, as shown in Figure 19.5. Note that a question is not asked. Rather, a clear statement is made and the respondent is asked to indicate whether the statement reflects his or her views. One secret to having effective Likert scales is to observe the following rules for sentencing:

●   Use single sentences containing only one complete thought.
●   Statements should be short, rarely exceeding twenty words.

Figure 19.5: Sample Likert scale item

	Strongly Disagree	Disagree	Not Sure	Agree	Strongly Agree
I use research methods in my job.	☐	☐	☐	☐	☐

- Statements should not be in the past tense.
- Statements should cover the entire range of expected responses; those which are likely to be endorsed by almost everyone or by almost no one should be avoided.
- Avoid statements that are factual or capable of being interpreted as factual.
- Avoid statements that may be interpreted in more than one way.
- Avoid the use of universals such as all, always, none and never.
- Words such as only, just, merely should be used with care and moderation.
- Avoid the use of words that may not be understood by the intended respondents.
- Do not use double negatives.

While Likert scales can have many response points (three to seven being most common), five-point scale is the most practical for most common purposes. It is easy to respond to, straightforward to analyze and sufficient for most needs. Young children, however, are more comfortable with a three-point or even two-point scale. The issue of whether or not to have a neutral mid-point is often debated. I lean to having a neutral position for two reasons. Without one, some people will leave the item blank or mark a mid-point anyway, and secondly research has shown that the proportion of people responding to non-neutral positions when there is no neutral position is similar to the proportion so responding when there is a neutral point and the neutral responders are discarded. In certain forms of these items, a 'not applicable' or 'don't know' category is sometimes added as a sixth response option at the right or left side of the other five boxes.

Likert scales provide an excellent means of gathering opinions and attitudes and they can relate to terms other than agree or disagree. Other useful scales in the Likert form are shown in Figure 19.6.

Likert scales provide a great deal of information in a short period of time and the number of people choosing each response is a simple and effective form of analysis. It is also possible to use such techniques as factor analysis to look for underlying patterns of responses.

Figure 19.6:   Alternate examples of Likert scales

Strongly Approve .... Undecided .... Disapprove .... Strongly disapprove

Probably
right .... Right .... Doubtful .... Probably wrong .... Certainly wrong

Much
greater .... Somewhat greater .... Equal .... Somewhat less .... Not at all

Very high .... A little above average .... Average .... A little below average .... Very low

Practically
all .... Many .... About half .... A few .... Practically none

Like very much .... Like somewhat .... Neutral .... Dislike somewhat .... Dislike very much

Everyone .... The majority .... Quite a few .... A few .... None

Strongly
urge .... Approve .... Neutral .... Slightly Disapprove .... Strongly Disapprove

Favor in
all aspects .... Favor in most aspects .... Neutral .... Favor in a few respects .... Do not favor at all

Absolutely
true .... Probably or partly true .... In doubt; divided; open question .... Probably or partly false .... Absolutely false

---

When using a Likert scale, you need instructions for completing the scale. Typical instructions are included with the sample questionnaire in Figure 19.9. In earlier times, much more extensive instructions were given, but today most respondents are familiar with Likert scales and how to complete them.

Rank

In this type of question the respondent is given a list of items such as priorities or causes, and is asked to rank them in order of importance (see Figure 19.7). An alternative form sometimes used is to ask the respondent to check all answers that are felt to be weaknesses. The true rank-order item is a more powerful form than asking the respondent to check all those that apply since the act of ranking forces some difficult decisions. It is better to know that most people considered a certain problem the most serious with the training program rather than just one of ten problems. In ranking questions one should not normally present more than ten or twelve items to rank since people can become confused. If more items are needed it is possible to modify the question by asking people to rank the five most important from the whole list and ignore the remainder, but this can present difficulties.

Figure 19.7:   Sample rank item

Rank in order of importance the following five weaknesses of the training program. That is, place a 1 beside the weakness you consider most important, a 2 beside the next most important weakness and so forth, until you have ranked all five weaknesses.

	Rank
The training program was too short.	___
The content did not suit my needs.	___
The content was too theoretical.	___
The training group was too large.	___
The training methods were poor.	___

Be sure in any items with a list of responses not to split the list between pages or you will get many response errors. Keep each item on a single page.

Sequence the Items

Good questionnaires, unless they are very short, generally contain sub-sections. If questionnaire items are based on research questions and their sub-questions, they will already be grouped to some degree. You should attempt to refine the groupings into areas with common dimensions. The process is not unlike writing a report with sub-headings and corresponding sections. Such sections give structure to the questionnaire and communicate a sense of purpose and order to the respondent. Within the sections you will have to sequence the questions to accommodate two different principles. A common debate about questionnaire writing is whether or not to group questions on the same topic one after the other, or disperse them throughout the questionnaire. My experience indicates that questions on the same topic should be grouped together and questions of similar form should also be grouped.

The latter principle is particularly relevant for Likert scale items since one does not want to repeat the instructions too often. Since these two principles are not always compatible, you may have to re-write some questions or perhaps change the sectioning of the questionnaire so that question types are not constantly shifting back and forth.

Sometimes it is necessary to use what are called filter questions. These filter out people with given characteristics and send them to a different branch from the others. Thus, those who attended a particular management training course will be asked to answer questions about it; those who did not take the course will skip those questions. It is necessary when designing branches to make a flow chart from the filter questions. Extensive page flipping should be avoided and the respondent should always move forward through the questionnaire.

Another consideration is the overall organization of the questionnaire. It should begin with easy, non-threatening questions (see Sudan and Bradburn, 1982). Questions about age, gender, annual income can be threatening and are generally best asked at the end rather than the beginning. Never start a questionnaire with an open question that requires much writing, as this will discourage people and lower the response rate. The various sections should be organized in logical fashion generally progressing from descriptive type information to more involved attitudes and opinions.

Proper sequencing will involve question editing and should lead to removal of questions that are redundant or unnecessary. The questionnaire should be as short as possible to achieve its purpose. The permissable length is related to the respondents and their vested interest in the questionnaire. Typically, questionnaires should be limited to two to four pages unless the respondents are highly motivated, in which case up to sixteen pages are possible. Respondents will be motivated when they believe the results will affect them or something they believe in. Sometimes respondents can be motivated by the promise of a reward for returning the questionnaire. Remember, too, that lengthy questionnaires require lengthy analyses.

Design the Questionnaire

The format of a questionnaire is extremely important because it is a major factor in determining whether the questionnaire will be completed. An attractive, well laid-out and easy-to-use questionnaire is taken more seriously than one which is thrown together with a minimum of thought. There are two important aspects to design: individual questions and the whole questionnaire. For individual questions, certain types of questionnaire layouts can reduce confusion and contribute to valid reponses. As noted earlier, response options for multiple choice, rank or list formats should be in a single column following the questions stem. Fill-in-the-blanks or response boxes should follow the question rather than precede it. Likert scale responses can follow the sentence being rated or appear at the right of it.

The second aspect is to format the whole questionnaire. Years of experience have proven that a booklet format is best. The questionnaire can then be printed on both sides and will apppear more slender and less onerous to complete than one which is printed on one side and stapled in the corner. A booklet is simple to use, and with a little thought, is easy to produce. It can be made in a range of sizes depending on its purpose but will need to be four, eight, twelve or sixteen pages. If there are more than four pages, it should be stapled in two places along the fold in the manner of a magazine. Because it has to be in four page multiples, the page size needs to be chosen so that the information will fit into a four page combination. Some tolerance regarding this restriction is afforded by the back cover, front cover and even the back and front inside cover pages.

Unless the questionnaire is short (four pages or less), it is advisable to use the first page as a cover. Whether or not a cover is used, the questionnaire should have a suitable title and there should be an introductory paragraph. The paragraph not only introduces the purpose of the questionnaire, but it should mention whether the responses are confidential, it should indicate that all questions are to be completed and, in the case of mailed questionnaires, where the completed questionnaire is to be returned.

The various sections and questions should be organized to make appropriate use of the available space. Where possible, sections should be self-contained and begin at the top of a page. Care must be taken to ensure that individual questions are not split but are intact on a single page. As with any layout, there should be a visually pleasing amount of white space. Questions must not appear crowded. Open ended comment questions can serve to open spaces and the space for responses can be expanded so that the whole page is filled. Generally, questions are numbered sequentially throughout the questionnaire.

In Canada, in some situations, the questionnaire will be sent to both French and English speakers. In such cases the questionnaires should be in two languages, one on the flip side of the other and both working into the centre. Other approaches, such as sending one copy in each language of a unilingual questionnaire, are often offensive to some respondents and will bias results. Respondents, regardless of linguistic preference, should be treated identically and should be able to respond in their language of choice.

Sometimes questionnaires are pre-coded. That is, they include numbers in small print adjacent to each possible answer. This is to aid the keypuncher. Personally, I generally avoid the use of pre-coding as I feel that it de-personalizes an instrument which is already somewhat cold. The procedure is not all that necessary when there are only 100 or 200 questionnaires. Once numbers get into the 1,000s, pre-coding is probably necessary.

Decide to Construct Questionnaire

1   Determine your research questions
    ● what do you intend to find out?
    ● how will the information be helpful?
    ● which issues will relate to the questionnaire?

2   Specify your sub-questions
    ● list all the things you want to find out
    ● indicate those sub-questions to be included in the questionnaire
    ● refine your list

3   Draft the items
    ● translate questions into items
    ● formulate fill-in-the-blanks, multiple choice, comment on, list, Likert scale and rank questions

4   Sequence the items
    ● group into topic sections
    ● group by question type
    ● rewrite as necessary

5   Design the questionnaire
    ● order and number questions
    ● layout booklet format
    ● arrange questions on pages

6   Pilot-test the questionnaire
    ● clarify wording with respondents
    ● group test the draft questionnaire
    ● discuss the questionnaire with the group
    ● revise and re-test if necessary

Administer questionnaire

Pilot Test the Questionnaire

It is always difficult to criticize your own written work and in developing questionnaires it is essential to obtain comments from at least a small group of the intended respondents. Pilot testing will identify ambiguities in the instructions; it will help clarify the wording of questions and it may indicate omissions or previously unanticipated answers in multiple choice or ranking questions. Normally, individual questions will be vetted before the draft questionnaire is assembled. The pilot testing permits overall reactions including comments on the length of the questionnaire.

A good method of pilot testing a questionnaire is to assemble a group of six to twelve volunteers. Have them complete the questionnaire individually and write marginal comments on it, then discuss the questionnaire as a group. Completed questionnaires should be collected and marginal comments reviewed.

Following the pilot testing, the whole questionnaire needs to be re-edited and suggested changes incorporated. If major changes are necessary a second pilot testing may be advisable.

Conclusion

By following the six steps in Figure 19.8 you should be able to produce an effective questionnaire for your research project.

Fundamentals of Educational Research

Figure 19.9   Canadian International Development Agency: Graduates Questionnaire

The Canadian International Development Agency (CIDA) provided support for the construction and development of the Natural Resources College (NRC). As part of its ongoing evaluation activities, CIDA is interested in learning more about NRC graduates and their present activities. Please assist us by completing and returning this questionnaire. You do not need to sign your name and your answers will be confidential to CIDA.

BACKGROUND INFORMATION

1   In which NRC programme were you enrolled? (Please tick)

agriculture science	☐	parks and wildlife	☐
farm home science	☐	surveying/cartography	☐
veterinary science	☐	upgrading course	☐
fisheries management	☐		

2   In what year did you graduate from NRC?

1985	☐	1987	☐
1986	☐	1988	☐

3   How old are you? _____ years.

4   What is your gender?

male   ☐
female   ☐

5   What were you doing the year before you went to NRC?

full-time student	☐	full-time employment	☐
part-time employment	☐	unemployed	☐

other (specify) _____

EMPLOYMENT

6   Where are you currently employed?

a) Within an ADD		b) Outside an ADD	
Karonya	☐	Research	☐
Mzuzu	☐	Malawi Young Pioneers	☐
Salima	☐	Central Vet lab	☐
Kasungu	☐	Fisheries	☐
Lilongwe	☐	Parks and Wildlife	☐
Liwonde	☐	Surveys	☐
Blantyre	☐	Other (specify) _____	
Ngabu	☐		

7   Approximately what proportion of your time is spent working:

		Proportion of Time				
		Little or None	Some Time	About Half Time	More Than Half	Most or All
a)	with rural women	☐	☐	☐	☐	☐
b)	in a laboratory	☐	☐	☐	☐	☐
c)	with government officials	☐	☐	☐	☐	☐
d)	on environmental problems	☐	☐	☐	☐	☐
e)	in farmer training centers	☐	☐	☐	☐	☐
f)	with farmers	☐	☐	☐	☐	☐
g)	in a teaching or training function	☐	☐	☐	☐	☐
h)	to demonstrate new methods	☐	☐	☐	☐	☐
i)	to organize groups of rural people	☐	☐	☐	☐	☐
j)	with ADMARK	☐	☐	☐	☐	☐

8   To what extent is your NRC training generally useful to you in your present job?

useful on a daily basis	☐	occasionally useful	☐
useful on a weekly basis	☐	rarely useful	☐

Figure 19.9: *(cont.)*

NRC TRAINING

For each of the following statements tick the box which indicates the extent to which you agree or disagree. For example, if you strongly agree, tick the box under that column. If you agree, but less strongly, tick the box under agree, and so forth.

NRC General

		Strongly Disagree	Disagree	No Opinion	Agree	Strongly Agree
9	I considered it a great privilege to attend NRC.	☐	☐	☐	☐	☐
10	I would have preferred to attend some other institution instead of going to NRC.	☐	☐	☐	☐	☐
11	The facilities at NRC are among the best in Malawi.	☐	☐	☐	☐	☐
12	The NRC teaching staff are competent.	☐	☐	☐	☐	☐
13	There were sufficient library books.	☐	☐	☐	☐	☐
14	I had sufficient access to text books and course materials at NRC.	☐	☐	☐	☐	☐
15	Food and living accommodations were satisfactory.	☐	☐	☐	☐	☐

NRC Training

		Strongly Disagree	Disagree	No Opinion	Agree	Strongly Agree
16	The content of my NRC training was appropriate to my present needs.	☐	☐	☐	☐	☐
17	Courses at NRC were too theoretical.	☐	☐	☐	☐	☐
18	Courses at NRC should include more practical work.	☐	☐	☐	☐	☐
19	The teaching methods were suitable.	☐	☐	☐	☐	☐
20	The level of training was too elementary.	☐	☐	☐	☐	☐
21	As a result of my training, I can now perform tasks that I was unable to do before I attended NRC.	☐	☐	☐	☐	☐
22	My training has helped me continue to learn as I do my job.	☐	☐	☐	☐	☐
23	My training is helping me to develop and manage the natural resources in my district.	☐	☐	☐	☐	☐
24	My training is helping me to contribute to the National Rural Development Programme.	☐	☐	☐	☐	☐
25	My training is helping me to improve agricultural practices in my district.	☐	☐	☐	☐	☐
26	My training is helping me to assist rural people.	☐	☐	☐	☐	☐
27	My training is helping me to upgrade the quality of living in my district.	☐	☐	☐	☐	☐
28	Overall, the training at NRC was worth the time and resources invested in it.	☐	☐	☐	☐	☐
29	I would recommend NRC training to a fellow worker.	☐	☐	☐	☐	☐

Figure 19.9:   (cont.)

CONCLUSION

30   My overall evaluation of my educational experience at NRC is:
excellent   ☐   fair   ☐
very good ☐   poor   ☐
good   ☐   a waste of time ☐

31   List the 3 major strengths of your training at NRC:
1. _____
2. _____
3. _____

32   List the 3 major weaknesses of your training at NRC:
1. _____
2. _____
3. _____

33   What other comments do you have about NRC? _____
1. _____
2. _____

Thank you for your cooperation.

Please return your questionnaire in the enclosed envelope to:
Canadian International Development Agency (CIDA)
Project Support Unit
P.O. Box 1257
Lilongwe, Malawi

Figure 19.9 provides an example of a questionnaire developed by the author as part of the evaluation of a training institution in Malawi (CIDA, 1989). My major concern was to trace the graduates and find out the degree to which the training was being used and its perceived effects. Before finalizing the questionnaire, the author made a special trip to Malawi sepecifically to pilot-test the instrument and ensure its relevance, cultural appropriateness and feasibility. Most of the draft items had to be modified extensively. Other components of the study included a questionnaire for supervisors of graduates and selected site visits and interviews to complement the questionnaire data.

While developing questionnaires requires thought and care, the end product can be satisfying and the results of the questionnaire can facilitate the tasks of organizing the data, analyzing it and writing it into a research report.

For Further Study

SUDAN, S. and BRADBURN, N.M. (1982) *Asking Questions*, San Francisco, Jossey-Bass Publishers.

Reference

CIDA (1989) *Malawi Natural Resources College Impact Evaluation*, Hull, Author.

Chapter 20

Using Interviews for Successful Data Collection

The interview is probably the most widely used method of data collection in educational research. Interviews can be conducted on all subjects by all types of interviewers and they can range from informal incidental sources of data to the primary source of information used in a research study. When used with care and skill, interviews are an incomparably rich source of data, but seldom are inexperienced researchers sufficiently familiar with the requirements for a good interview or sufficiently practiced in the requisite interviewing skills. Perhaps the commonness of the interview is its major downfall. We use interviews in all walks of life for a wide range of purposes and to use it for research purposes requires more care and skill than is commonly exercised. While everyone conducts interviews to some degree, few do it well. This chapter discusses various types of interviews, describes the planning requirements and how to structure an interview protocol.

An interview is defined as a specialized form of communication between people for a specific purpose associated with some agreed subject matter. Thus, the interview is a highly purposeful task which goes beyond mere conversation. There are many advantages to the interview as a method of data collection. People are more easily engaged in an interview than in completing a questionnaire. Thus, there are fewer problems with people failing to respond. Secondly, the interviewer can clarify questions and probe the answers of the respondent, providing more complete information than would be available in written form. It is this opportunity for in-depth probing that makes the interview so attractive when dealing with informed respondents. Thirdly, interviewing enables the interviewer to pick up non-verbal cues, including facial expressions, tones of voice and, in the case of interviews conducted on the respondent's turf, cues from the surroundings and context.

There are also disadvantages. It is often difficult to record responses, particularly if the interviewer is also responsible for writing them down. Secondly, the quality of responses, that is their reliability and validity, is dependent on the interviewer. Different interviewers may obtain different answers, particularly if questions, procedures and techniques are not standardized. Thirdly, the context, which has the advantage of providing useful non-verbal information, has the disadvantage of sometimes affecting responses due to interruptions and pressures of time.

Types of Interview

There are basically two types of interviews categorized according to purpose: normative and elite. **Normative** interviews are used to collect data which is classified, and analyzed statistically. Common examples of normative interviews are those used in mass surveys by pollsters and researchers intent on finding the views of large numbers of people to fairly straightforward questions. In essence, these routine interviews are little more than a questionnaire but in oral form. Questions are always worked out carefully in advance and the interviewer codes the responses on a form.

The other type of interview is called an **elite** interview and is for a different purpose. The researcher is not interested in statistical analysis of a large number of responses, but wants to probe the views of a small number of elite individuals. An elite interview is one directed at a respondent who has particular experience or knowledge about the subject being discussed. The person might be a school principal who has in-depth knowledge of what goes on in the school or it could be a head of state or other significant person who is unique. In the latter case, there may be only one respondent in the sample and the elite interview becomes of prime importance in collecting the necessary data. This is frequently used in historical research where someone involved with the history discusses it.

Normative interviews often include many interviewers all of whom are trained to ask questions in a similar way. Their own knowledge of the subject is of far less consequence than is their ability to interview for reliable and valid responses. On the contrary, with elite interviews the interviewer should be expert in the subject under discussion. He or she must be in a position to grasp new information and use it to pursue new directions. The interviewer is interested in building understanding and in this sense the elite interview is a teaching situation in which the respondent teaches the interviewer about events and personal perspectives. Unless the interviewee is unique, researchers generally combine approaches by collecting normative data on a modest-size group and continuing the interview to obtain more elite-type information on questions requiring more personal and conceptual perspectives.

Interview Contexts

There can be many contexts for interviews which may encompass a variety of settings and from two to a large number of participants. The typical interview includes two people, and when face-to-face, most often takes place at the respondent's place of work, whether home, office or school. While I have interviewed busy people over lunch or on airplanes, it is preferable to conduct the interview in a setting where one's full attention can be devoted to the interview. My own research has included interviews in the Canadian bush, in mud huts in Africa and in the offices of prime ministers and many other highly placed government officials. All of these settings work, providing that the session is relatively uninterrupted and seating can be arranged to provide for the process needs of the interview as discussed later.

Interviewing by telephone is one of the most commonly used research techniques because it is quick and economical. No other data collection technique can provide such a fast return of data from geographically dispersed people. Sampling can be precisely targeted. One knows the refusal rate which is generally as low as 7 per cent in popular surveys and polls. People who are often difficult to reach in person can sometimes be reached by telephone and the fact that one is not on view often facilitates people answering honestly. Of course, people require a telephone to be interviewed in this way. There are other disadvantages as well. The interview must be shorter for telephone use than for personal interviewing. Complicated explanations and visual aids such as response cards or diagrams cannot be used to aid the respondent nor can the interviewer depend on visual cues from respondents that might reveal a misunderstanding of the question or boredom with the interview. The effectiveness of research interviews by telephone can be greatly enhanced when there is precontact, either by letter or phone, arranging a precise time for the telephone interview to take place. In some cases, written information can be sent to the respondent in advance and it can be reviewed and considered prior to the phone call. With good planning and good techniques, there should not be a major difference between the validity of data obtained in telephone interviews and those obtained face to face.

In some cases, there might be more than one interviewer and there can be more than one respondent. Elite interviews are often highly effective when there are two interviewers who are experienced in working together and who can bounce the questioning back and forth so that one can pick up things that the other would have missed. When there is more than one respondent, one has the advantage of synergy within the group. The responses of one person trigger responses of another and one can get more complete data than if each individual were interviewed alone. Of course, in this case the responses within the group also bias what other people might have said and one must be careful to ensure that the overall group response is valid. One of the major difficulties when there are several respondents is the problem of recording responses. Often the responses come fast and furious and it is difficult for one person to record them, particularly when the interviewer is also responsible for pursuing points of interest and generally guiding the process.

Focus groups occur when a group of people focus on a particular topic and discuss it fully with the leader. I have sometimes used the technique following a fifteen minute pre-session in which each participant completes a short written questionnaire. For example, in conducting a follow-up study on the effectiveness of a job-related training course, I was able to use such a procedure to obtain both normative and focus group data. On that occasion, I observed that the normative data in the written questionnaire disagreed with the central thrust elicited by the group, presumably because of the group sanction of critical and negative feedback.

One of the most challenging settings is in developing countries where government officials are being interviewed with respect to development assistance programs. There are generally several problems to overcome. In these cases, the interview may be highly formal, sometimes including a whole delegation of officials from the researcher's embassy and an equal number from the host government. The challenge for the team leader in such settings is to control the questioning and not let unbriefed members of the embassy team interrupt the flow by asking questions which do not relate to the purpose of the visit. Of course, there is an added difficulty in that the respondents have a stake in the result and will try to portray things in a way that furthers their interests. The process itself is also a concern as it often follows official protocols and may not allow for a free and relaxed dynamic. Generally, the most senior person does most of the talking and one must direct questions to technical and support people through the senior official. Thus, the responses tend to be guarded rather than candid. At the extreme, such interviews are conducted in two languages and the exchange is filtered through a translator. Also, these are cross-cultural interviews in which for both linguistic and cultural reasons people may not easily understand one another's perspectives. Finally, there can be technical difficulties. I have found in Africa and the Caribbean that the low bass voice of many respondents, coupled with the din of an air conditioner makes it difficult to hear what the respondent says. Numbers are particularly problematic with fifteen and fifty sounding identical. The only defense is to sit close, but even that is subject to social custom. On several occasions I have saved the day by inviting people to lunch where the central air conditioning, being less noisy, allowed for interpretable conversation.

Planning for a Successful Interview

The next chapter discusses the important step of developing an interview protocol. After the protocol has been developed and tested, several factors need to be considered in order to carry out an actual interview. One needs to arrange the appointment giving some idea of the interview's purpose and how long it is expected to take. On the question of length, most interviews should not exceed forty minutes. Elite interviews, however, can last hours and may even be phased over several sessions. However, for normative interviews if you can't cut through to the substance in that length of time then there is probably a problem with planning or interviewing technique.

The location is important. If the interview is to be conducted in a busy office where there are many interruptions, the interview process could be affected profoundly. It is best then to find a quiet, uninterrupted place and time for the interview, or failing that, ask the respondent to hold phone calls and other interruptions. I once conducted an interview in Swaziland which was interrupted by five entrances of other people and seven phone calls! Needless to say, the process was more than a little discontinuous.

A second consideration is the physical arrangement of furnishings and seating. My experience includes an interview with a senior Permanent Secretary in Asia where we were seated at opposite ends of a small couch while photographers shot flash pictures throughout the interview. On many other occasions large desks or tables found themselves between me and the interviewee. In such instances protocol dictates that the senior official determine where people sit, so there is not much that can be done to control it. If one meets on neutral territory or the situation otherwise allows it, it is best to sit facing the interviewee.

Effective communication requires a degree of trust between interviewer and interviewee. It helps in establishing this trust to be like the person being interviewed. A common background of age, education, social class, employment status and manner of speech is helpful. It is very difficult for a 20-year-old researcher to interview a senior manager in his sixties. Be sure to dress the part. Few school principals would welcome being interviewed by someone wearing jeans and a T-shirt. School children might relate better if you weren't wearing a tie. As a general rule, wear something similar to what you presume your interviewee will wear.

Conducting Effective Interviews

Effective interviewing relies on sound planning, skills which can be developed by practice, a cooperative interviewee and sometimes considerable good luck. For effective interviewing the interviewer needs to control both the content and the process of the interview. The content is controlled largely by the protocol and the nature of the questions (see Chapter 21). If the objectives are clear and one uses appropriate techniques there should be few occasions when you leave without the content you need. To help ensure validity and to accomplish the task pleasurably and efficiently, good process skills are required.

The basic structure of the interview lies in the messages sent and the responses obtained about a particular subject and as such the two major roles are those of the interviewer and the interviewee or respondent. The interviewer and the respondent enter into a kind of interactive relationship in which communication becomes a two way street. The interviewer sends a message which the respondent receives. The respondent processes the message and sends a response. The response is received and processed by the interviewer and so on. Both interviewer and respondent act as senders and receivers. It is this passing of messages from one party to the other which offers the greatest challenge for reliability and validity. As we all know, much distortion can occur when messages are communicated verbally. Sometimes the cause is in the way message was sent and sometimes it is in the manner in which it is received. The researcher must be particularly sensitive to this source of error and must take steps to ensure valid responses.

Initial attitudes may influence the rapport between the interviewer and respondent. If a respondent dislikes an interviewer or has any negative feelings towards the interviewer, it is unlikely that the respondent will be open to the questions being posed. It is also important for the interviewer to know that he or she may reflect a particular attitude simply because of the tone that is used in phrasing a question. If as an interviewer, you are self-assured or lack confidence, these dispositions may also send certain messages to your respondent. The interviewer must be aware of the many ways that attitudes can shape an interview.

Effective communication is also affected by expertise. Perhaps the greatest hallmark of effective communication is one's facility to use language. All of us have experienced a situation where we couldn't quite get someone to see a situation as we saw it. We weren't able to make the description of a situation as vivid to our audience as it was to us. This was probably due to the fact that we could not find the proper words to serve us adequately. In the interview process, it is extremely important that questions are understood. Checks for clarity must be made to ensure the respondent's interpretation is correct. In the same way, the interviewer must also check whether he or she has understood the message that has been sent.

Basic Interviewing Skills

Active Listening

It is important to attend or listen actively to the respondent. Good attending behavior demonstrates respect and that you are interested in what the respondent has to say. By utilizing attending behavior to enhance the individual's self-respect and to establish a secure atmosphere, the interviewer facilitates free expression thereby enhancing validity.

In order to attend to the interviewee, the interviewer should be physically relaxed and seated with natural posture. A comfortable interviewer is better able to listen to the person being interviewed. Also, if the interviewer is relaxed physically, his or her posture and movements will be natural, thus enhancing a sense of well-being. This sense of comfortableness better enables the interviewer to attend to and to communicate with the interviewee. Relax physically; feel the presence of the chair as you are sitting on it. Let your posture be comfortable and your movements natural; for example, if you usually move and gesture a good deal, feel free to do so at this time. Do not be overly relaxed however. By leaning forward occasionally you signify your attention.

The interviewer should initiate and maintain eye contact with the person. However, eye contact can be over done. A varied use of eye contact is most effective, as staring fixedly or with undue intensity usually makes the respondent uneasy. If you are going to listen to someone, look at them.

The final characteristic of good attending behavior is the interviewer's use of comments which follow directly from what the person is saying. Follow what the other person is saying by taking your cues from what is said. Do not jump from subject to subject or interrupt. If you cannot think of anything to say, go back to something the person said earlier in the conversation and ask a question about that. There is no need to talk about yourself or your opinions when you are interviewing. By directing one's comments and questions to the topics provided by the individual, one not only helps develop an area of discussion, but reinforces the person's free expression, resulting in more spontaneity and animation.

In summary, the interviewer's goal is to listen actively and to communicate this attentiveness through a relaxed posture, use of varied eye contact, and verbal responses which indicate to the person that the interviewer is attempting to understand what is being communicated.

Openness and Empathy

Your purpose in an interview is to allow the interviewee to share his or her information with you. You should be open in posture and expression, willingly accepting the information offered. You should empathize, but in a non-leading way. Avoid value judgments and agreeing or disagreeing with the respondent. Accept what is said, but do not lead the person being interviewed further than he or she wants to go voluntarily. If you don't understand, get the message clarified, but resist taking sides. For example:

Respondent: The principal is a bastard.
Interviewer: Why do you say that?

> *Respondent*:   Because he says one thing to your face and another behind your back.
> *Interviewer*:   He's pretty inconsistent, then?

Being open should not mean that you are not assertive. You must control the interview while not condoning the opinions expressed. Be firm and direct while at the same time open.

Paraphrasing

Paraphrasing takes what the interviewee has just said and repeats it back in different words. It acknowledges your attention and it increases validity by checking whether what you heard the interviewee say was the intended message. Paraphrasing crystallizes comments by repeating them in a more concise manner. When your paraphrase differs from the interviewee's intent, he or she will clarify the statement and you will not have obtained an invalid response.

Summarization of Content

Summarization attempts to recapitulate, to condense and to crystallize the essence of what the interviewee has said. While a summary thus resembles a parahrase, it differs in one fundamental respect — the period covered by a summary is substantially longer than that of a paraphrase. The latter deals with the individual's last few sentences or a short paragraph. A summary puts together a number of his paragraphs, or an entire section of an interview. It may cover even an entire interview.

A summary serves at least these three major functions: it may crystallize in a more coherent and integrated manner what the interviewee has been talking about; it may help the respondent put facts together; it may serve as a stimulus for further exploration of a particular topic or area. Because it pulls together materials discussed over a substantial period of time, it frequently serves as a necessary perception check for the interviewer.

Summarizations are frequently used when the interviewer wishes to structure the beginning of a conversation by recalling the high points of a previous interview; when the interviewee's presentation of a topic has been either very confusing or just plain lengthy and rambling; when an interviewee has seemingly expressed everything of importance on a particular topic; when at the end of an interview, the interviewer wishes to emphasize what has been learned within it.

Controlling the Process

In my view, the interviewer must know how to control the interview, its process and its pace. By controlling, the interviewer need not always take the lead. Indeed, many elite interviews are successful because the person being interviewed is so skilled at communicating and knows exactly what to say. You merely give a lead and the interviewee picks it up and carries on, often answering many of your other questions on the way. It can be many minutes before you probe or nudge the process in a new direction. However, you must be able to regain the lead at any time or the interview will no longer be yours and it may no longer suit your purpose.

In order to assume and maintain leadership in the interview it is important to set the stage right up front. Your introduction will do much to establish where you will be in the process. If you are insecure and unsure of where you are going you may easily get sidetracked into a friendly conversation or discussion which doesn't do much to produce the data you need. I find it helpful to outline an agenda for the interview which states the three or four major themes or sections and provides a lasting frame of reference to which you can refer later. This helps prevent the respondent from moving ahead of you as he or she knows that there will be a time later to make some point on that topic. The agenda also helps you speed up the interview when required using the interjection, 'that is very interesting, but as you know, we have three more topics to cover, so perhaps we should move on'.

Once the interview begins, you should shape the behavior you expect by cutting off a response which gets too long. Once you establish how much you want on each question most interviewees learn to go to that level of detail and no more. At first this can seem awkward, but with practice, you should be able to do it authoritatively while not throwing cold water on the process. My advice is to study skilled T.V. interviewers and learn how they do it.

The opposite problem also presents itself. Sometimes the respondent does not respond, at least not easily or fully. In these cases you must invite a response. Learning to live with silence is fundamental. Many interviewers from the Canadian culture find this difficult, so end up doing all the talking themselves. Ask the question and wait patiently. If the respondent doesn't understand, he or she will eventually ask for clarification. Sometimes you should talk in an attempt to engage the respondent in conversation. This is all right, but it should not persist. Do it a little and then go back to silent waiting.

Humor is one of the most effective process tools if you know how to use it. I often get people laughing and then find that their natural resistance disappears. It can build trust and disarm the respondent. I use it frequently in cross-cultural settings and consider it an indispensable tool.

Conclusion

A data collection interview is a marvelous challenge and is always a test. No two interviews are ever alike and every interview teaches new lessons. I find that unless I am up for an interview, well briefed on what I need to know and conscious of the need to work at the process, I lose a unique opportunity for data collection. Plan each interview as carefully as possible, practice your interviewing skills, and analyze each experience once it is over.

For Further Study

Downs, C.W., Smeyak, G.P. and Martin, E. (1980) *Professional Interviewing*, New York, Harper and Row Publishers.

McCracken, G. (1988) *The Long Interview*, Qualitative Research Methods, Volume 13, Beverly Hills, Sage Publications.

Chapter 21

Developing Effective Interview
Protocols

Interviewing for research purposes must follow a plan related to the objectives one wants to achieve in the data collection. It is not sufficient merely to meet with people and conduct an informal chat. One should plan the interview in great detail and write down the questions in modified questionnaire form. Such a data collection tool is called an interview protocol or schedule. The purpose of this chapter is to provide guidance on how to develop an interview protocol.

Effective protocols vary greatly in detail and in the amount of research and development they require. An elite interview with a head of state may have relatively few planned and written questions, but these will be supported by weeks or months of careful research and planning on the part of the interviewer who is also the person intimately involved with preparation of the protocol. On the other extreme, a relatively routine protocol for a normative interview might require considerable planning and detailed instructions, including standardized replies for the interviewer and coding sheets to record the responses. Such interviews are frequently undertaken by a team of interviewers, so there needs to be standardization as well as a natural but explicit flow that suits all types of interviewers.

Unlike a questionnaire, the interview protocol must address process issues as well as just content. It also is not typically shared with the respondent (though sometimes a summary of headings or list of issues is exchanged), so the respondent does not know what questions are coming later. One advantage for the interviewer is the ability to gain the respondent's confidence before asking what might otherwise be threatening questions. A disadvantage is the tendency of many respondents to get ahead of the interviewer and take the lead, destroying the sequence which has been prepared, resulting in a disjointed interview in which the interviewer may leave without critical information. You will have to judge the amount of detail your protocol requires, but these seven steps should help organize the process and guide you through the requirements for an effective interview protocol.

Determine your General and Specific Research Questions

As with all types of structured data collection one must have a clear idea of the objectives for the interview and the data needs of the researcher. As was the case with construction of a questionnaire, your information needs can be determined effectively with a research framework which includes your questions and sub-questions. If you have not done so, review steps 1 and 2 in Chapter 15 on questionnaire construction.

The interview is generally a one-time event, so if you miss essential data the first time you may not have a chance to get it later. Every part of the interview has a purpose and you should think about the reason for asking every question before you include it. At this stage you are focusing on the content concerns of the interview only. Process concerns will be addressed later.

Draft the Interview Questions

Using a similar process to that involved in questionnaire construction, you can begin drafting the interview questions. Here, however, the form of questions may differ from those used in a written question-naire. As in the case of the written questionnaire, all questions must be carefully drafted and worded so that ambiguity is minimized. It is useful when drafting questions for an interview to distinguish between open questions and closed questions.

Open questions ask for broad or general information. They put few restrictions on how the interviewee might answer. For example, 'How do you feel about the merger of the two schools?' Such open questions have a great value in many circumstances. They help dis-cover the respondent's priorities and frame of reference. They give recognition to the respondent and satisfy a communication need by letting the individual talk through his or her ideas while you listen. They tend to be easy to answer and pose little threat since there are no right or wrong answers. They also reveal the depth of a person's knowledge and might enable you to evaluate the degree of emphasis to put on their response. These open questions are the major type used in elite interviews. Open questions also have distinct limitations. They consume a lot of time and energy. They make it difficult to control the interview placing more stress on the interviewer's skill, and recording and tabulating answers is more difficult.

Closed questions, on the other hand, are specific and frequently restrict the options available to the respondent. There are three types of such questions: The multiple-choice question provides for a list of answers. The bipolar question essentially gives a yes or no option. Thirdly, is a specific factual question to which the interviewer does not know the possible response. For example, 'Where did you complete your undergraduate degree?' The advantages of closed questions is that they save you time and energy, they enable you to classify and record easily. They also apply well when there are multiple interviewers dealing with a large sample. Of course, these closed questions are limited in that they do not let you know how much information the respondent really has about the question and in some cases the respondent may not like the available options and cannot easily respond. In general, open and closed questions are complimentary and often work together to provide a balanced, smooth-flowing yet controlled interview.

In some cases it is helpful to present the respondent with a rating scale or other device. In the case of a face-to-face interview, one can use cards made up as visual aids to show the respondent the rating scale, or to enable the respondent to sort options into choice-categories or otherwise to convey in-depth information. Such techniques are useful only with normative interviews.

There are various possible problems in how the questions are phrased. Figure 21.1 provides examples of five of the most common problems in interview questions.

Sequence the Questions

Variety of questions is essential if an interview is to be interesting and natural. Generally, it is best to organize the questions into blocks on various themes. Just like a questionnaire or research paper, each section stands on its own with its own inherent structure and integrity. Within such a section you may vary the question types though in some sections it will make more sense to keep them all closed. It is generally a good rule to mix closed questions with open-format questions. By organizing the questions into sections you will also be in a position

Figure 21.1: Tips on asking questions

Interviewers often get into trouble because they violate basic rules. The following problems should be avoided:

Double-barrelled questions
Example: Have you ever experienced burn-out and what do you do to prevent it?
Avoid double-barrelled questions. Ask one question at a time. Do not combine questions and expect an answer.

Two-in-one Questions
Example: What are the advantages and disadvantages of working in a private school?
Do not combine opposite positions in one question. Separate out the parts and things will be much clearer.

Restrictive Questions
Example: Do you think that female school administrators are as good as male school administrators?
The phraseology of this question eliminates the possibility that females might be better.
Avoid questions which inherently eliminate some options.

Leading Questions
Example: Bill 101 which forces 'immigrant' children into French schools in Quebec has been challenged in the courts on the grounds that it violates the Canadian charter of Rights and Freedoms. What do you think of Bill 101?
Do not precede questions with a position statement. In this type of question, the interviewer states a view or summarizes the position of a current or recent event and then asks for a response. This tends to lead the respondent in a given direction.

Loaded Questions
Example: Would you favor or oppose murder by agreeing with a woman's free choice concerning abortion?
Avoid questions which are emotionally charged and use loaded words.

to convey the major themes to the interviewee and will be able to judge your timing.

Sometimes special question sequencing techniques are used for a particular purpose. Many structured interviews use funneling techniques, moving from general questions to specific questions, or vice versa. A funnel sequence, moving from the general to the specific, will help develop a logical progression for responses, and it will help the respondent to communicate pieces of information in a loosely connected fashion. If an inverted funneling sequence is used, the interviewer will begin with specific questions and then move to general questions. This type of sequence is often used with respondents who exhibit shyness. By answering specific questions, the respondent may gain confidence which will enhance the possibility for greater expression later.

As with questionnaires, interviews also frequently incorporate branches. Various filter questions are used to direct the interview along various paths. For example, a person might be asked which university program he or she has completed. A graduate in engineering might then be asked different questions than a graduate in the arts.

You will, of course, have to try various orders among and within the sections in order to provide a natural flow to the interview.

Consider your Process Needs

The interviewer must manage the interview process, and the protocol may also reflect this concern. A question as simple as 'How are you?' is asked for a reason. If you forget the reason, you might spend the whole afternoon discussing the respondent's state of health!

Between each block of questions you will need a transition which moves from one theme to the next. Transitions are useful in giving both the interviewer and interviewee a constant reminder of where the interview is going. Abrupt transitions leave the interviewee questioning whether you might not have liked the responses. Essentially, transitions provide a summary of where you have been, where you are going and perhaps why.

At various places in the protocol it is often helpful to place reminders to yourself to paraphrase or summarize. It is also sometimes useful to list standard probes, or questions, to move along the process, clarify what is intended and so forth.

Prepare the Introduction and Closing

The protocol begins with an introduction. It states the purpose of the interview, who the interviewer is and why the interview is taking place. It clarifies any questions about the research and informs the respondent about confidentiality and the use of data. Permission to use recording devices is obtained at this stage. The introduction indicates how long the interview will be and sometimes provides an overview of the major topics to be discussed. The issue here is to provide this relevant information quickly and efficiently, yet without cutting off the respondent's questions. It is very important in setting the tone of the interview and in establishing a rapport with the respondent.

Finally, the interview contains a closing. All interviews should be brought to a definite close so that the interviewee does not wonder whether this is the end. A verbal statement can be used to signify the end and a non-verbal gesture such as rising, shaking hands or opening the door will surely convey the message. The closing should be reinforcing and leave both people with a sense of accomplishment. A final summary or reference to a particularly helpful contribution will do this. Finally, the interviewer should thank the respondent, confirm any arrangements for follow-up or sharing the results of the research and enable the researcher to exit easily, presumably to conduct another interview.

Prepare for Recording the Responses

A final consideration is what is to be done about a record of the interview. If the interview is with an elite respondent whose every word has potential significance, it would be wise to tape record the interaction. If you do so, be sure to get permission, preferably in advance of the session, and use an unobtrusive recording device. Such things are easily forgotten and ignored whereas a microphone in the center of a table can put some interviewees on edge and affect their responses. The major difficulty with tape recording is the inordinate amount of time required to listen to the tapes. My preference is to record responses during the interview on the interview protocol or in a stenographic notebook. The latter is easy to use on one's knee and the spiral binding reduces it to a single page in front of you at any time. For normative interviews, the interview protocol can be organized with check off boxes and space for efficient data recording.

Remember too, that taking copious notes may slow down the interview considerably. It is probably best to take brief notes and to reconstruct the interview later. My preferred method is to take written notes and immediately following the interview, dictate a summary into a portable mini-cassette recorder. The facts and perspectives are then fresh and can be dictated and forgotten, keeping the mind unencumbered for the next interview. If you wait until the end of the day and have done several interviews, the responses become blurred and impossible to separate. On a couple of recent occasions both in Asia and Southern Africa, I brought a portable lap-top computer and typed in a summary immediately following each interview. Two interviewers are a great advantage for re-constructing and validating what the interviewee said and intended.

Pilot Test the Interview Protocol

While it is important to test a questionnaire to ensure that the wording will be understood, it is doubly important to validate an interview

Figure 21.2:   *Tips on asking questions*

Decide to Develop Interview Protocol

1   Determine your general and specific research questions
   o what do you intend to find out?
   o what information is essential from the interview?
2   Draft the Interview Questions
   o group into topic sections
   o draft closed questions
3   Sequence the questions
   o group into topic sections
   o vary question type
   o arrange sections in sequence
4   Consider your Process Needs
   o prepare suitable transitions
   o prepare probes, process questions
5   Prepare the Introduction and Closing
   o record verbal statements
   o note non-verbal actions
6   Prepare for Recording the Responses
   o decide on general method
   o organize protocol for written responses
7   Pilot test the Interview Protocol
   o pilot test
   o revise as necessary

Conduct the Interview

---

protocol. Here, as well as the content, you also have to validate the flow, the physical utility of the form of the protocol and the arrangements you have made to record the responses.

If you are using interviewers other than yourself, you have the added problem of ensuring that they can deal with your protocol. Such interviewers will need to be trained to use your protocol and ideally, they should be monitored in its use over several interviews or simulations.

Conclusion

By following the seven steps in Figure 21.2, you should be able to develop an effective interview protocol. Appendix II provides a sample protocol developed for an evaluation of linkages between universities in Canada and in Thailand. This particular protocol was used to conduct telephone interviews with university officials from across Canada. It was also used in face-to-face interviews in Montreal.

A good interview schedule won't eliminate all the problems in this form of data collection, but it helps. I recently returned from a field mission in the Caribbean where I conducted many interviews. I began the trip with my protocols carefully pasted into my field notebook. The first interview is always the hardest because you are not yet immersed into the subject and its jargon. I arrived for my first interview and discovered that I had left my notebook at the hotel! On that occasion I was saved by good planning: a second set of protocols in my briefcase.

For Further Study

FREY, J.H. (1983) *Survey Research by Telephone*, Vol. 150, Sage Library of Social Research, Beverly Hills, Sage Publications.
SUDAN, S. and BRADBURN, N.M. (1982) *Asking Questions*, San Francisco, Jossey-Bass Publishers.

Chapter 22

Focus Groups

As early as the 1930s, social scientists expressed concern about the interview as a data collection technique. Interviews were judged to be overly dominated by the questioner, and criticized as not leading to the true feelings of the respondents. Various approaches were attempted in response to this criticism, leading to such innovations as Carl Rogers' non-directive therapy, and later, invention of the T group. Another approach became known as the Focus Group. A focus group is a group comprised of individuals with certain characteristics who focus discussions on a given issue or topic. Since the 1960s, the technique has been adopted by market researchers who use it to determine what consumers think of products, or potential products. In the last decade, serious applied and scholarly researchers have also discovered the technique and are now using it for data collection on a wide variety of issues and topics.

The focus group has advantages over other approaches to data collection such as the questionnaire or the interview. The use of questionnaires in data collection permits no input, other than that of the individual respondent. There is no opportunity to clarify questions or for the respondent to expand his or her own perceptions by sharing and comparing them to those of others. In the case of interviews, there is some opportunity for clarification and other input in that the interviewer might probe and suggest ideas which give rise to views and opinions which the respondent may not have shared in a written questionnaire. The focus group goes one step further. It not only discloses what is important to individual respondents, but it attempts to provide a situation where the synergy of the group adds to the depth and insight. Thus, the group strives to provide in-depth qualitative data which could not be obtained as efficiently any other way. In this sense, focus groups have something in common with brainstorming techniques.

Focus groups have many uses, most of which relate to program planning, program improvement and program evaluation. They are often used before the introduction of a new social or educational program in order to determine needs, to test reactions to possible program offerings and to examine the factors which help make people decide to enroll in programs or not. They are also used in the development of research procedures to test reactions to possible evaluation, questions and procedures to be used later using quantitative methods. They are particularly useful in helping develop specific research questions and issues for further exploration. Focus groups are sometimes used during an ongoing program in order to provide formative evaluation. They are increasingly being used after programs are conducted in order to provide a basis for evaluation and analysis. They provide a useful complement to other methods of summative program evaluation.

Why do focus groups work? Focus groups work because they provide a setting in which individuals are comfortable in self-disclosure and, furthermore, where the group dynamics create a chain of reactions designed to exhaust the views on the issue or topic. They work, in part because of the skill of the leader in planning and conducting the group, in part because of the group composition, and also because the participants are in some way motivated to focus on the issue at hand.

Planning the Focus Group

As with all types of research and data collection, one must have a clear idea of the purpose of the exercise. In planning to use focus groups, you need a clear idea of what specific information is needed, who will use the information, and you should also have some notion of why the information is important.

It is vital to select an appropriate category of individuals to be included in the focus groups. It would be fallacious for the market researcher to involve people who do not use the product being researched. Similarly, in focus groups used for your research, you must decide who are in the best position to give the information you require. Sometimes one single category of people can give you what you need, but be sure not to restrict your focus groups to only one target population when several may relate to the problem. In examining a training program, for example, you might like to involve participants in the program, those involved in instructing, and perhaps even those who choose not to attend the program.

One of the difficult tasks with focus groups is to construct the questions. When you finish, the questions are deceptively simple, but in practice, they take considerable energy to develop. Good answers dictate the need for good questions and as is the case with interviews, the questions have both a content and a process function. With respect to content, many focus groups include only five or six questions, but because of the group process, a great deal of discussion and elaboration can take place — much more than would be possible through interviewing any of the group participants alone. Focus group questions are always open-ended. For example, in an evaluation activity you might ask such questions as: 'What did you think of the program?' 'What did you like best about your training?' 'Have you been able to use any of your training back on the job?' Be sure to keep your questions of a qualitative nature, and avoid quantifiers such as 'how much?' These qualifiers tend to restrict answers, rather than provide for the full range. Also, avoid questions that have a possible 'yes' or 'no' answer. Ironically, while the main purpose of focus groups is to discover why people hold certain views, the 'why' question is rarely asked in the focus group session. You are not interested in a rational answer to the question 'why'. Instead, you want to determine why from a less directive approach obtained from questions based in how people feel about what is being discussed. It is often useful as part of your planning to brainstorm a large list of questions and systematically reduce and refine them, until you have the core. The questions must then be sequenced, and the sequence must ensure a natural flow and transition from one to the other. Participants should not feel that they have finished one question and are then being asked another. Instead, they should feel that the session is an overall discussion, exploring a variety of related issues and leading logically through the various topics.

Group Composition

Group composition is fundamental to good focus-group technique. First, the participants must have some common characteristic related to what is being focused upon. For example, participants in a training program have that as a common characteristic, regardless of gender, background, education or experience. This becomes the glue that bonds the group together, and it is advisable not to confuse this by having too many other common characteristics. It is a mistake, generally speaking, to involve people who know one another outside the group context. Such people will not benefit as much from the ideas of colleagues as they would from those of complete strangers. In some types of evaluation, however, this is hard to avoid since those who participated in a program have generally come to know one another. There is particular danger dealing with intact groups, which have evolved a life and personality of their own, which is rarely conducive to the focus group purpose. Wherever possible, one should involve a mix of relative strangers who will feel comfortable sharing their views without having to wonder what their friends and colleagues might think about their responses.

Focus groups generally range from six to twelve participants. You need enough people to achieve synergy and facilitate group dynamics, but not so many as to prevent everyone from having a full say. In practice, it is difficult to control groups greater than twelve, which tend to break apart into various factions. Groups smaller than six generally don't have enough to provide the synergy required. The exception is where the topic needs to be explored in great depth, and where people have had lengthy experiences related to it. In those cases, mini-focus groups are often best.

Participants are typically pre-screened to ensure that they have the required characteristic, and are telephoned or written a letter to pre-screen them and to invite their participation. You don't invite people to attend a 'focus group', but merely to join a group discussion on the topic of interest. As with any method, you must make clear arrangements concerning the time of the group, its purpose and how long it will last. It is best to meet in some neutral but convenient place, where the intended participants can be expected to feel comfortable.

You will need more than one focus group. In practice, researchers typically collect data until they stop getting appreciable new information. In most situations, the first two groups give considerable new information. Thereafter, the new insights rapidly diminish. In my experience, by the third or fourth session, the topic has generally been exhausted unless, of course, the groups have some inherent difference. For example, in examining national training programs, I have conducted focus groups on the training program, but have also been interested in regional differences. In such cases, groups in various settings across the country permit insights into regional variations.

Conducting the Focus Group

To be effective, the focus group procedure requires a moderator, skilled at leading groups. Such a moderator should have sufficient group dynamics skills and techniques to be able to exercise control over the group, yet do so unobtrusively. The skilled moderator will be able to draw out silent individuals, and control those who dominate the conversation. Such a moderator will be skilled at asking the questions, and keeping the flow directional, animated and relevant. The moderator has to be a good listener, and know how to empathize. In my experience, it is most effective to have an assistant as well. The assistant frees up the moderator to focus entirely on the process, while the assistant is instrumental in overcoming logistical difficulties and is occupied with taking notes and sharing in the analysis phase.

It is advisable to begin the session with some transitional period. For example, one can provide coffee and refreshments for those who arrive early, and the moderator and assistant can engage in appropriate small-talk. You will want to use this to put the participant at ease, but avoid talking about the issues until the group formally begins. This also provides an excellent context to assess who is in the group, and the skilled group leader will identify the dominant individuals who, whenever possible, should be seated at the moderator's side. Once the expected number of participants have arrived, it is best to seat them so that all members of the group have eye contact. Be sure to avoid the 'head table' approach as the moderators should always be seen as part of the group. As a moderator, beware of other people arranging the setting for you as they may not understand your requirements in arrangement of furnishings.

Begin the group by thanking the participants for coming, and briefly state its purpose. You might also inform people why they were selected. Be sure to emphasize the rules of confidentiality, and provide an opportunity for people to ask questions about why they are there. Tell the participants how the information will be recorded and reported. They generally ask whether or not they will receive the results, so this question should be anticipated. The first question should be an ice-breaker, designed to engage people in the process. As the process develops, the moderator will introduce relevant questions, provide probes, pauses, involve people in discussion, always without expressing any value on the answers received. Avoid closing a response with agreement or head-nodding. Even comments as innocuous as 'yes' imply a value to the response received.

The purpose of the focus group is not to achieve consensus but to exhaust an exploration of the various perspectives held. For this reason, I conclude by thanking the participants, rather than providing any form of summary. It is important to ask whether you have missed anything to give everyone the feeling that all their contributions have been heard. You might, of course, give some sort of comment on the great value of the contributions, then thank the participants and dismiss them. In my experience, most focus groups can be conducted in an hour and a half to two hours. A good rule of thumb is to allow about a half hour per question and slightly more for groups of more than eight.

Recording the Responses

Because of their intensity, focus groups lend themselves to tape recording. If you use a tape recorder, be sure to inform the participants and obtain their permission to tape-record. The advantage of tape recording is that it gives you a full record of a potentially rich source of data. Its disadvantage is that it is time-consuming to listen to the tape. As with all such techniques, it is preferable to use an unobtrusive recording device. Use tapes of sufficient length so you do not have to make a change midway through the session, as this may destroy the group atmosphere. Whether or not you tape-record, detailed notes are indispensable, if only to assist in providing the location of information on the tape. The assistant moderator should copy down copious notes of the relevant material. In doing so, the recorder must avoid giving cues to participants about the value of their contributions by noting only the 'best' ones. In general, the recorder should be writing things at all times, or at least appear to be doing so. In recording the notes, it is useful to jot time references in the margin so that specific points can be located easily on the tape. It is also useful to underline or otherwise highlight particular reference points which appear at the time to be significant contributions. In some instances you can pre-define categories and organize a page of your notebook to accommodate comments in the anticipated categories. Some people use shorthand or codes in order to prevent the participants from peeking at what was recorded.

Data Analysis

Data analysis should take place as soon as possible after the group session concludes. The moderator and other researchers present should be involved in the analysis. You should systematically go through your data record, be it a tape recording or detailed notes. In doing the analysis you must constantly keep in mind the purpose of the focus group. At the next level, first look for the big ideas and concepts and make a list of these, later to be refined and organized. In conducting the analysis, you must consider the words used, the context which gave rise to those words, whether people changed their views, or held them constantly throughout the session, and you need to assess the intensity of the responses; that is, the enthusiasm a participant holds for a given idea. As you explore the data, you should try to organize the big ideas into a framework. The research and focus group questions provide one type of framework. You might also use content analysis procedures to record the dominant themes and big ideas. In this, you must strive for a balance between detail and being concise. The extent to which you carefully refine the written analysis will depend on how you intend to report the findings.

Reporting on Focus Group Findings

Some focus groups have little or no written report. In marketing research, the client is sometimes invited to observe behind a one-way mirror or view a video of highlights of the session. In assessing consumer reaction to a product, typical responses of this type are an ideal way of communicating the reactions of potential consumers. For other purposes a briefing and oral report is prepared.

For most research purposes, however, a written analysis is required. In general, there are two extremes to written forms of reporting focus group data. One is to conduct the analysis and report summaries of the major ideas and themes. The other is to use the participant's words verbatim. Which route you choose will depend on your purpose and the intended reader. Personally, I like to combine narrative summaries with actual quotes that illustrate views in the participant's own words. In doing so, be sure to avoid extreme views and attempt to select typical statements for your quotations. It is alright to edit them, laundering the swear words and correcting the grammar if you wish, as long as the intent is clear. Remember that you are trying to obtain insight and understanding about the theme, and why people hold the views they hold. It is often possible to distill this information into a concise form, not withstanding the great depth of data collection and analysis which precedes it.

Conclusion

Like all data collection techniques, focus groups are an indispensable tool for certain types of issues and questions. Focus groups are intended strictly for qualitative data, and to help you understand why people hold the view they hold. For their purpose they are a good tool, and in the hands of trained researchers provide valid and reliable data. Focus groups can be an efficient data collection technique and with relatively little investment can often help us avoid asking the wrong questions, or embarking on things which are guaranteed to fail. Focus groups also provide a timely response and can suggest the futility of more elaborate forms of research. They may also help you sharpen your questions for complementary forms of data collection and analysis. Remember, however, that quality data requires trained and experienced researchers. Focus groups may have inherent appeal because they are in vogue, but only if used properly.

Appendix I Terms of Reference

Statement of Services
Consulting and Professional Services

1.0 *BACKGROUND*

Human resource development and institution building in the priority sectors of energy, natural resources and rural development, constitute the main objectives of Thailand's program. Institution strengthening is recognized as one of the principal areas of CIDA's cooperation program with Thailand. Over the years, through bilateral programming and the responsive mechanism of the Institutional Cooperation and Development Services (ICDS), projects have been undertaken in support of these objectives.

Presently there has developed increasing communication and mutual interest between the two countries that has led to the development of university linkages based on the prospect that these can be of national benefit to both countries. To enable Thai universities to carry out their mandate of contributing to the development of Thailand, all linkage arrangements are designed and coordinated within the context of the National Development Plan. The university community, ICDS and the Thailand Desk collaborate in the establishment of linkage projects as developmental tools, in support of clear developmental and institutional objectives in the targeted sectors of concentration.

2.0 *OBJECTIVES OF THE MID-TERM EVALUATION*

The project approval documents require that an evaluation be conducted at the end of the second year of project implementation. The objectives of the evaluation are:

2.1   to assess the extent to which the ILP Project is achieving its objectives;

2.2   to assess the efficiency and effectiveness of the processes and administrative arrangements of the ILP Project;

2.3   to make recommendations to CIDA, as deemed necessary, on the management of the project over the remaining term;

2.4   to determine whether a second phase of the ILP Project should be planned, based on the results to date.

3.0 *PROJECT DESCRIPTION AND COMPONENTS*

3.1   The current Institutional Linkage Program (ILP) Project which commenced in July 1985, is scheduled to terminate in 1989/90. It is designed to assist Thai and Canadian universities undertake linkage arrangements consistent with the priorities of the Royal Thai Government (RTG) and CIDA's Thailand Program. The ILP Project will establish a mechanism whereby the priorities of both Canadian and Thai universities are addressed, initial contacts between institutions facilitated and adequate funds made available to effectively plan for and implement successful institutional linkage projects. The Association of Universities and Colleges of Canada (AUCC) is the Canadian Executing Agency of the project, with responsibility for financial administration, information dissemination, communication activities and monitoring and review functions.

The objectives of the Project are:

— to increase capabilities in the areas of energy, natural resources and institutional development in Thai universities in support of development objectives;

— to foster collaboration among Thai universities and with Canadian universities;

— to improve the knowledge and understanding in Canada con-

cerning Thailand, its development priorities and possible opportunities;
— to strengthen the capacity of Thai universities to contribute to the development of Thailand.

3.2   The ILP Project is mainly a process to promote and fund individual projects designed and undertaken by participating Thai and Canadian universities. While the Thailand Desk undertakes the management and coordination of the overall process, in collaboration with ICDS, the management of individual linkage projects is the responsibility of the participating universities, adopting standard ICDS procedures. All linkage arrangements are designed to meet particular development and administrative criteria and a set of guidelines specifying the types of linkages and priority areas of involvement acceptable to the RTG.

3.3   The Project includes the following components:

— Management Activities
— Planning Missions
— Individual Linkage Projects

The management activities encompass information activities which include the preparation of information packages and information dissemination in cooperation with ICDS and the Canadian Executing Agency.

Planning Missions make provision for exchange visits between the universities. The missions are governed by specific guidelines entitled: Institutional Linkages Program (ILP) Project-Thailand-Revised Guidelines For Institutions, Revision of May 1986 The guidelines provide detailed information concerning development objectives, priority sectors, types of activities and the criteria to be used in assessing proposed linkage arrangements. Requests are recommended by the Sub-Committee for Thai-Canada Institutional Cooperation (STIC) and subsequently reviewed by the CIDA project team.

Detailed linkage proposals are prepared by the universities based on the guidelines. Proposals are reviewed in Thailand by STIC to ensure compliance with Thailand's development objectives. Final approval of individual linkage projects comes from CIDA. To date, nine linkages have been extablished, involving eighteen projects.

4.0 DESCRIPTION OF SERVICES

4.1 General
For purposes of this contract the Consultant shall provide the services of Gary Anderson to conduct an evaluation of the project, assessing it in terms of the processes and the likelihood of the project achieving the stated goals and purposes as outlined in the attached Logical Framework Analysis (LFA) Exhibit 1, dated April 1985. The review shall include an assessment of the universities' appraisal of individual linkage projects, AUCC's effectiveness in administering the project and recommendations on whether a second phase of the project should be planned.

4.2 Specifics
Without limiting the generality of the foregoing, the Consultant shall:

4.2.1   spend the first two weeks of the evaluation reviewing project documents, including the Plan of Operation and progress reports, holding discussions with the Project Team and officials of AUCC;

4.2.2   prepare a work plan, an evaluation design and an outline for the evaluation report;

4.2.3   spend twelve days visiting the Canadian institutions and fifteen days visiting the Thai institutions upon acceptance of the work plan, the evaluation design and report framework by CIDA;

4.2.4   assess the extent to which project goals and purposes are being realized or are likely to be achieved. Report on what can be realistically accomplished by the present project over the remaining term;

4.2.5   determine whether the original assumptions outlined in the LEA are still valid with respect to achievement of the goals and purposes;

4.2.6   determine whether the linkages established under the project are in line with the goals, purposes and priority areas of the project;

4.2.7 assess the efficiency and effectiveness of the processes of the ILP for the establishment of linkages and the efficiency of the mechanisms established for the management and administration of the project, particularly,

4.2.7.1 the generating of Linkage proposals;

4.2.7.2 the review and selection of proposals for ILP support.

4.2.8 identify any factors that have hindered or facilitated the processes. Suggest what steps can be taken to overcome or minimize those which adversely affect project performance;

4.2.9 comment on the universities' monitoring, control, reporting and evaluaton of individual linkage projects;

4.2.10 assess the degree of commitment of the participating institutions to a long-term cooperation program, independent of CIDA support;

4.2.11 assess AUCC's monitoring, control and reporting of the ILP Project;

4.2.12 determine the number of linkages established to date. Comment on the nature and quality of the linkages in terms of compliance with stated goals and purposes and Thailand's priority areas;

4.2.13 comment on the work and activities of the following, including a review of their roles and responsibilities:

— The International Division Office (IDO) of the AUCC;
— The CIDA Project Team;
— The Sub-Committee for Thai-Canadian Institutional Cooperation (STIC);
— The Thai Ministry of University Affairs (MUA);
— ICDS/CIDA (Thai Desk);
— The Canadian Embassy, Bangkok.

4.2.14 comment on the adequacy and effectiveness of other support mechanisms, particularly the following:

— The Guidelines for the Institutions (attached);
— ICDS' Proposal Format;
— Monitoring and Reporting Mechanisms;
— Project Review Visits.

4.2.15 report on the efficiency of the general financial administration of the project, including the provision of inputs from CIDA and the participating institutions, and the timely disbursement of funds;

4.2.16 identify any necessary changes and practical improvements required to enhance the efficiency and effectiveness of the program in the next three years of implementation;

4.2.17 report on the need for the development of a second phase of the ILP Project, based on the results to date.

5.0 *Reporting*

5.1 The evaluation report shall be succinct, clearly organized and approximately 30 (1 1/2 spaces) pages in length. Lengthy technical analyses shall be attached as appendices, including the terms of reference, instruments, references and other pertinent material. Recommendations shall be clearly identified and enunciated in a brief executive summary.

5.2 The Consultant shall prepare and submit for CIDA's comments and recommendations a draft report approximately two (2) weeks after the Consultant's return to Canada.

5.3 The Consultant shall prepare and submit a final report, in light of CIDA's comments and recommendations, in ten (10) copies, no later than March 31, 1988.

Appendix II

ILP CANADIAN UNIVERSITY TELEPHONE INTERVIEW PROTOCOL

Project Number: _____
Person Contacted: _____   Interviewer:_____
University: _____   Date: _____
Phone: _____   Time Begun: _____

Introduction

My name is _____ , from Universalia, a management consulting firm. We have been engaged by CIDA and AUCC to conduct a mid-project evaluation of the Canada-Thailand Institutional Linkages Program. We are interviewing university professors who have been responsible for projects and requests, whether their initiatives have led to funded projects or not.

Would you be willing to answer a few questions about this, or would you prefer that I call back at another time? If you would prefer another time, what would be convenient for you?

Date:_____ Time: _____ Phone: _____
If you like, I could mail you a copy of the questions in advance
Yes ☐   No ☐
Address _____ Fax _____
            _____
            _____

I. Background
I would like to begin with a few background questions on your involvement.

2. Before this initiative, had you previously been involved in any work in or for developing countries?
   No   ☐   go to Q.3
   Yes   ☐

   If yes:
   a) In how many countries had you been involved? _____
   b) Have you had any previous involvements with Thailand?
   No   ☐
   Yes   ☐
   If yes, please describe:

   _____

   _____

3. How did you learn about the ILP program?
   - AUCC newsletter or contact   ☐
   - AUCC information session   ☐
   - through university colleague   ☐
   - Thai university colleague/contact   ☐
   - contact with CIDA   ☐
   - other (specify) _____

   _____

4. Following that first exposure, did you seek additional information before applying?
   No   ☐   go to Q.8
   Yes   ☐
   From where:
   - within your university   ☐
   - AUCC   ☐
   - from CIDA   ☐
   - other (specify) _____

   _____

5. What type of information did you receive?

   _____

   _____

6. How did you get information on possible Thai universities for a linkage?
   - AUCC advice   ☐
   - Thai university visit   ☐

- CIDA advice ☐
- Personal acquaintance ☐
- Other: (describe) _____

_____

7. How did you select the Thai university for a linkage?

_____

_____

_____

8. Did you seek advance clarification from AUCC whether your proposed project concept was an appropriate endeavour for ILP?
No ☐
Yes ☐ (Describe) _____

_____

_____

II. Planning Mission Proposal
Let's talk about the planning mission request phase.

9. Did you develop a planning mission request?
No, not at all ☐ go to Q.20
No, but ILP proposal
was accepted as P.M.R. ☐ go to Q.20
Yes ☐ (Describe) _____

_____

10. Were you supplied with adequate information with which to make your planning mission request?
Yes ☐
No ☐ (What was lacking?)_____

_____

_____

11. Were the guidelines for preparation of planning mission requests adequate?
Yes ☐
No ☐ (What was missing?) _____

_____

_____

12. Did you make any contacts before making your planning mission request with people or institutions in Thailand?

No ☐

Yes ☐ (Describe): _____

_____

_____

13. Who was involved in preparing the planning mission request?
    • your alone ☐
    • you plus one or more other Canadian professors ☐
    • you plus Canadian university administrators ☐
    • you plus Thai university personnel ☐
    • AUCC/International development officer ☐
    • other: _____

14. Was your department and university supportive of your request?

No ☐ (Why not)? _____

_____

Yes ☐

15. Was the Thai university fully aware of the nature of the proposal?

No ☐

Yes ☐

16. How many weeks did it take to prepare your proposal? _____ weeks.

17. How long did it take after submission to receive a reponse? _____weeks

18. What type of feedback did you receive on your submission?

_____

_____

Was it adequate?

Yes ☐

No ☐ (What was missing?)_____

_____

_____

19. Do you feel you were fairly treated?
    Yes ☐
    No ☐ (If not, why not?) _____
    _____
    _____

III. Planning Mission to Thailand

20. Was your university involved in a planning mission to Thailand?
    No ☐ go to Q.30
    Yes ☐

21. Who from your university was involved in the mission?
    yourself? ☐
    yourself plus other professors? ☐
    yourself plus ILC ☐
    other? ☐_____

22. How long was the planning mission? ____weeks or ____days

23. How many Thai universities were visited? ____

24. Did you receive help from AUCC in planning the mission?
    No ☐
    Yes ☐ (Describe) _____
    _____
    _____

25. Did you receive a briefing on Thailand and Thai universities?
    No ☐
    Yes ☐ By whom? AUCC ☐
                    CIDA ☐
         Other _____

26. Did the planning mission provide for sufficient opportunities for the Canadian visitors to learn about Thais and Thailand?
    Yes ☐
    No ☐ _____
    _____
    _____

27. During your visit did you:
    engage in discussions about a linkage ☐
    attend formal meetings related to ILP ☐
    work with Thai colleagues on a project proposal? ☐
    attend a seminars/lectures/classes ☐
    deliver a seminar/lecture ☐

28. Were Thai counterparts involved with you throughout the planning mission in Thailand?
    No ☐
    Yes ☐

29. Do you feel there was sufficient compatibility between your department and that in the Thai university?
    Yes ☐
    No ☐

IV. Thai Visitation to Canada

30. Did counterparts form Thailand visit your university?
    No ☐ go to Q.33
    Yes ☐ How many? ____

31. How long did they stay? ____ weeks ____ days

32. During the visit, did they:
    engage in discussions about a linkage ☐
    attend formal meetings related to ILP ☐
    work with you on a project proposal ☐
    attend seminars/lectures/classes ☐
    deliver a seminar/lecture ☐

V. The ILP Proposal

33. Did you develop a full ILP proposal?
    No ☐ (Why not?) _____
    _____
    _____ go to Q.59
    Yes ☐
    At what point did you decide to develop a full proposal? _____
    _____
    _____

34. Were Thai colleagues involved in this development?
    No   ☐ go to Q.36
    Yes ☐ (Describe) _____
    _____
    _____

35. Would you say that the Thai university was equally involved?
    No   ☐
    Yes ☐

36. What procedure did you use for involving Thai colleagues in the final submission?
    Mailed a copy   ☐
    Mailed a copy and incorporated comments   ☐
    Other _____

37. Who else was involved is preparing the proposal?
    _____
    _____

38. Did your university support it?
    No   ☐ _____
    Yes ☐ _____

39. Did AUCC provide any support?
    No   ☐
    Yes ☐ _____
    _____

40. Who costed the proposal?
    You   ☐
    University administrators   ☐
    IDO   ☐
    Other _____

41. Was it viewed as
    full-cost recovery   ☐
    or subsidized by your university? ☐

42. Were people experienced in past proposals of this type involved in developing the proposal?
    No   ☐
    Yes   ☐ _____
    _____
    _____

43. Do you feel the proposal provided equal benefits to the Canadian and Thai university?
    Yes   ☐
    No   ☐ (explain) _____
    _____

44. How long did it take you to develop the proposal? ____ weeks

45. How long did it take to receive a response? ____ weeks

46. Did you receive feedback on the proposal submission?
    No   ☐
    Yes   ☐

47. Do you feel it was fairly reviewed?
    Yes   ☐
    No   ☐
    If not, why not? _____
    _____
    _____

48. Would you make another proposal under ILP?
    Yes   ☐
    No   ☐
    If not, why not? _____
    _____

V. Implementation

49. Are you currently implementing or about to implement an ILP project?
    No   ☐ go to Q.59
    Yes   ☐

50. Please list the dates (month/year) of the following milestones?
    a) feasibility request _____
    b) feasibility mission _____
    c) proposal submission _____
    d) proposal approval _____
    e) beginning of project _____

51. Has/will the implementation phase involved AUCC to any degree?
    No   ☐
    Yes   ☐ (Describe) _____
    _____
    _____

52. Who manages/will manage the financial aspect of the project?
    You   ☐   University financial officer ☐
    ILO   ☐   IDO   ☐

53. To what extent do you feel it is achieving its objectives?
    Considerably   ☐
    Somewhat   ☐
    Not at all   ☐
    Too early to tell   ☐

54. What are the major problems you have encountered?
    1. _____
    2. _____
    3. _____

55. What do you expect to be the three major benefits to your university?
    1. _____
    2. _____
    3. _____

56. What do you expect to be the three major benefits to the Thai university?
    1. _____
    2. _____
    3. _____

57. Do you anticipate development of a long-term relationship independent of CIDA?

    Yes ☐

    No ☐ _____

    _____

    _____

58. Would you apply again under similar circumstances?

    Yes ☐

    No ☐ Why not? _____

    _____

VI. Conclusion

59. As a result of your involvement in ILP, how many Canadian faculty members have had an opportunity to increase their understanding of Thais and Thailand?

    _____

60. As a result your involvement in ILP how many Canadian students have had an opportunity to increase their understanding of Thais and Thailand?

    _____

61. What would you say are the three major weaknesses of the overall ILP project?

    1 _____

    2 _____

    3 _____

62. In what ways could the ILP project be improved from your perspective?

    1 _____

    2 _____

    3 _____

63. What advice would you offer AUCC on the ILP project in general?

    1 _____

    2 _____

    3 _____

64. What advice would you offer CIDA regarding the ILP project in general?

    1 _____

    2 _____

    3 _____

65. Do you have any other comments or advice you wish to share?

    _____
    _____
    _____
    _____

    Thank you for taking the time to share these perceptions with us.

    Time interview ended: _____

Index

abstracts 52, 95
  see also reviews
Adair, J.G. 22, 27
administration 77
Adrien, M.H. 64, 75
adversary models 169
Ahola-Sidaway, J. 150, 156
Algranti, C.A. 36, 43
American Educational Research
  Association 53, 119
American Psychological Association
  19
  Style Manual 86–7, 88, 89, 96, 134
American Sociological Association 19
analysis 81–2
  content analysis 121–2
  correlational analysis 143–4
  discriminant analysis 140–1
  for meaning 149–50
  for program evaluations 183
  in case studies 162
  in ethnographic research 153–4
  interaction analysis 124
  of data from focus groups 245
  of previous research 102
  policy analysis 187
  statistical analysis 12, 110, 133
  units of 13–14, 145, 159
ancestry searches of literature 54, 56
Anderson, G.J. 30, 43, 64, 68, 71, 74–5,
  95, 122, 132, 137, 139, 146, 163, 168,
  169–70, 204–5, 217–21, 222
anonymity 24–5

anthropology 147–8, 153, 160
APA *see* American Psychological
  Association
appearance 227
appendices 95
Association of Universities and
  Colleges of Canada App. I, App. II
associations 53
assumptions 6, 11, 71–4, 122
attrition 135, 136
AUCC *see* Association of Universities
  and Colleges of Canada
axiological knowledge 4, 46–7, 49

Badia, P. 16
basic research 7, 9, 136
Bayley, S. 114, 119
Beach, M. 114, 119
Beals, 35, 43
Becker, H.S. 93, 96, 147, 156
behavior, studies of 131
  see also enthnographic research
behavior modification 131
behavioral sciences 127
Bernstein, B. 159
Best, J.W. 5, 16
bias 5, 11, 126
  analyzing 121–2
bibliographies 88, 100
Biklen, S.K. 147, 156
black box model 68
Blanchard, K.H. 162, 164
Bogdan, R.C. 147, 156